THE BEST OF **WOODWORKER'S JOURNAL**

JIGS & FIXTURES
for the Table Saw & Router

THE BEST OF **W**OODWORKER'S **J**OURNAL

JIGS & FIXTURES
for the Table Saw & Router

from the editors of *Woodworker's Journal*

FOX CHAPEL
PUBLISHING

Our friends at Rockler Woodworking and Hardware supplied us with most of the hardware used in this book. Visit *rockler.com*.

Woodworker's Journal
Publisher: Ann Rockler Jackson
Editor-in-Chief: Larry N. Stoiaken
Editor: Rob Johnstone
Art Director: Jeff Jacobson
Senior Editor: Joanna Werch Takes
Field Editor: Chris Marshall
Illustrators: Jeff Jacobson, John Kelliher
Contributing Writers: Rob Johnstone, Bill Hylton,
Chris Inman, E. John DeWaard, Jeff Greef, Ralph Bagnall,
John English, Ian Kirby, Rick White, Carol Reed, Jim Dolan,
Jack Gray, Chris Marshall and Barry Chattell

ISBN 978-1-56523-325-6

Publisher's Cataloging-in-Publication Data

　　　　Jigs & fixtures for the table saw & router. -- East Petersburg, PA :
　　Fox Chapel Publishing, c2007.

　　　　　　p. ; cm.

　　　　　　(The best of Woodworker's journal)
　　　　　　ISBN 978-1-56523-325-6

　　　　　　1. Jigs and fixtures. 2. Jigs and fixtures--Design and
　　construction. 3. Machine-tools. 4. Routers (Tools) 5. Woodwork.
　　6. Woodworking machinery. I. Jigs and fixtures for the table saw &
　　router. II. Series. III. Woodworker's journal.

TJ1187 .J54 2007
621.9/92--dc22   0705

To learn more about the other great books from Fox Chapel Publishing, or to find a retailer near
you, call toll-free 800-457-9112 or visit us at *www.FoxChapelPublishing.com*. For subscription information
to *Woodworker's Journal* magazine, call toll-free 800-765-4119 or visit them at *www.woodworkersjournal.com*.

Note to Authors: We are always looking for talented authors to write new books.
Please send a brief letter describing your idea to Acquisition Editor, 1970 Broad Street, East Petersburg, PA 17520.

Printed in China
Fourth printing

INTRODUCTION

The table saw and router are the most versatile of all woodworking machines. Known when invented as the variety saw and the universal saw, the table saw is, at its essense, a steel platform with a howling toothy blade sticking up through a slot. In the same vein, a router is little more than a one-pound coffee can with an amazingly sharp bit furiously spinning at one end. The table saw allows woodworkers to cut solid wood and sheet materials into precisely sized pieces. The router helps make grooves, joints, and molded edges on those pieces. Together, these two machines are the heart of today's woodworking shops.

Because they are so important, woodworkers have spent a great deal of time and effort perfecting them and augmenting them with helpful fixtures and jigs. Technically, a fixture takes hold of the workpiece and controls its path. A jig controls both the path of the blade or cutter as well as of the workpiece. The distinction, these days, is academic—woodworkers tend to use the two terms interchangeably.

Thus in this book you will find table saw jigs to aid in the processes of crosscutting, mitering, tenoning, making box joints, breaking plywood down into manageable chunks, plus a very useful fixture that simply sits on the outfeed side of the machine, to catch the work as it moves beyond the blade. And you will find router jigs for making joints, fitting inlays, cutting circles, straightening edges and surfaces, and making flutes and reeds. You'll also find several ambitious router tables, designed to harness the handheld router and making it behave more like a stationary machine—that is, more like a table saw.

Woodworkers ostensibly make these devices as aids to accuracy, productivity, and safety. But you won't have to look far into this book to see beneath those bromides. The truth is, woodworkers mostly make jigs and fixtures as vehicles for displaying cleverness, ingenuity, and appropriate workmanship. Most everything else the craftsman makes leaves the workshop to go into the family home or the home of a customer. The apparatus that woodworkers make for themselves to use remains behind. When made thoughtfully and well, they are a comfort and joy.

Larry N. Stoiaken, Editor-in-Chief

ACKNOWLEDGMENTS

Woodworker's Journal recently celebrated its 30th anniversary—a benchmark few magazines ever reach. I would like to acknowledge both the 300,000 woodworkers who make up our readership and Rockler Woodworking & Hardware (rockler.com), which provided most of the hardware, wood and other products used to build the projects in this book. Our publishing partner, Fox Chapel, did a terrific job re-presenting our material, and I am especially grateful to Alan Giagnocavo, Gretchen Bacon, John Kelsey, and Troy Thorne for their commitment to our content.

Larry N. Stoiaken, Editor-in-Chief

CONTENTS

Table Saw Jigs & Fixtures 8

Router Jigs & Fixtures 54

74

TABLE SAW
JIGS & FIXTURES

AVOIDING KICKBACK AND BINDING

When readers ask: "What's the most dangerous tool in the shop?" our consensus is, the one you're sure won't hurt you. If you respect the power of woodworking tools, your caution will be rewarded with safe, precise work. With that in mind, let's look at four problems in basic table saw operations.

by Rob Johnstone

Kickback During Ripping

Kickback means that the workpiece is kicked, or driven, back toward the operator. When most woodworkers hear the term, they think of a ripping operation coming to a sudden and dramatic stop. There are two interrelated causes for this: an underpowered saw and incorrect blade height.

Forensic scientists have long known that a bullet causes its greatest damage as its velocity decreases (small entry/large exit). The same is true with kickback, which occurs when a saw blade is slowing down. If the saw has enough power to keep driving, it won't kick back. Not only does the sheer power of the saw come into play here, but the physical weight does too: if the motor, saw arbor and blade are heavy enough, their momentum should keep the blade spinning during a sharp impact.

The second cause of this type of kickback (and many other problems too) is a blade that's set too low. Your high school shop teacher may have told you to set the blade as low as possible—just above the top of the wood (see Figure 1). But that means the teeth are cutting more horizontally than vertically.

When the teeth do catch, they're traveling at the top of the blade's rotation. If the blade is set high (as shown in Figure 2), the teeth are traveling downward,

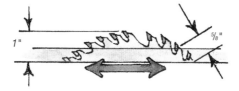

Figure 1: A blade set too low causes the teeth to cut more horizontally than vertically, which increases the chances of kickback.

Figure 2: When a blade is set high, the teeth are traveling downward as they enter the workpiece, forcing it safely onto the table.

forcing the workpiece onto the table, instead of back toward the operator. A low blade also causes motor drag because there are more teeth in contact with the

wood. Each tooth, instead of cutting through a little more than ¾" of stock, is cutting through more than twice that amount of material. With a ¾" board and

Never, Never, Never

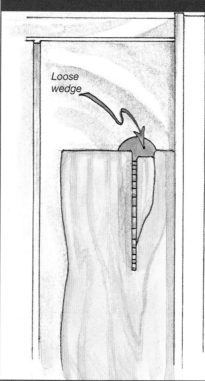

Loose wedge

No matter how rough things get, or how probable a kickback will be, don't ever let go of the wood! Even if you think you're Speedy Gonzales, you're simply not fast enough to get out of the way of a 50 mile-per-hour projectile. More often than not, by holding fast you actually will prevent the kickback. The trick is to train your reflexes not to panic and jump away so that you can hold on even tighter and even drive the piece forward if you can. Let go, and there's no telling where the wood will end up.

On long rips, *stand at the end of the board to the left and walk it through. This is not only safest, but it also produces a smoother cut.*

¼" of blade protrusion on a 10" blade, the teeth must cut through a full 1⅝" of material. This heats up the teeth and the wood, increases drag on the motor, and reduces the feed rate. Not only does heat cause metal fatigue, but it may cause some species of wood to expel oils that gum up the blade, further reducing its life. Since the blade is already slowing down and the motor is operating close to its stall rate, kickbacks are far more likely.

Over-the-Top Kickback

One reader reported that the first shop he worked in had a slab of plywood mounted on the wall with the boss's name written on it. This piece had a distinctive semi-circular gouge out of one face. The boss wouldn't tell what caused it, only that it "had to stay on the wall until someone else makes one like it." He could have explained that the culprit was over-the-top kickback.

Over-the-top kickback is most dangerous because the wood is thrown

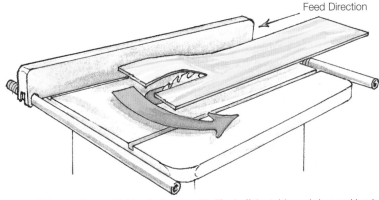

Feed Direction

Figure 3: With over-the-top kickback, the wood is lifted off the table and dropped back on top of the blade, which then throws it toward the operator at about 50 mph.

toward the operator at close to blade speed (about 52 mph!). The workpiece catches the rear teeth of the blade (Figure 3), which lift the wood off the table. As the saw teeth travel up and forward, they drive the wood toward the operator. Speed increases and the blade cuts less while digging in like baseball cleats, throwing the wood.

Ripping Lumber and Sheet Products

I've seen woodworkers rip a long board by standing close to the saw and pulling the workpiece through in short choppy spurts.

To them I say the best method for ripping a long board is to stand at the back left side of the board and walk it into the saw. This will result in a smooth, continuous rip. Keeping your left hand fairly far forward during this operation helps push the edge of the board safely toward the fence.

On sheet products, it can help to deliberately hold the sheet very slightly crooked with only the front corner touching the fence (full sheets or long rips). Slowly ease the sheet forward until you hear the blade make its first contact. Then immediately straighten the sheet tight to the fence. This ensures that the rip starts with the front of the sheet tight to the fence. As the sheet is straightened, the blade holds the front in place and you can exert pressure with your left hand to keep the workpiece against the fence.

...Never Let Go of the Workpiece!

YIKES!

Switch

A reader told us he once was ripping some oak for face frames and either didn't notice the end check (a split at the end of the board), or didn't think much of it. But this check was unusual: it ran diagonally at about 20°, perhaps 6" into the wood. When the blade hit the end of the check, it cut off a wedge-shaped piece that got jammed into its own slot. This increased pressure on the side of the blade. At the moment, he was eight feet behind the saw's OFF switch, so his only choice was to hold tight until the thermal overload tripped. He had to ask himself if it was more important to have

the saw motor burn out or end up with a three-pound chunk of oak sticking out of his ear. Had he let go, the small wedge would surely have been free to fly.

Keep in mind that, although some circumstances may leave you no choice but to bail out, the majority of sawing problems are best handled by holding onto that wood, no matter what.

Crosscut Binding

Often you'll need to cut a piece of wood that's wider than it is long. Regardless of grain direction, this is a cross-cut. The safety issue here is binding, which occurs when the workpiece twists away from the fence. This is one of those operations where things can go wrong very quickly. Don't attempt it if you're not comfortable with your saw. The safest way to tackle this cut is to use a sliding cutoff jig. And keep the saw table waxed and the rip fence properly aligned with the blade.

SIMPLE CROSSCUT SLED

Table saws and crosscut sleds are a marriage made in heaven. A crosscut sled will add accuracy, ease of operation and safety to your work. Here's a great sled design you can build in a couple hours.

by Bill Hylton

We all need a little help in the shop now and then. Sometimes it's just an extra pair of hands, but often what we need is a device of one sort or another that helps improve the accuracy of our work. That's when jigs come to the rescue, and the best of them tend to be the ones that are easy to build.

Even if you love your table saw, chances are the standard miter gauge that came with it sometimes disappoints. Most miter gauges just can't support workpieces longer than a couple feet for making accurate crosscuts. In these situations, a crosscut sled is the perfect solution. It cradles long workpieces and slides over the saw table along the saw's miter slots. A fence in back

holds workpieces securely for dead-on crosscuts every time.

You'll run across many different crosscut sled designs in books and magazines, but this sled fulfills three important functions: It rides in both miter gauge slots instead of just one to keep it tracking accurately without slop. Second, it immobilizes the workpiece on a platform mounted to those slides, against a sturdy fence. And third, this sled isn't adjustable, so it won't get out of square. Here's how to build it.

Getting Started

Your first order of business is to rough out the two slides (pieces 1). They must be straight and made of stable stock.

Quartersawn oak or hard maple make excellent slides, but be sure to use hardwood if you don't have either of these options in your scrap bin. You'll want to cut the slides to rough size, then let them acclimate for a day or two. Now rejoint and thickness them to final dimensions so the slides move along your saw's miter slots easily but without excess play.

While the slides settle, complete the machining of the base and fence parts (pieces 2 through 6). The back fence and its extension are straightforward, but the front subassembly is more involved; see the Elevation Drawings, next page. The extensions, which are glued into place later, reinforce the fences where the blade

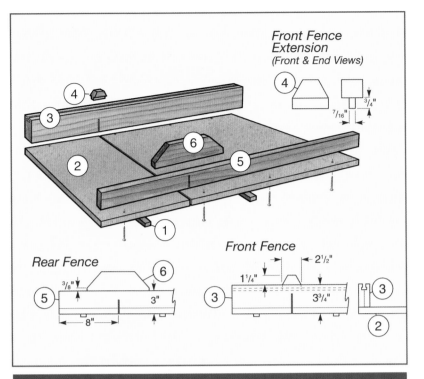

Front Fence Extension
(Front & End Views)

3/4"
7/16"

Rear Fence

3/8"
8"
3"

Front Fence

2 1/2"
1 1/4"
3 3/4"

Material List - Crosscut Sled

	T x W x L
1 Slides (2)	3/4" x 3/8" x 18"
2 Base (1)	3/4" x 18" x 28"
3 Front Fence (2)	3/4" x 3" x 28"
4 Front Fence Extension (1)	1 1/2" x 2" x 2 1/2"
5 Rear Fence (1)	1" x 2 1/4" x 28"
6 Rear Fence Extension (1)	1" x 2 1/2" x 8 3/8"

cuts through so they'll remain strong even when you cut through them with your blade at full height.

Next, drill four or five counterbores and pilot holes in each slide and install the slides on the base as shown in the first two photos below. You need to do this with the slides fitted in the miter slots.

Before mounting the fences, switch on the saw and raise the blade up through the base about midway across its width. Don't split the base yet; the blade is needed to square the front fence, as shown in the right photo, below. Drive a mounting screw up through the base into the end of the fence closest to the blade. Use this as a pivot while you align the fence to the blade with a square. Drill an oversized pilot for a screw at the far end of the fence and secure the fence. Now make a test crosscut with the sled on a piece of scrap and check the scrap for square. Tweak the fence position as needed and make additional test cuts until the sled fence is perfectly square to the blade. Then secure the fence to the base with additional countersunk screws.

The rear fence doesn't need to be exactly square. Just screw it to the base along the opposite edge. Use glue and clamps to install the extensions. Apply some paste wax to the slides, and you are ready to let that puny miter gauge gather some dust for awhile.

Assembling the Sled

1. After tacking the slides from above (inset), slide the assembly partway off the saw table to drive screws up through the slides into the base. Do a couple of screws at the back of the saw, then repeat the process at the front.

2. Carefully raise the blade through the sled's base. This provides a reference with which to square the front fence.
An absolutely 90° relationship between the blade and fence is essential, or the jig will never yield accurate cuts.

3. When you're ready to attach the fence, start with a single screw (on the fence end closest to the saw blade). This provides a pivot point as you adjust the other end of the fence to a perfect 90°.

PRECISION CROSSCUTTING JIG

Spend a day or two making this classic workshop project and the results will improve your woodworking accuracy for years to come. The sled makes it easier to perform crosscuts on long or heavy stock and panel material. Our design also includes a mitering fence for dead-on angle cuts and a micro-adjustable stop block.

By Chris Inman

Woodworking is an exercise in precision. A fine joint that crisply mates two pieces of wood into a single, strong unit depends on a craftsman's ability to make the cuts accurately. It's possible to carry this to ridiculous limits (as when people talk about tolerances in thousandths of an inch), but in woodworking, differences under 1/64" are generally acceptable. Trimming a board to the correct length with square ends lays the foundation for all subsequent layout and joint-cutting steps. It's essential, therefore, to make these first cuts as perfect as possible, and there's no better tool for getting this done than a crosscutting jig for your table saw.

While 90° cuts are the first priority of a crosscutting jig, it's a bonus if it handles miters as well. My crosscutting jig has a mitering accessory for cuts from 0° to 65°, with positive stops at 22½° and 45°.

This jig works great for trimming all kinds of panels, including the raised-panel shown here.

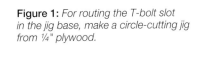

Figure 1: *For routing the T-bolt slot in the jig base, make a circle-cutting jig from ¼" plywood.*

Building the Jig Base

The core of the crosscutting jig is a piece of ½"-thick Baltic birch plywood (piece 1). The jig described here was made for a Delta Unisaw. You should size your jig for your saw—a good rule of thumb is to cut the plywood the same size as the saw table. Make sure the plywood is perfectly flat, then cover both faces with plastic laminate (pieces 2) for a durable, long-lasting surface. Choose a light color that allows you to see any pencil marks drawn on the jig.

Trim the laminate with a flush-cutting router bit, then lay out the entry holes and the pivot hole for the miter fence accessory (see the Jig Base Elevation Drawing on page 17). Use a drill press and a ¾" Forstner bit to bore ⅜"-deep entry holes for the T-bolt slot, then flip the panel over to drill a ¼"-deep counterbore at the pivot hole location. Now switch to a ⁵⁄₁₆" bit to complete the pivot hole.

Cutting the curved T-bolt slot in the base requires a simple circle-routing jig (see Figure 1). Make the jig and attach it to your plunge router. Chuck a ⅜" straight bit in the collet and align the pivot hole in the jig with the pivot hole in the crosscutting jig base. Press a ⁵⁄₁₆" bolt through the holes and adjust the bit so it touches the bottom of the entry holes. Now rout a slot to connect the two entry holes, then switch to your T-slot cutter, adjust its cutting depth, and complete the slot.

The runners (pieces 3) must fit the miter gauge slots in your saw table yet not be so tight that the jig binds. Using wood runners is common, but wood changes with airborne moisture.

A better choice is to use a stable, self-lubricating plastic, like polyethylene.

To install the runners, first cut shallow dadoes in the underside of the base so they're laid out just like the miter gauge slots in your saw table. Clamp the jig base squarely on your saw table and mark the miter gauge slots, then measure the width of your slots and install a dado blade of matching size. Now set your rip fence to align each set of marks with the blade and cut ¹⁄₁₆"-deep dadoes. These cuts must be as accurate as possible to keep the jig runners from binding.

Rip your plastic stock to the exact width of your dadoes, then place the two runners in the dadoes and drill ⁵⁄₃₂" countersunk pilot holes. Use #8-¾" screws (pieces 4) to secure the runners. Test the jig base on the table saw and, if the runners bind in the slots, use a cabinet scraper to shave them until they operate smoothly.

Installing the Fences

Now that the jig base is constructed, build the three fences (pieces 5, 6 and 7). Cut your stock to size and shape following the Material List and Elevation Drawings on the next two pages, then set the rear fence aside so you can rout T-bolt slots in the front fence and miter fence for mounting the stop block.

For each slot, make your first pass with a ⅜" straight bit routing ⁵⁄₁₆" deep,

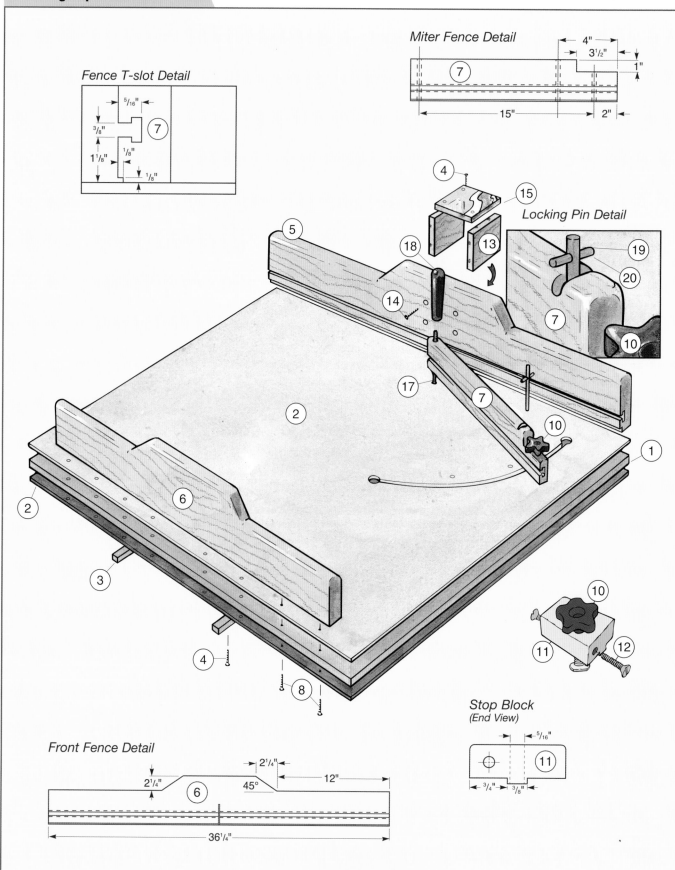

Fence T-slot Detail

⁵⁄₁₆"

³⁄₈" ⑦

1¹⁄₈" ¹⁄₈"

¹⁄₈"

Miter Fence Detail

4"
3¹⁄₂"
1"
⑦
15"   2"

④

⑮

Locking Pin Detail

⑤   ⑱

⑬   ⑲

⑭   ⑳

④   ⑦
⑩

⑰   ②
⑦   ⑩

②   ①

⑥

③   ⑩

④   ⑪   ⑫

⑧

Stop Block
(End View)

⁵⁄₁₆"

Front Fence Detail

2¹⁄₄"   2¹⁄₄"
12"
⑥   45°   ⑪
³⁄₄" ³⁄₈"

36¹⁄₄"

Material List

		T x W x L
1	Plywood Core (1)	½" x 27" x 36¼"
2	Plastic Laminate (2)	1⁄16" x 27" x 36¼"
3	Runners (2)	⅜" x ¾" x 27"
4	Flathead Screws (16)	#8 - ¾"
5	Front Fence (1)	1½" x 5⅝" x 36¼"
6	Rear Fence (1)	11⁄16" x 5⅝" x 32¼"
7	Miter Fence (1)	11⁄16" x 3½" x 17¾"
8	Flathead Screws (16)	#8 - 1½"
9	Short T-bolts (2)	5⁄16" x 1¾"-18
10	Hold-down Knobs (3)	5⁄16"-18
11	Wood Block (1)	¾" x 1¾" x 5"
12	Micro-adjust Bolts (2)	¼" x 1½" - 20
13	Guard Walls (2)	¾" x 4" x 4"
14	Flathead Screws (4)	#8 - 2½"
15	Plastic Shield (1)	¼" x 4" x 4"
16	Long T-bolt (1)	5⁄16" x 3½"
17	Carriage Bolt (1)	5⁄16" x 4" - 18
18	Post Handle (1)	5⁄16" - 18
19	Locking Pin (1)	⅜" x 5"
20	Cross Dowel (1)	⅛" x 1"
21	Wood Block (1)	¾" x 2" x 2"
22	Toggle Clamp (1)	Right-angle Type

Jig Base Elevation
Exact dado locations for runners depend on your table saw

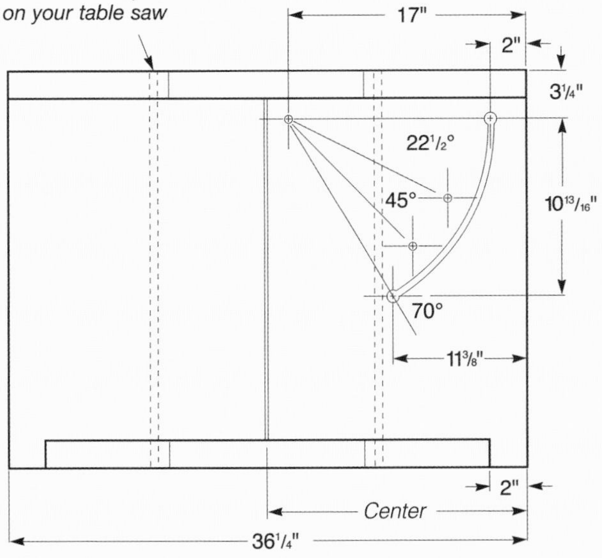

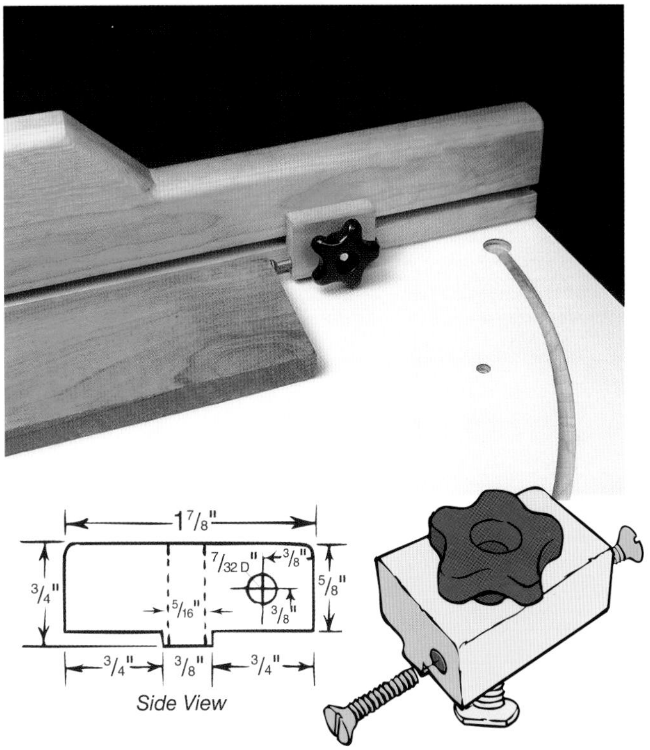

Figure 2: *The micro-adjustable stop block brings great precision to your jig, especially when cutting many pieces to the same length.*

then follow with the T-slot cutter routing to the same depth. After routing the slots, rip a ⅛" x ⅛" rabbet along the bottom inside edge of both fences for dust relief. Next, drill the three holes in the miter fence for the hold-down bolts and pin lock, and pass the fence over the table saw blade to cut a ⅜"-deep kerf at the pin hole lock location (see Miter Fence Detail on the previous page). Finally, rout the top edges of all three fences as well as the pivot hole end of the miter fence, with a ½" roundover bit.

Installing the back fence to the base isn't critical, but mounting the front fence requires accuracy. Clamp the back fence so it's aligned with the edge of the base and drill countersunk pilot holes to secure the assembly with #8-1½" screws (pieces 8). Clamp the front fence to the base and drill one countersunk pilot hole to secure the right end of the fence (leave the left end free for now).

The micro-adjustable stop block (pieces 9, 10, 11 and 12) is really great for accurately setting repeat crosscuts (see Figure 2), but it also comes in handy for precisely setting the front fence. Make the jig and slip it into the T-slot in the jig base, then use a framing square to adjust the fence square to the blade. Now slide the stop block up to the fence and tighten the hold-down knob. Clamp the fence to the stop block (see Figure 3) and make your first pass completely through the crosscutting jig.

Test the accuracy of the front fence by crosscutting a scrap piece that has perfectly parallel edges. After cutting

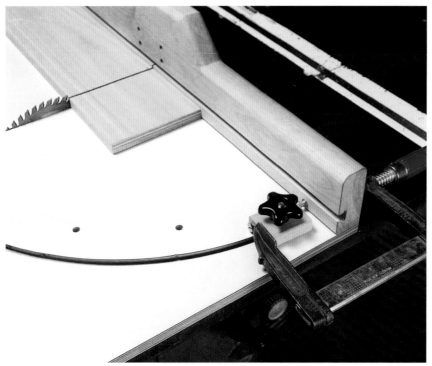

Figure 3: *When you're ready to install the front fence, use your new stop block and a clamp for making fine adjustments to get perfect 90° cuts.*

the scrap, flip one piece over and slide the freshly cut ends of the two pieces together, holding both pieces firmly against the jig fence. If the ends don't match perfectly, loosen the clamp to turn the micro-adjustment bolt a tiny bit; then reclamp the fence and cut another piece of scrap material. Continue this process until the cut ends match perfectly, at which point you can drill countersunk pilot holes and screw the front fence in place.

Completing the Jig Accessories

The guard on the front fence helps protect you as the jig passes beyond the blade. Cut the material and clamp the walls (pieces 13) to the front fence 1¼" from the blade kerf, then drill ⁵⁄₃₂" counterbored pilot holes. Secure the walls with long screws (pieces 14), and complete the guard by drilling pilot holes

---

QuickTip

Sanding Jig for Multiple Boards

When you need to sand several boards of the same size, clamp two fences to your bench, leaving one at a very slight angle to the other. Then load up the boards and wedge them in place with a piece of scrap. It makes for quick board changes, which is great on big jobs. Just make sure the fences and wedge are thinner than the boards being sanded.

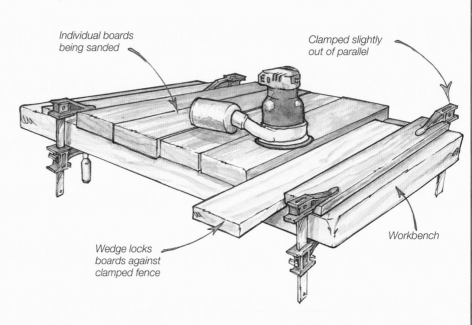

Individual boards being sanded

Clamped slightly out of parallel

Wedge locks boards against clamped fence

Workbench

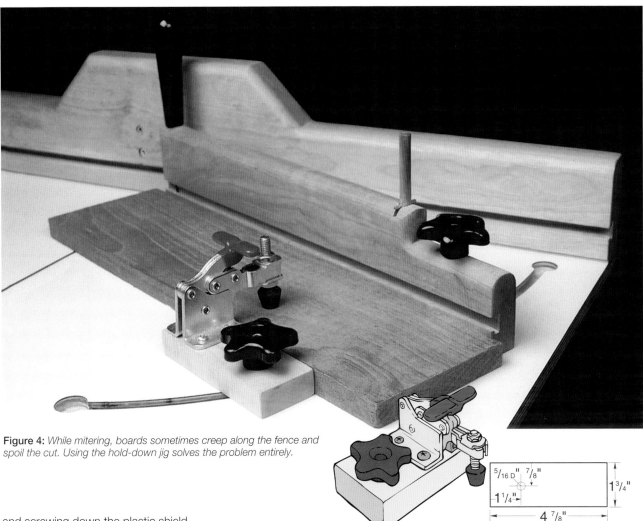

Figure 4: *While mitering, boards sometimes creep along the fence and spoil the cut. Using the hold-down jig solves the problem entirely.*

Top View

and screwing down the plastic shield (pieces 4 and 15).

Now install the miter fence to the base with a long T-bolt (piece 16) and a carriage bolt (piece 17). Slip the miter fence onto the bolts and spin on the hold-down knob and post handle (pieces 10 and 18).

Setting the miter fence lock positions at 22½° and 45° requires the help of an artist's adjustable triangle (available at art supply stores). First set the triangle to 45° and slip it between the front fence and the miter fence. When you have the angle dead-on, slip a ⅜" brad-point bit in the miter fence pin lock hole and use a hammer to tap it lightly against the laminate. Next, move the miter fence out of the way and drill a ⅜"-deep hole at the mark with the ⅜" bit. Reset the triangle to 22½° and

follow the same procedure for marking and drilling this hole.

Make a locking pin (pieces 19 and 20) by cross drilling a ⅜" dowel with a ⅛" bit (see Locking Pin Detail, page 16), then glue a short piece of ⅛" dowel in the pin. Sand the pin so it slips through the hole. When you insert the pin and align the cross dowel with the saw kerf you cut earlier, the pin will reach into the locking holes in the base.

To use the stop block you've already made, slide it into a fence slot and use a tape measure to set it a particular distance from the saw kerf. If the length is off, just give the stop block bolt a turn and make another cut.

The hold down jig (pieces 9, 10, 21 and 22) is designed to lock a workpiece onto the jig base during a cut. It's especially effective at preventing creep while mitering. Make the jig shown in Figure 4, above, and install it in the T-bolt slot in the jig base. Adjust the toggle clamp to work on ¾"-thick stock, since that's probably what you'll cut most often. If you frequently cut thicker stock, you may want to make a second hold-down jig suited for this material.

Now that the crosscut box is complete, oil all the wood parts to keep them free of glue and dirt. Or apply a clear hard finish of your choice for even greater durability.

THE MITER CLAMP JIG

Attach this jig to your miter gauge, and you can clamp workpieces
in place for making extremely accurate and safe angle cuts.

by E. John DeWaard

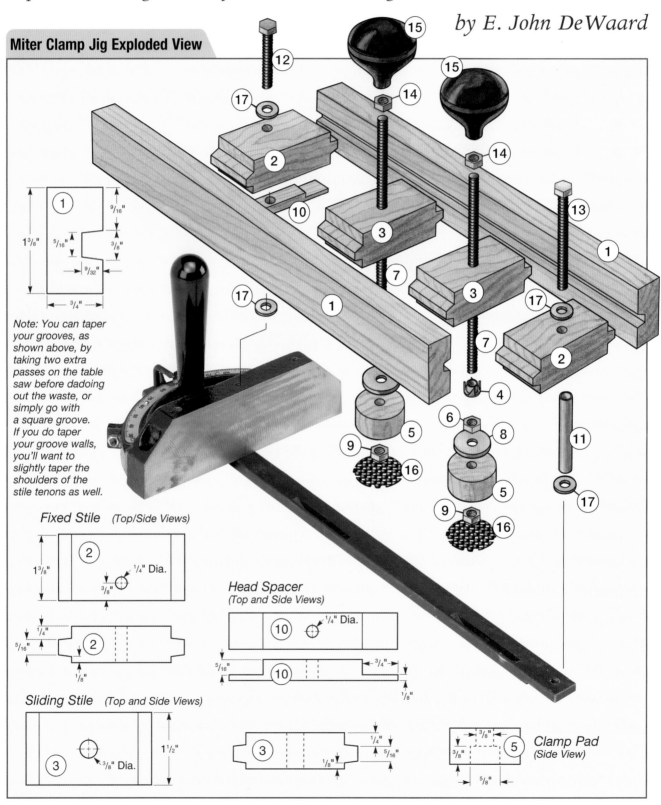

Miter Clamp Jig Exploded View

Note: You can taper
your grooves, as
shown above, by
taking two extra
passes on the table
saw before dadoing
out the waste, or
simply go with
a square groove.
If you do taper
your groove walls,
you'll want to
slightly taper the
shoulders of the
stile tenons as well.

Fixed Stile (Top/Side Views)

Sliding Stile (Top and Side Views)

Head Spacer
(Top and Side Views)

Clamp Pad
(Side View)

Material List

	T x W x L
1 Rails (2)	¾" x 1⅜" x 14"
2 Fixed Stiles (2)	¾" x 1⅜" x 2¾"
3 Sliding Stiles (2)	¾" x 1½" x 2¹¹⁄₁₆"
4 T-nuts (2)	⁵⁄₁₆" - 18
5 Clamp Pads (2)	¾" x 1¾" Dia.
6 Upper Pad Nuts (2)	⁵⁄₁₆" - #18
7 Clamp Bolts (2)	⁵⁄₁₆" - #18 x 5"
8 Pad Fender Washers (2)	⁵⁄₁₆" I.D. x 1¼" O.D.
9 Lower Pad Locknuts (2)	⁵⁄₁₆" - 18
10 Head Spacer (1)	¾" x ⁷⁄₁₆" x 3⅝"
11 Toe Spacer (1)	⅜" x 2⅝"
12 Head Bolt (1)	¼" - 20 x 1½"
13 Toe Bolt (1)	¼" - 20 x 3½"
14 Knob Stop Nuts (2)	⁵⁄₁₆" - 18
15 Knobs (2)	⁵⁄₁₆" - 18 x 2" Dia.
16 Pad Liners (2)	1¾" Dia.
17 Washers (4)	¼" I.D.

Here's the miter clamp jig in action. It eliminates creep and adds another level of safety, especially on cuts like the one shown above.

Start by ripping a 30" length of hardwood for the rails (pieces 1) to the dimensions shown. Plow a groove with slightly angled walls in one of the wider faces (it takes three passes on the table saw), then crosscut the rails to length.

Make the fixed stiles (pieces 2) and sliding stiles (pieces 3) from a single 1 x 8 board crosscut to 2¾" long. Mill a tongue on each end to the dimensions in the Drawing: a tenoning jig on the table saw works well for this. (Taper the tenon sides slightly so they'll slide even easier.) Rip the board to produce two fixed and two sliding stiles (check the Materials List, above, for the dimensions), then trim a hair off each end of the sliding stiles. This will allow them to move in the rail grooves. If they still bind, trim their shoulders slightly with a block plane or sanding block. Be sure to label all four parts to avoid confusion.

Using diagonal lines, find the center of each sliding stile and bore a ⅜" through hole. Slip a ⁵⁄₁₆", #18 T-nut (pieces 4) into the bottom of each hole and hammer it flush.

Assemble the jig body by gluing one fixed stile between the rails and clamping it, then add the sliding stiles and glue and clamp the second fixed stile in place at the other end. Set the assembly aside to cure while you make the clamp pads (pieces 5).

Forming the Clamp Pads with a Hole Saw

With a 1¾" hole saw chucked in the drill press, select the slowest speed and drill halfway into a piece of 1 x 3. Make sure the saw's ⅜" guide bit slightly penetrates the bottom face. Replace the saw with a ⅝" Forstner bit, increase the speed and drill ⅜" deep to counterbore the earlier hole.

Now flip the 1 x 3 and re-chuck the hole saw. Free the clamp pad by drilling through, using the hole produced by your first cut as a guide. Follow the same sequence for the second pad.

Drilling a Hole in Your Miter Gauge

Disassemble your miter gauge and turn the head over to locate the pivot hole. Transfer the center of this hole to the top of the head and chuck a #7 drill in your press. Drill and tap the hole with a ¼ x #20 tap, and clean off the new threads.

Complete the clamping pad subassemblies next. Begin by running an upper pad nut (pieces 6) up each clamp bolt (pieces 7). Add a fender washer (pieces 8), the clamp pad and the lower pad Nyloc® nut (pieces 9). Tighten it until the rod is flush with the opening, then tighten the top nut until the washer is trapped.

Joining the Bar

Bore a ¼" hole in the fixed stile nearest to the head of the miter gauge, at the location shown in the Drawings. Then, using the bar from the miter gauge as a pattern, mark and drill a ¼" hole for the toe bolt in the other fixed stile. Notch the head spacer (piece 10) as shown in the Drawings and glue and clamp it to the bottom of the fixed stile, flush with the end. When the glue has set, drill down through the fixed stile to produce a through ¼" hole. Next, chuck a ⅜" drill in your press and counterbore the bottom of the other fixed stile ¼" deep. This will accommodate the toe spacer.

Reassemble your miter gauge, then cut the toe spacer (piece 11) to length (this will depend on your miter gauge). Fit the spacer into the counterbore on the fixed stile. Thread the clamp bolts into the T-nuts in the sliding stiles, and you're ready to attach the bridge to the miter gauge with the head and toe bolts (pieces 12 and 13). Run the knob stop nuts (pieces 14) down each clamp bolt, followed by the knobs (pieces 15). Tighten the knobs, then tighten the nuts back up against the knobs to lock them in place.

Apply epoxy to the bottom of each fender washer on your clamp pads and screw the pads down. The jig acts as a clamp here. When the epoxy has set, apply Loctite® to the three threads above the nuts. Use rubber cement to attach pieces of router pad (pieces 16) to the bottom of the pads. Now your miter gauge is safer and more accurate than ever.

TABLE SAW TENONING JIG

Here's an indispensable table saw accessory for cutting tenons, bridle joints and spline slots. It allows workpieces to be held safely on end, and a micro-adjust feature ensures pinpoint blade accuracy. Best of all, you can build this jig from scrap and save more than $100 over the cost of buying a commercial tenoning jig.

By Jeff Greef

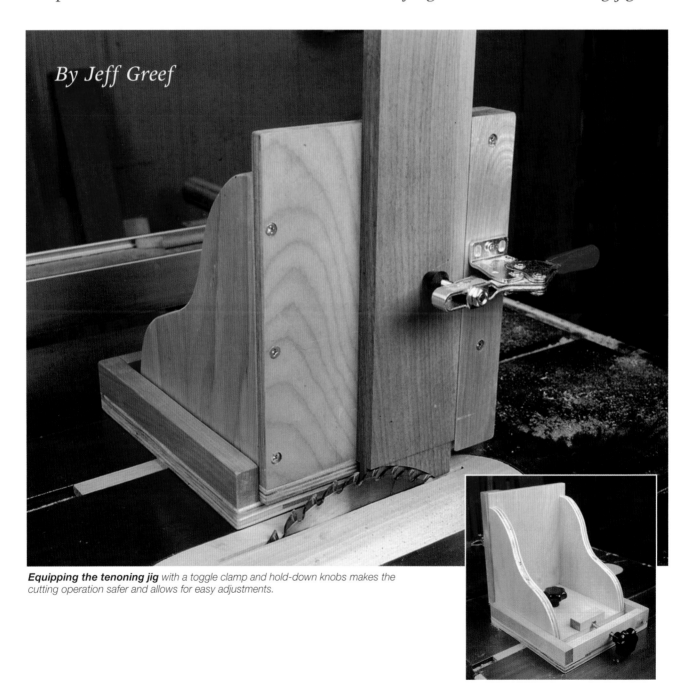

Equipping the tenoning jig with a toggle clamp and hold-down knobs makes the cutting operation safer and allows for easy adjustments.

There are many ways to cut tenons, but one of the easiest and most accurate methods is with a table saw and tenoning jig. Some tenoning jigs are quite elaborate, but the fact is, the simpler the jig the more it gets used. Complicated jigs take longer to build and set up, and the additional capabilities just aren't needed that often. Building a simple jig, on the other hand, takes only an hour or two and, when it's done, will provide a means for precisely cutting tenons as well as open mortises for bridle joints and spline slots.

This basic tenoning jig has two subassemblies: the base and the carrier. The base rides in the table saw's miter gauge slot to keep the jig parallel with the blade. The carrier slides back and forth in the base so you can adjust the distance between the blade and the workpiece. The knobs and bolts provide the fine-tuning control and a hold-down lock that keeps the jig in place.

Building the Jig

Begin by cutting the base (piece 1) to size and centering a counterbored pilot hole on the underside of the panel for a T-nut (pieces 2), as shown in the T-nut Detail on the next page. Install the T-nut, then rip hardwood for outlining the base. Screw two of the hardwood strips (pieces 3) along opposite edges of the base (make sure the strips are parallel to each other) and cut the third strip (piece 4) so it fits between the first two. Drill a pilot hole through the center of the third strip, as shown in the Top View Elevation, and install a T-nut in the hole. Screw the strip along the back edge of the base.

Now cut ½" plywood for the fence and the carrier plate (pieces 5 and 6)—the plate should slide easily on the base, but without any slop. Next, lay out and

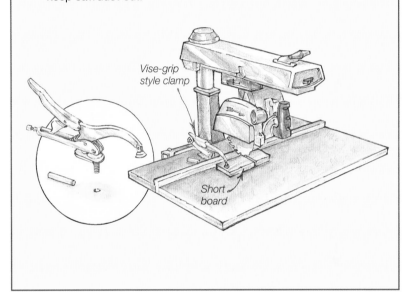

QuickTip

Radial Arm Saw Holddown Clamp
Cutting small pieces with a radial arm saw is inherently dangerous because you have to put a hand too close to the blade for comfort. A better holddown solution than your hand is to use a vise-grip style clamp that bolts to the tabletop. Drill a hole adjacent to the saw blade, just large enough for the threaded part of the clamp. Sideways pressure may be enough to keep the clamp in place, but for safety's sake, secure the clamp to the table with a nut from below. Plug the hole with a loose dowel when you're not using the clamp to keep sawdust out.

Vise-grip style clamp

Short board

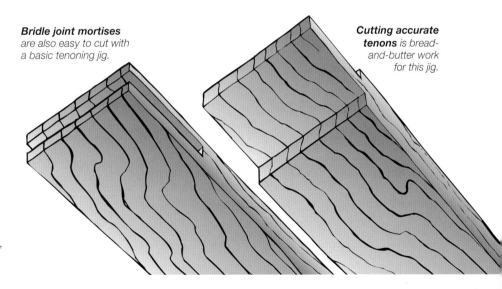

Bridle joint mortises are also easy to cut with a basic tenoning jig.

Cutting accurate tenons is bread-and-butter work for this jig.

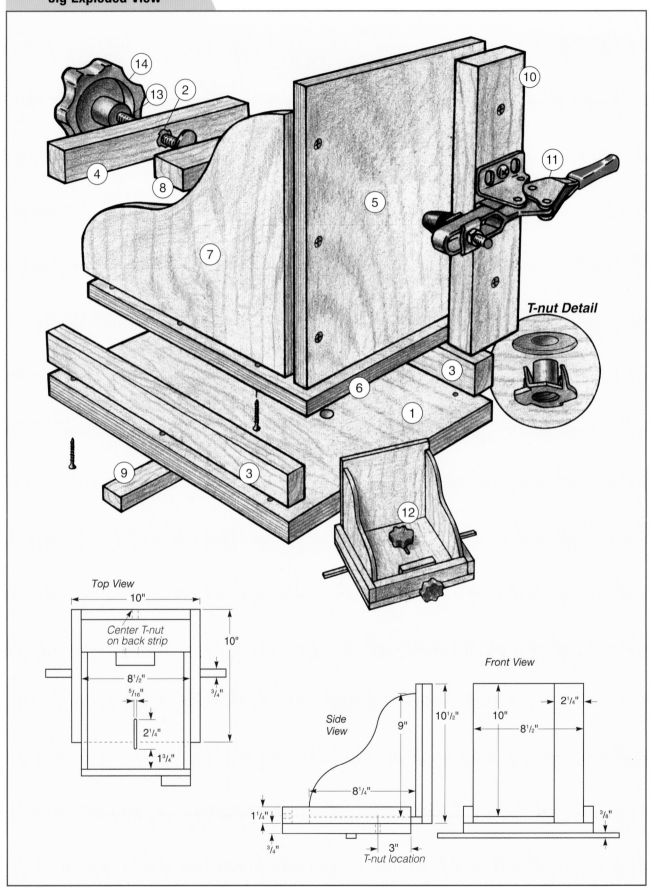

T-nut Detail

Top View

10"

*Center T-nut
on back strip*

10"

8¹/₂"

³/₄"

⁵/₁₆"

2¹/₄"

1³/₄"

Front View

*Side
View*

9"

10¹/₂"

10"

8¹/₂"

2¹/₄"

8¹/₄"

1¹/₄"

³/₄"

3"

T-nut location

³/₈"

Material List - Tenoning Jig

		T x W x L
1	Base (1)	¾" x 10" x 10" (Plywood)
2	T-nuts (2)	⁵⁄₁₆"-18
3	Side Strips (2)	¾" x 1¼" x 10" (Hardwood)
4	Back Strip (1)	¾" x 1¼" x 8½" (Hardwood)
5	Fence (1)	½" x 10" x 8½" (Plywood)
6	Carrier Plate (1)	½" x 8½" x 8¾" (Plywood)
7	Fence Supports (2)	¾" x 8¼" x 9" (Plywood)
8	Bearing Block (1)	¾" x 1" x 3" (Hardwood)
9	Guide (1)	⅜" x ¾" x 14" (Hardwood)
10	Stop (1)	¾" x 2¼" x 10" (Hardwood)
11	Toggle Clamp (1)	Post Handle Type
12	Hold-down Knob (1)	Handle with ⁵⁄₁₆"-18 Bolt
13	T-bolt (1)	⁵⁄₁₆" x 3½"-18
14	Knob (1)	Handle with ⁵⁄₁₆"-18 Nut

rout the slot in the middle of the plate for the hold-down knob (see Top View Elevation).

Next, lay out the curved fence supports (pieces 7). When you cut these pieces to shape, make sure the corner of each one is truly 90° (you could make a jig for cutting angled tenons and mortises by cutting these corners at different angles). Now screw the fence to the supports, then screw the carrier plate to this assembly.

Cut hardwood to size for the bearing block (piece 8) and screw it flush with the back edge of the plate. The bearing block provides a footing for the fine-tuning bolt to press against.

Carefully fit a hardwood guide (piece 9) to the miter gauge slot in your table saw, then clamp the guide to the bottom of the base. Since each table saw is a little different, you'll want to position the guide specifically for your machine. Clamp the guide so the front

edge of the base will fall about 1" from your table saw blade—be sure the guide is parallel with the carrier fence—then drill countersunk pilot holes and screw it to the base.

Screw a stop (piece 10) to the fence so it's 90° to the saw surface—drive the screws above the blade's path. Next, secure a toggle clamp (piece 11) to the stop for holding your workpiece. Now set the carrier on the base and install the hold-down knob and the fine-tuning T-bolt (pieces 12 and 13). Spin the knob (piece 14) onto the T-bolt, then take the jig apart and coat it with varnish. You'll improve your jig's performance by waxing the base and guide regularly.

While this jig won't do everything, it will do a few things very well. Woodworkers who cut lots of tenons will appreciate the accurate, repeatable results, and they won't get bogged down building a jig that's over-designed and difficult to set up.

QuickTip

Magnetic Push Sticks

Push sticks are essential safety items when using a table saw or jointer, but they're easy to misplace. Here's a simple solution: Drill shallow holes in all your push sticks and cement small, round rare earth magnets in the holes. These rare earth magnets are amazingly strong, and your push sticks will stay put wherever you place them.

ADJUSTABLE BOX JOINT JIG

On a standard-style box joint jig, setting up the pin to match the dado blade and getting the spacing just right makes the jig a fussy, single-use item. Here's an adjustable, reusable box joint jig that will suit any joint. It's the last one you'll ever make.

by Ralph Bagnall

Box Joint Jig Exploded View

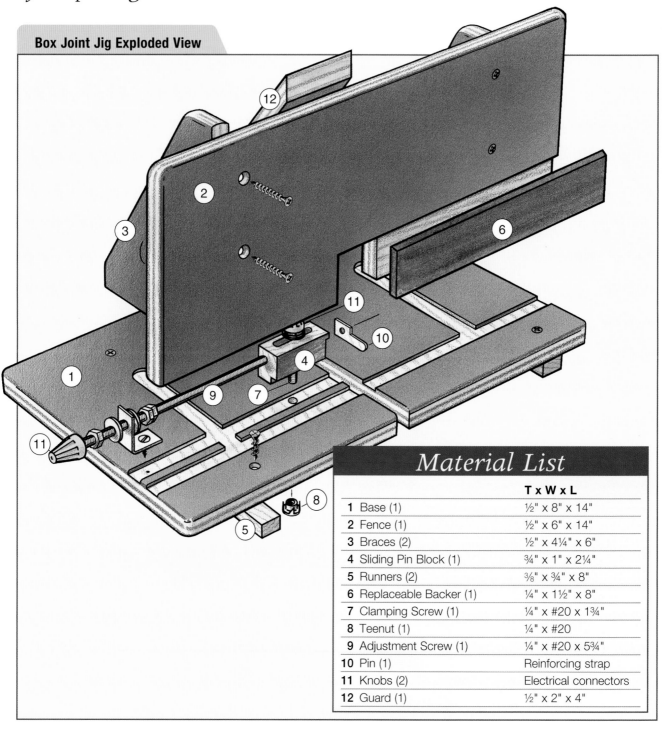

Material List

		T x W x L
1	Base (1)	½" x 8" x 14"
2	Fence (1)	½" x 6" x 14"
3	Braces (2)	½" x 4¼" x 6"
4	Sliding Pin Block (1)	¾" x 1" x 2¼"
5	Runners (2)	⅜" x ¾" x 8"
6	Replaceable Backer (1)	¼" x 1½" x 8"
7	Clamping Screw (1)	¼" x #20 x 1¾"
8	Teenut (1)	¼" x #20
9	Adjustment Screw (1)	¼" x #20 x 5¾"
10	Pin (1)	Reinforcing strap
11	Knobs (2)	Electrical connectors
12	Guard (1)	½" x 2" x 4"

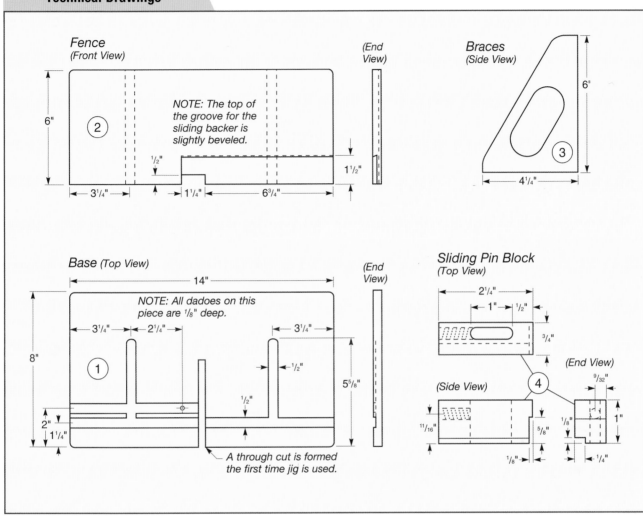

Fence
(Front View)

(End View)

NOTE: The top of the groove for the sliding backer is slightly beveled.

Braces
(Side View)

Base (Top View)

NOTE: All dadoes on this piece are 1/8" deep.

(End View)

A through cut is formed the first time jig is used.

Sliding Pin Block
(Top View)

(End View)

(Side View)

One of the significant benefits of this jig over fixed-style jigs is that the pin doesn't have to precisely match the dado blade. Only the leading edge is used to set the spacing. And, since it's mounted on a sliding block, you can make micro adjustments to the pin.

Machining the Parts

Cut the larger pieces of this jig from 1/2" MDO. Mill shallow dado slots into the base (piece 1) for the fence, braces, and sliding pin block (pieces 2 through 4).

Cut two matching dadoes into the rear face of the fence to receive the braces. Cut the runners next (pieces 5), which must fit snugly into your saw's miter slots. It also helps to cut openings in the braces to provide a safe place for your hands.

The fence needs a wide slot to accept the replaceable backer (piece 6). Bevel the top of this slot to keep the backer in place. The bottom edge rides in the dado milled into the base. Use 1/4" hardboard for the backer. It is important

that the face of the backer is flush with the face of the fence.

Maple is a good choice for the jig's other hardwood parts. Make a rabbet on the bottom of the sliding pin block to create a step that rides in the dado in the base; then cut a 1/4" slot through the block for the clamping screw (piece 7). Next, drill a 5/16" clearance hole in the base and counterbore it on the bottom. This hole houses the Teenut (piece 8), for the clamping screw.

Drill one end of the sliding pin block and tap threads into it for the adjustment screw (piece 9). Mortise the other end to accept the pin (piece 10). Make all these cuts on a longer stick for safety, and trim off the short block last.

For hardware, you'll need a ½" x 3" reinforcing strap (for the pin), a ½" x 1"

corner strap and about 12" of ¼" #20 threaded rod with a few ¼" #20 nuts. Everything is easy to find at a home center.

The corner strap simply holds the end of the adjustment rod, so bore out one of the existing screw holes to ¼". You can make your own knobs (pieces

11) for the threaded rods by dabbing a little quick-set epoxy into electrical wire connectors and screwing these onto the ends of the rods.

If your dadoes are snug, you can dry-fit everything together. You are going to need to cut a notch in the fence to allow for index pin adjustment, so mark the required opening. Drill a hole in the right side brace now, as well, for the threaded rod to pass through. Follow the drawings on page 27 to establish these locations.

Assembling the Jig

Time to glue and assemble the jig. This is also when you should add the runners for the miter slots. Set them into the

QuickTip

Straightening Twisted Lumber

Rough lumber with a diagonal twist can be difficult to straighten, unless you use this trick. Joint the edges of the board and set it on a flat surface. Shim the two high corners, then rip two guide rails from scrap stock: their height should be the same as the highest spot on the shimmed board, and they should be cut from straight hardwood. Finish-nail these in place, keeping the nails as close to the center of the guide rails as possible, so they never come in contact with the planer knives. Then run the assembly through the planer, alternating the sides: the top should be up on the first pass, down on the second, and so on, until the board is flat. The guide rails will keep the board perfectly aligned. You can use the same technique for flattening lumber on a wide belt sander.

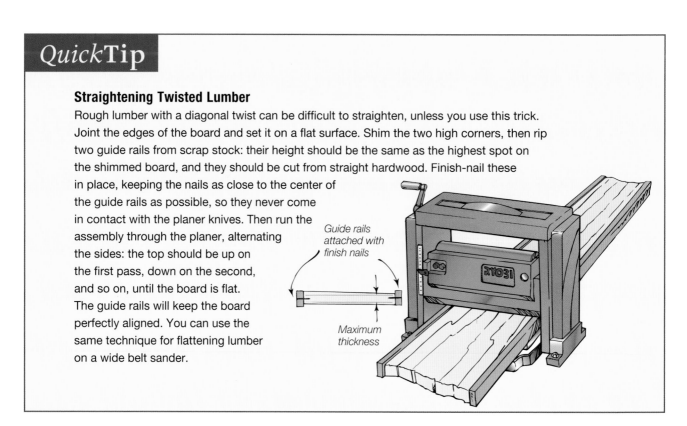

Guide rails attached with finish nails

Maximum thickness

Once the pin is adjusted properly, the first series of pins and slots can be cut across the first workpiece (left photo, above).

After the last cut, clamp this piece to the jig fence and use it to index the first cut on the mating part, as shown in the right photo, above.

We used electrical connectors (wire nuts) as knobs on these adjustment screws.

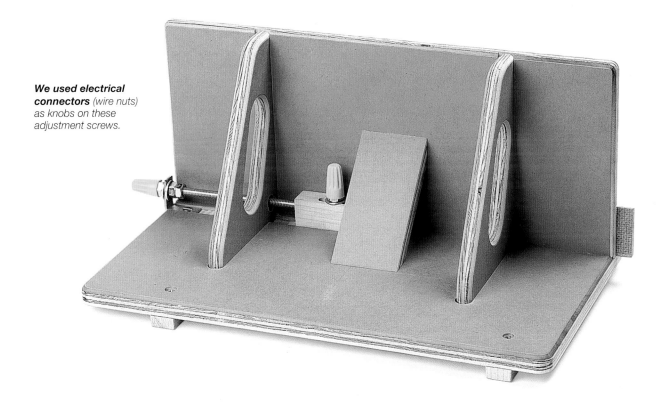

miter slots, and use a square against the saw's fence to ensure the jig and runners will be square to the blade. For safety, add a guard (piece 12) where the blade comes through the fence to keep the blade covered during use.

Cutting Box Joints

Using the jig couldn't be simpler. Set up your dado blade to match your desired pin and slot thickness, and raise it to the correct slot depth. Slide the backer out of the way, loosen the clamping knob on the pin block, and turn the adjusting knob until the pin is the proper distance from the dado blade. (It helps to fit a spacer between the pin block and blade that matches the joint pin thickness.) Retighten the clamping knob and slide the backer up to the pin. Cut a pair of test parts from the same thickness wood you'll use for the finished joints. If the spacing is off, re-adjust the pin slightly.

From here on, use the jig just like any other box joint jig. The next time you need to set up a different joint spacing, simply trim off the cut end of the backer (you can do this several times) and slide it back into place.

OUTFEED/ASSEMBLY TABLE

A must for every shop with space limitations, this project is an outfeed table for your saw that transforms into a low-height assembly table for your larger projects. It also provides plenty of storage for blades and saw accessories. The design is perfectly suited for contractor's saws with motors that extend behind the base.

by John English

Working in a one-man shop can have its drawbacks. We all know what handling large sheets of plywood or MDF alone on a table saw is like: It's not only awkward, it can be dangerous. An outfeed table is essential, but it takes up a lot of room, especially in a small shop situation.

Most of us don't have a comfortable place to assemble large projects, either. Your workbench may be too high while the floor is too low. This outfeed table unit solves both problems: it does double-duty as outfeed support for your table saw while also being a low assembly bench. Dual functionality makes it perfect for a small shop.

The outfeed/assembly table has a pair of extra-deep drawers for storing saw accessories such as push sticks, earplugs and table inserts. But my favorite feature is the blade storage caddy that includes a special space for a dado set. This portable caddy is a safe and convenient device for carrying blades to the sharpener's shop.

Making the Tabletop

I used white oak with walnut accents to build this piece, but any stable hardwood would do. To make the tabletop, cut all the parts to size according to the dimensions given in the Material List on page 32, then install a ⅜" dado cutter in your table saw. Using a 12" high auxiliary fence, create spline slots on the ends of the side aprons (pieces 1). Now use your miter gauge to make matching dadoes in the faces of the front and back aprons (pieces 2) at the locations indicated on the Technical Drawings (see page 38). Glue your apron splines (pieces 3) in place and check the subassembly for squareness by measuring diagonally. When both measurements are the same, tighten your clamps.

The next step is to create the rabbet for the particleboard tabletop (piece 4) with your router. Run a ¾"-deep by ⁷⁄₁₆"-wide rabbet all the way around the inside edge of the frame. Round the corners of the tabletop to match, then glue top into place.

As an outfeed table, this dual-purpose project keeps large panels or long boards from tipping off the saw. Dropped down into an assembly station, it brings larger projects within easier reach and saves a lot of backache.

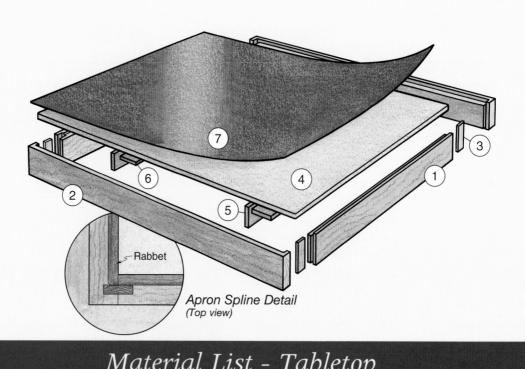

Rabbet

Apron Spline Detail
(Top view)

Material List - Tabletop

	T x W x L		T x W x L
1 Side Aprons (2)	1¼" x 3⅞" x 27½"	**5** Tabletop Supports (2)	¾" x 2⅞" x 24"
2 Front and Back Aprons (2)	1¼" x 3⅞" x 42"	**6** Support Cleats (2)	¾" x 2⅞" x 24"
3 Apron Splines (4	⅜" x 1¼" x 3⅞"	**7** Tabletop Laminate (1)	1⁄16" x 31" x 43"
4 Tabletop (1)	¾" x 28⅜" x 40⅜"		

Applying Plastic Laminate

Working with laminate is not too complicated, but you should keep in mind that the adhesive is very unforgiving. The plastic must be positioned correctly the first time. Once contact is made, it can't be repositioned.

Use dowels or thin sticks to separate the two surfaces while positioning laminate on the substrate. Remove them one at a time, starting in the center.

Expose as little of the bit as possible for a clean, safe, error-free cut. Work in a counterclockwise direction at a constant speed to avoid burning or chatter marks.

Next, install the tabletop supports (pieces 5) and their cleats (pieces 6). Screw and glue the cleats to the supports and position them on the underside of the tabletop as shown in the Technical Drawings. Screw the cleats to the underside of the top using 1¼" wallboard screws. Countersink the heads, but don't go too deep or the screws will interfere with installing the laminate. Also make sure that the screws don't fall where the miter slot extension grooves will be cut in later.

Applying the Plastic Laminate

If you haven't worked with laminate before, the process may sound more difficult than it really is. The first thing you need to do is check that the joint between the aprons and the tabletop is flat, and sand it if necessary.

You can use a brush to apply your contact cement, but we've had much better luck using a serrated trowel. Spread a coat of cement on the tabletop and your laminate (piece 7), and let it dry to the touch. Place dowels or thin sticks about every eight inches along the tabletop as shown in the tint box on the previous page, and gently lay the laminate in position, centering it over the top. If you followed the Material List, you'll notice that the laminate is 1" longer and wider than the tabletop to allow for trimming. Remember that the adhesive bonds on contact, so there is no room for mistakes: You must have everything lined up right the first time.

Working from the center out, remove the dowels and press the laminate down firmly. When the last dowels are removed, roll the entire surface with a 3"-wide hand roller, applying heavy pressure from the center out to the edges.

Before trimming, it's important to use a scraper to remove any adhesive that ran down the sides of the tabletop: The laminate-trimming bit in your router must have a clean surface to run against. Keep in mind that a minimum amount of the bit's cutting edge should be exposed to reduce the possibility of damage in case the router tips.

Making the Base Frames

The front and back of the base are frames with floating panels. Their stiles and rails receive ¾"-wide grooves (see Technical Drawings) that house both the panels and splines. Forming those ⁷⁄₁₆"-deep grooves is the first milling process and it is done with a dado set in the table saw.

The front and back rails (pieces 8) are milled along their full length, as are the short stiles (pieces 9). However, the cuts on the long stiles (pieces 10) are stopped at the 14" mark. This is because these two stiles extend beyond the bottom rails and become the assembly table's legs. After the grooves are made, square their ends with a sharp chisel.

Now chamfer the bottoms of the long stiles, and you're ready for assembly.

Assemble the frames and panels using the base splines (pieces 11) and glue, but don't glue the panels (pieces 12) in place—they float freely to allow for expansion and contraction. Be sure to check for squareness as you tighten the clamps.

QuickTip

Flush your Dust!
A commode floor flange fits a 4" dust collector hose perfectly. Screw one to a piece of ¾" plywood in order to hook up your contractor's saw to your dust collection system. This low-cost coupling will cost you about $5.

Plywood with hole

Commode floor flange

Base Exploded View

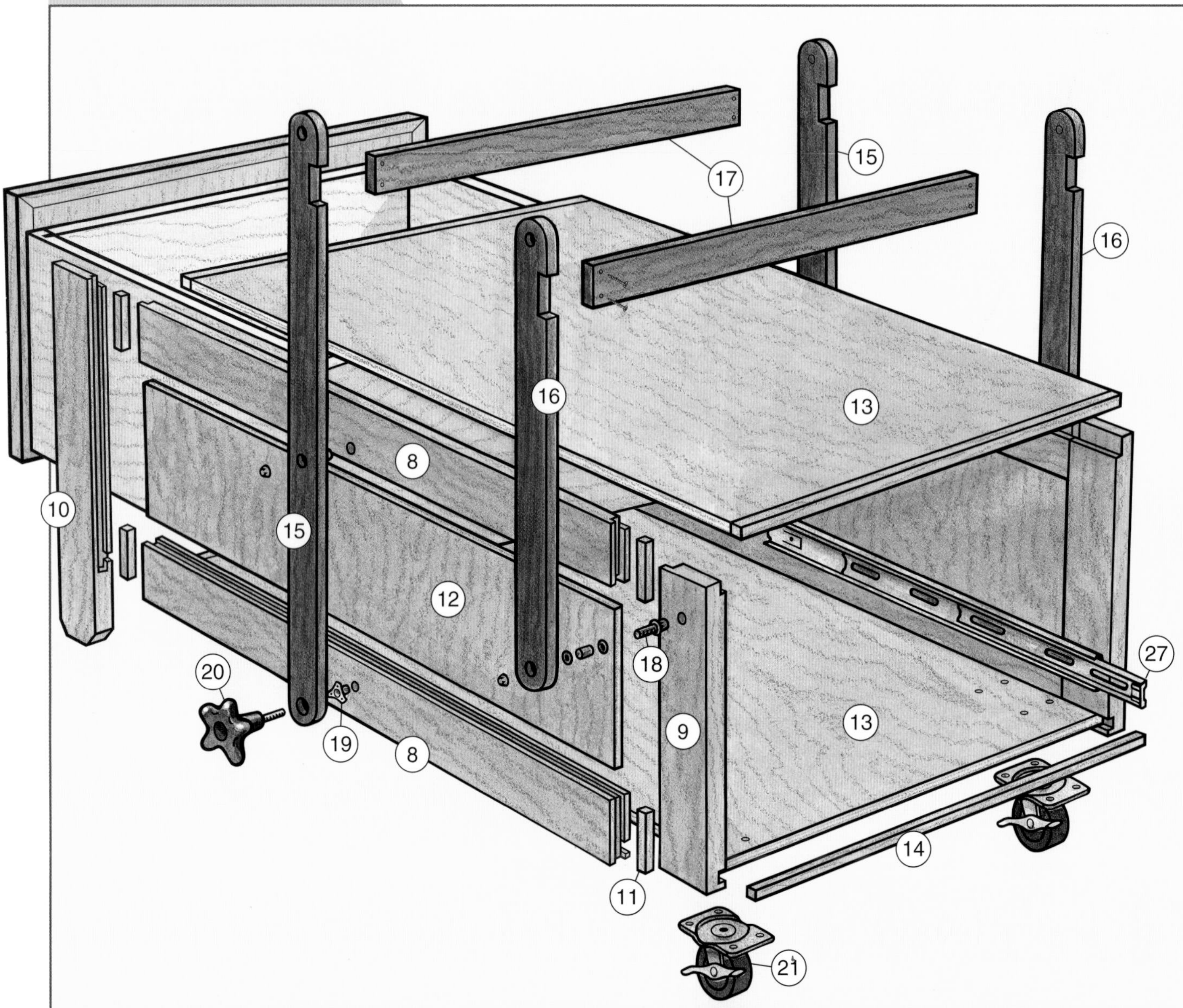

Material List - Base

	T x W x L		T x W x L
8 Front and Back Rails (4)	1¼" x 3" x 32"	**18** Pivot Hinges (4 pairs)	Rust-resistant
9 Short Stiles (2)	1¼" x 3" x 14"	**19** Threaded Inserts (2)	Screw-on T-nuts
10 Long Stiles (2)	1¼" x 3" x 17¾"	**20** Star Knobs (2)	5⁄16" x 1" Stud
11 Base Splines (8)	¾" x ¾" x 2⁹⁄16"	**21** Heavy-duty Locking Casters (2)	3" Dia.
12 Front and Back Panels (2)	¾" x 32¾" x 8¾"	**22** Drawer Sides (4)	¾" x 10½" x 17¾"
13 Base Top and Bottom (2)	¾" x 23⅝" x 36½"	**23** Drawer Fronts and Backs (4)	¾" x 10½" x 21⅛"
14 Top and Bottom Edging (1)	¾" x ¾" x 96"	**24** Drawer Bottoms (2)	¼" x 21¹⁄16 " x 16¹⁵⁄16 "
15 Long Pivot Arms* (2)	¾" x 2½" x 29⅛ "	**25** Drawer Faces (2)	¾" x 21¼" x 10¾"
16 Short Pivot Arms* (2)	¾" x 2½" x 18⅝"	**26** Drawer Face Edging (1)	¾" x ¾" x 144"
17 Stretchers (2)	¾" x 2½" x 27¼"	**27** Drawer Slides (2 pairs)	18" Full Extension

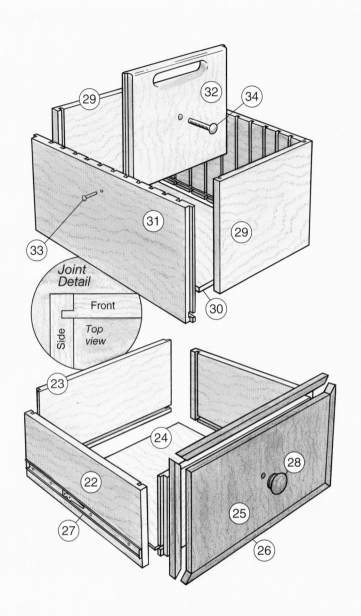

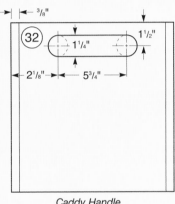

Caddy Handle
Elevation

Material List - Drawer/Caddy

		T x W x L			T x W x L
28	Drawer Knobs (2)	2" Dia.	**33**	Handle Locking Pins (2)	2⅜" x ¼" Tie Pegs
29	Caddy Sides (2)	¾" x 11" x 10¾"	**34**	Dado Blade Holder (1)	½" x 2" Carriage Bolt and Nut
30	Caddy Bottom (1)	½" x 9¹⁵⁄₁₆" x 19"			
31	Caddy Front and Back (2)	¾" x 11" x 19⅛"			
32	Caddy Handle (1)	¾" x 9¹⁵⁄₁₆" x 10"			

* Lengths shown are for a 34"-high table saw.
Adjust this dimension to fit your saw.

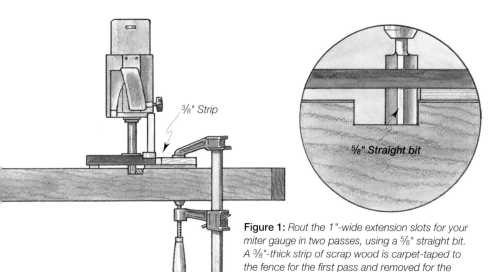

Figure 1: *Rout the 1"-wide extension slots for your miter gauge in two passes, using a ⅝" straight bit. A ⅜"-thick strip of scrap wood is carpet-taped to the fence for the first pass and removed for the second pass.*

⅜" Strip

⅝" *Straight bit*

Once these two subassemblies are dry, go back to the dado cutter and mill the rabbets for the base top (piece 13) and the grooves for the base bottom (also piece 13) as shown in the Technical Drawings. To prevent chip-out, be sure to back up these cuts with some scrap.

Attach edging (piece 14) to the base top and bottom with glue and finish nails, drilling pilot holes through the oak for the nails. Set the nail heads, fill the holes and sand the edging flush. Complete the base carcass by gluing and clamping the top and bottom to the front and back, checking for squareness as you go.

Building the Drawers

I used aspen to make the drawer sides (pieces 22) and the fronts and backs (pieces 23). Cut them to size and mill the ¼"-wide by ⅜"-deep grooves that hold the bottoms (pieces 24). Stop the grooves on the fronts and backs ⅜" from each end.

Now create a ¼"-thick by ⅜" tongue on each end of the drawer fronts and backs. These tongues fit into the dadoes on the drawer sides (see

Technical Drawings for locations). Cut these dadoes on your table saw, and you are ready to assemble the drawers with glue and clamps. Remember to measure diagonally for squareness, and don't glue the drawer bottoms.

The drawer faces are plywood panels (pieces 25) that are edged with mitered solid oak (piece 26). Make the faces now, but don't attach them until the drawers have been installed—that way you can align them perfectly. Installing the drawers is a matter of following the instructions that come with the drawer slides (pieces 27). However, before you can install them, you'll need to attach the casters (pieces 21), so that you're working on a level surface.

Once the drawers are in, align the faces and secure them from the back with screws. Install the knobs (pieces 28) next and you're ready to make the removable blade caddy.

Constructing the Blade Caddy

Making the caddy is fairly easy because it uses the same dado setup several times. It is sized for ten 10" blades and an 8" dado set, but you can change that to suit your own saw or collection of blades.

With the parts cut to size, plow two vertical dadoes on the inside face of the sides (pieces 29), using a ¼"-wide dado head set for a ⅜"-deep cut (see Joint Detail on page 35). Next, cut the dadoes for the blades and handle. The first two cuts run down the inside center of the front and back (pieces 31), then additional cuts are made to the left and right, each 1½" on center from its neighbor.

The last operation to perform with this setup is making the grooves on the bottom of the front and back to hold the caddy bottom (piece 30). Because you're using a ¼" dado, you'll have to take two passes. The corresponding grooves in the sides are best done on a router table, as these are stopped at each end.

Now it's time to make the tongues on the ends of the front and back. Raise the blade height to ½" and set the fence for a ⅜" cut, making two passes with the miter gauge.

With the same setup, create the rabbets on both ends of the caddy handle (piece 32). Now use the elevation drawing on page 35 to create the cutout for the handle. This handle slips into the center groove and is held in place with two wooden locking pins (pieces 33). Inserting the pins allows you to take the caddy out of the drawer (perhaps for a trip to the sharpener). Your dado set mounts on the handle with a carriage bolt and nut (pieces 34).

Making the Pivot Arms

Making the pivot arms (pieces 15 and 16) the correct length is not really as complicated as it seems. The dimensions given in the Material List are for a saw that is 34" high, so adjust that measurement to suit your saw. For example, if your saw is 36" high, add 2" to each arm. With that length

Connecting the Table to the Base

With all the parts made, there's still one step left—connecting the top to the base. Since saw heights vary, some of the hinge locations have to be determined during assembly. But first, check the Technical Drawings for the known hinge and scribed line locations. Transfer these to the inside of the table aprons and the upper base rails, drill the holes and install the pivot hinges (see illustration, right) and arms.

To find the location for the lower hinge on the long arm, center the table on the base and move the arm in an arc until the hole for the hinge intersects the scribed line on the base rail. Mark this location, repeat the procedure on the other side, drill the holes in the rails and install the hinges, as shown in Step 1.

To establish the threaded insert location, begin by elevating the top to its full outfeed height, as shown in Step 2. Keeping the top level, use an awl to mark the insert location on the bottom rail. Use a framing square to keep the arm perpendicular during this operation. Drill the holes, install inserts and lock both arms in the up position with the star knobs.

The pivot hinge is one of the most versatile pieces of hardware available for shop projects.

the

To find your final pivot hinge location on the inside of the table apron, simply measure the distance between the two hinges on the base rail (shown as A below) and transfer this measurement to the scribed line on the inside of the apron. With that point established, you can drill for the final hinges.

The last step is to glue and screw the two stretchers (pieces 17) in place to stabilize to the assembly.

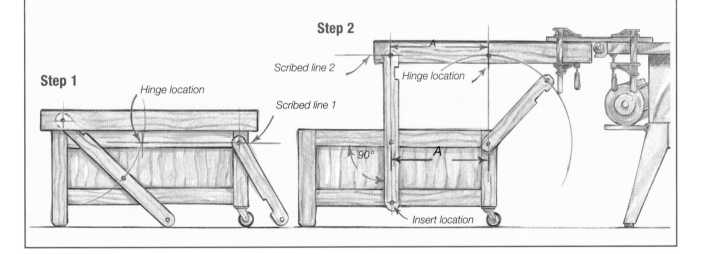

Step 1

Hinge location

Step 2

Scribed line 2

Scribed line 1

Hinge location

90°

A

A

Insert location

determined, cut the arms to size. Use your bandsaw to round both ends of each arm, then sand the kerf marks. You can now use the Pivot Arms detail on page 39 to mark the drilling locations for your hardware. While you're at it, lay out the cuts for the two stretchers (pieces 17).

Follow the instructions that come with the pivot hinges (pieces 18) and drill the arms at the locations you just marked. Remember that the top hinges are installed on the outsides of the arms, while the bottom ones are located on the insides. Then, using your bandsaw, make the cuts that house the stretchers.

Refer to the sidebar, above, for your final assembly instructions. Once the table is all together, roll it over to your saw to lay out and cut the miter slot extensions, as shown in Figure 1, page 36. With that done, you can wrap up your outfeed/assembly table with three coats of a durable finish, then go to work on all those large projects your small shop couldn't handle. Now you've got support to spare.

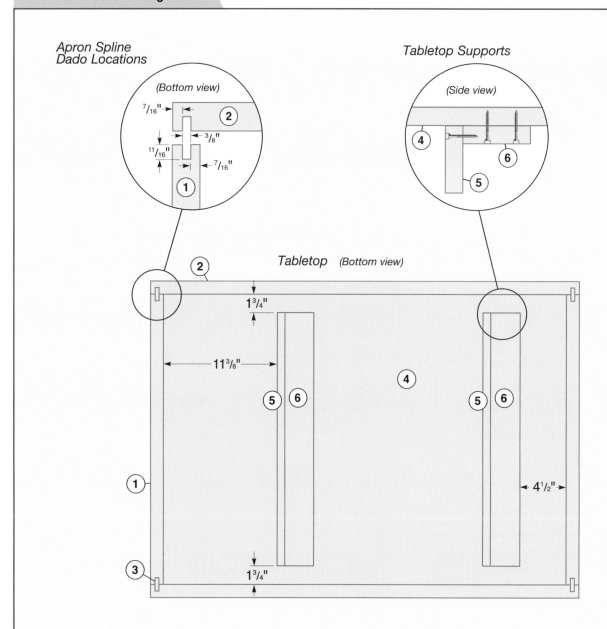

*Apron Spline
Dado Locations*

(Bottom view)

$^7/_{16}$"

$^3/_8$"

$^{11}/_{16}$"

$^7/_{16}$"

Tabletop Supports

(Side view)

Tabletop (Bottom view)

1$^3/_4$"

11$^3/_8$"

4$^1/_2$"

1$^3/_4$"

Drawer Assembly

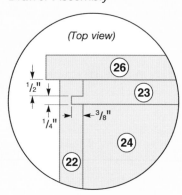

(Top view)

$^1/_2$"

$^1/_4$"

$^3/_8$"

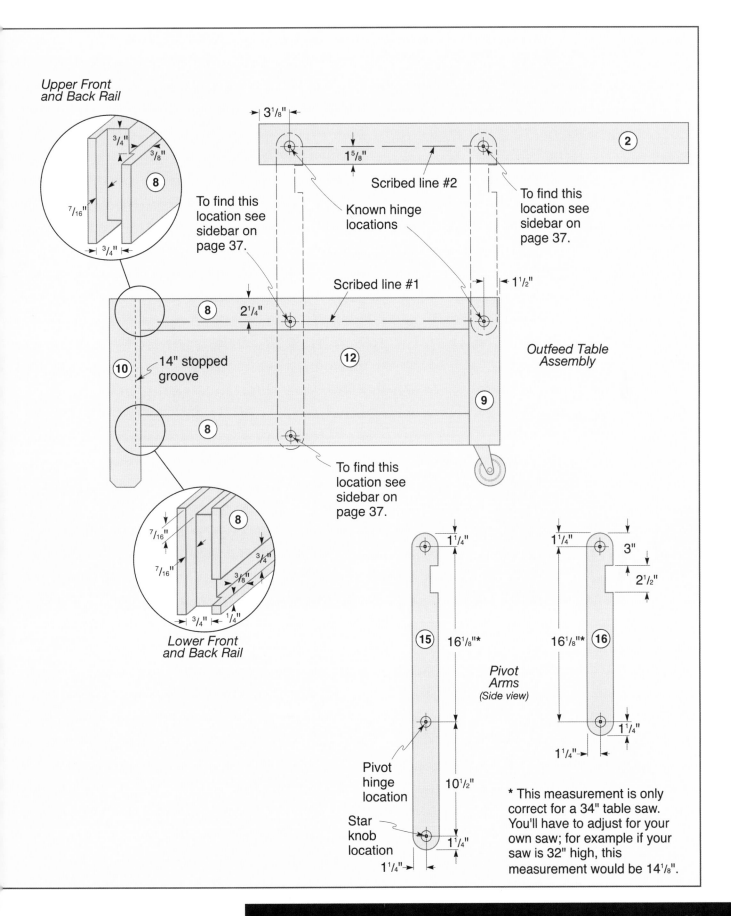

Upper Front and Back Rail

3/4"
3/8"
7/16"
3/4"
⑧

3 1/8"
1 5/8"
②
Scribed line #2
To find this location see sidebar on page 37.
Known hinge locations
To find this location see sidebar on page 37.
Scribed line #1
1 1/2"

To find this location see sidebar on page 37.

⑧ 2 1/4"
⑩ 14" stopped groove
⑫
Outfeed Table Assembly
⑨
⑧

To find this location see sidebar on page 37.

7/16"
7/16"
3/4"
3/8"
3/4"
1/4"
⑧
Lower Front and Back Rail

1 1/4"
⑮ 16 1/8"*
Pivot hinge location
10 1/2"
Star knob location
1 1/4"
1 1/4"

1 1/4" 3"
2 1/2"
16 1/8"* ⑯
1 1/4"
1 1/4"

Pivot Arms (Side view)

* This measurement is only correct for a 34" table saw. You'll have to adjust for your own saw; for example if your saw is 32" high, this measurement would be 14 1/8".

by Rob Johnstone

SHOP-BUILT PANEL SAW

Get the accuracy the pros are used to at less than half the cost.
Our aluminum sliding system is the key to success.

While renovating my 1906 home, I realized that what I really needed on site was a panel saw. Every job I tackled seemed to involve cutting large panels on the table saw. Working on my own, this was gruelling and dangerous work. But panel saws aren't cheap: basic models run about fifteen hundred dollars. The only realistic option was to build one of my own, and now you can, too.

One of the big advantages to a panel saw like this one is you move the circular saw, not the workpiece, making it much easier for one person to handle large sheet materials. You can crosscut panels in the standard mode, or rotate the saw 90° to rip sheets of plywood. Any 7¼" circular saw will work with this design except worm drive saws. They won't fit the carriage.

By making an additional mounting plate for the sliding carriage, you'll be able to install a portable router in your panel saw as well. This opens the door to cutting grooves, rabbets, dadoes and even decorative designs for doors and cabinet panels. I recommend dedicating one mounting plate to a saw and another to a router. You'll soon wonder how you ever got along without a panel saw.

Easel Does It

The main component of the panel saw is a plywood frame, rather like an artist's easel, that supports both the work being cut and the saw carriage. For this frame I chose appleply, a voidless, veneer-core product that is durable and dimensionally stable. It's sometimes also called Baltic birch plywood.

After cutting all the parts to size (see the Material List on page 43), get started by attaching the column returns (pieces 3) to the edges of the center and side columns (pieces 1 and 2) with glue and screws. Next, glue the base (piece 4) to the base plate (piece 5) and secure it with screws driven though from the back.

Sawdust accumulation is a problem with some panel saws, and I dealt with this by providing a series of dadoes in the bed beam (piece 6), through which excess dust can escape. Cut these dadoes on your table saw using a ¾" dado head, following the locations given on the drawings on page 42. Then glue and screw the bed (piece 7) to the bed beam.

With the ¾" dado head in your saw, go ahead and plow a groove in the lower cross support (piece 8) for some T-track that will be installed later (see drawings on page 42). Stop the groove 48" into the piece. The upper cross supports (pieces 9) are not grooved. Rip the cross trim (pieces 10) from ¾" walnut stock, then glue and clamp them in place. Scrape the excess cured glue and sand the faces of all the pieces, then glue the two halves of the top stretcher (pieces 11) together.

Build the Body

As you assemble the body of the saw, it's important to keep all structural members absolutely square. Begin the process by marking center lines across the back of the top stretcher and the base assembly, then lay both pieces face down on a flat floor, edge to edge with their center lines matched up. Mark the locations of the columns on both pieces (see drawings on page 42), then separate the parts and set the columns in place. Square up all five pieces using a large square, then glue and screw the columns to the top stretcher and base assembly, as shown in Figure 1.

After the glue dries, set this assembly upright to attach the bed beam and cross supports (see drawings on page 42 for locations). Drive the screws in from the back of the columns and use scrap spacers (see Figure 2) as you glue, clamp and screw them in place.

Temporarily clamp the angle supports (pieces 12) in place at the

Figure 1: *When working on larger assemblies like this panel saw, keep a square handy as you glue and screw each piece together.*

Figure 2: *Spacers are an absolute necessity when aligning the horizontal members on a frame this large. To ensure accuracy, be sure your spacers are true along their full length.*

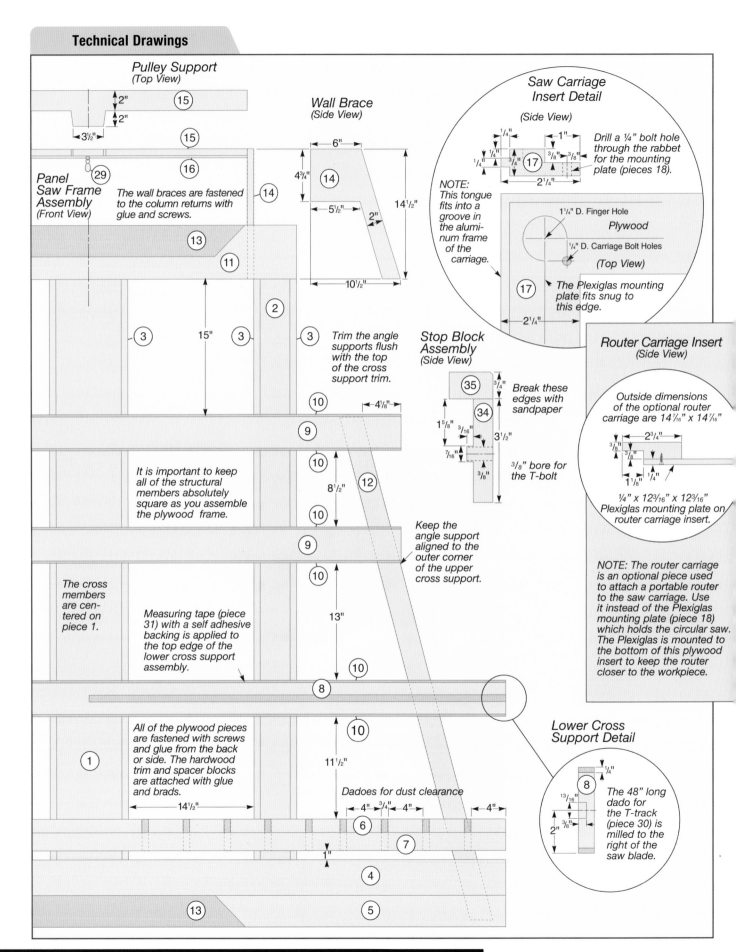

Pulley Support
(Top View)

2"
2"
3½"

15

15

16

**Panel
Saw Frame
Assembly**
(Front View)

29

The wall braces are fastened to the column returns with glue and screws.

13

11

Wall Brace
(Side View)

6"

4¾"

14

5½"

2"

14½"

10½"

14

2

3

3

3

15"

Trim the angle supports flush with the top of the cross support trim.

10

4⅛"

9

It is important to keep all of the structural members absolutely square as you assemble the plywood frame.

10

8½"

12

10

9

Keep the angle support aligned to the outer corner of the upper cross support.

The cross members are centered on piece 1.

10

Measuring tape (piece 31) with a self adhesive backing is applied to the top edge of the lower cross support assembly.

13"

10

All of the plywood pieces are fastened with screws and glue from the back or side. The hardwood trim and spacer blocks are attached with glue and brads.

1

8

10

11½"

14½"

Dadoes for dust clearance

4" ¾" 4"

4"

6

7

1"

4

13

5

**Saw Carriage
Insert Detail**
(Side View)

¼"
¼"
¼"
¾"
1"
⅜" ⅜"

17

Drill a ¼" bolt hole through the rabbet for the mounting plate (pieces 18).

2¼"

NOTE: This tongue fits into a groove in the aluminum frame of the carriage.

1¼" D. Finger Hole

Plywood

¼" D. Carriage Bolt Holes

(Top View)

17

The Plexiglas mounting plate fits snug to this edge.

2¼"

**Stop Block
Assembly**
(Side View)

35

¾"

34

Break these edges with sandpaper

1⅝" 3/16"

7/16"

3½"

⅜"

⅜" bore for the T-bolt

Router Carriage Insert
(Side View)

Outside dimensions of the optional router carriage are 14 7/16" x 14 7/16"

⅜"

2¾"
3/16"

1⅛" ¼"

¼" x 12 3/16" x 12 3/16" Plexiglas mounting plate on router carriage insert.

NOTE: The router carriage is an optional piece used to attach a portable router to the saw carriage. Use it instead of the Plexiglas mounting plate (piece 18) which holds the circular saw. The Plexiglas is mounted to the bottom of this plywood insert to keep the router closer to the workpiece.

**Lower Cross
Support Detail**

¼"

8

13/16"

2"

⅜"

The 48" long dado for the T-track (piece 30) is milled to the right of the saw blade.

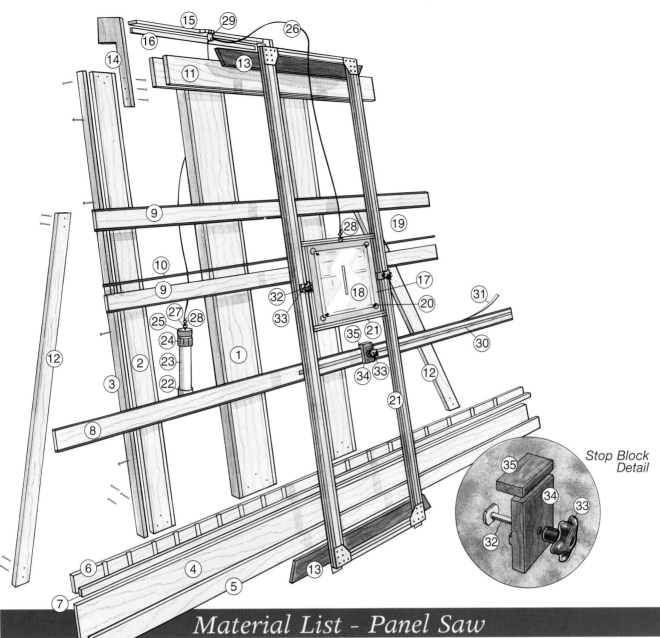

Stop Block Detail

Material List - Panel Saw

		T x W x L
1	Center Column (1)	¾" x 7½" x 78"
2	Side Columns (2)	¾" x 3½" x 78"
3	Column Returns (6)	¾" x 1½" x 78"
4	Base (1)	¾" x 7½" x 96"
5	Base Plate (1)	¾" x 3½" x 96"
6	Bed Beam (1)	¾" x 3½" x 96"
7	Bed (1)	¾" x 2" x 96"
8	Lower Cross support (1)	¾" x 3½" x 96"
9	Upper Cross Supports (2)	¾" x 3½" x 72"
10	Cross Trim (6)	¼" x ¾" x 96
11	Top Stretchers (2)	¾" x 6" x 48"
12	Angle Supports (2)	¾" x 2½" x 58½"
13	Spacer Blocks (2)	½" x 3½" x 36"
14	Wall Braces (2)	¾" x 10½" x 14½"
15	Pulley Support (1)	¾" x 4" x 36½"
16	Support Brace (1)	¾" x 1" x 36½"
17	Carriage Insert (1)	¾" x 17¼" x 17¼"

			T x W x L
18	Mounting Plate (1)	Plexiglas	¼" x 14⁷⁄₁₆" x 14⁷⁄₁₆"
19	Carriage Bolts (4)		1" x ¼" x 20
20	Easy Grip Knobs (4)		⅞" x ¼-20
21	Extruded Alum. Kit (1)		Instructions with kit
22	Cap (1)		2" pvc
23	Pipe (1)		2" x 12" pvc
24	Coupling (1)		2" threaded pvc
25	Threaded Cap (1)		2" threaded pvc
26	Cable (1)		⅛" x 96" braided
27	Eye Bolts and Nuts (2)		¼"
28	Cable Clamps (2)		small
29	Pulley (1)		2"
30	T-Track (1)		40"
31	Measuring Tape (1)		Self adhesive
32	T-Bolt (1)		¹⁵⁄₁₆" x 1½"
33	Star Knob (1)		¹⁵⁄₁₆" threaded
34	Stop Block (1)		¾" x 2⅞" x 3½"
35	Stop Top (1)		¾" x 1¼" x 3½"

Installing Threaded Brass Inserts

Brass inserts are easy to cross-thread or damage if you don't have a screwdriver large enough to fit the slot on top of the insert. One solution is to thread three inserts on a round-head, slotted machine screw as shown in the sketch.

Then drill a clearance hole through a piece of scrap that's twice as thick as one insert to act as a guide. Screw the entire assembly into the hole in the scrap, positioned over the hole in your workpiece. Stop driving the screw when the screw head reaches the block. Then back out the machine screw together with the two remaining inserts. The third insert remains perfectly embedded in your workpiece.

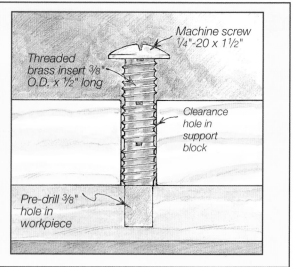

Machine screw ¼"-20 x 1½"

Threaded brass insert ⅜" O.D. x ½" long

Clearance hole in support block

Pre-drill ⅜" hole in workpiece

---

positions shown on page 42. Transfer the locations of the cross supports onto the angle supports, then disassemble them and trim them at these angles using your power miter box. Clamp the angle supports back in place and secure each piece with screws.

Supporting Cast

Two walnut spacer blocks (pieces 13) separate the frame from the aluminum track assembly that holds the saw. Cut these spacers from ½" stock, trim their ends at an angle with your power miter box (see drawings on page 42), then glue and clamp them in place. Next, cut the wall braces and the pulley support (pieces 14 and 15) to shape, and glue and screw them together. Glue and nail the support brace (piece 16) in place and install the entire brace subassembly onto the saw body.

A Carriage Built for Two

A plywood carriage insert (piece 17), installed in an aluminum frame, holds interchangeable Plexiglas™ mounting plates in place. Begin machining this insert by cutting ¼" rabbets on all its edges, then miter the corners (see drawings on page 42). Cut the center out by raising your table saw blade through it and complete these cuts with a handsaw. Drill finger spaces at the corners with a 1¼" Forstner bit and make the interior rabbet on your router table, following the dimensions provided in the drawings on page 42.

Drill a ¼" hole at each corner for carriage bolts (pieces 19) that hold the mounting plate (piece 18) in place. The mounting plate itself

Figure 3: *The plywood carriage insert fits a traveling aluminum frame. In turn, the saw is mounted to a Plexiglas plate, which is attached to the insert with threaded knobs.*

Figure 4: *After installing the pulley (inset), set the counterweight on a spacer and, with the saw at its highest position, attach the cable. Adjust the counterweight to equal the weight of the saw and carriage.*

is cut from ¼" thick Plexiglas™. Each corner receives a ⅜" hole to match the ¼" bolt holes on the carriage insert. Test fit the Plexiglas in the insert, then epoxy the carriage bolts in place.

I used Easy Grip knobs (pieces 20) to hold the bolts in place while the epoxy cured.

Follow the instructions provided with the Extruded Aluminum Kit, piece 21 (available from www.rockler.com, 800-610-0883), to assemble three sides of the aluminum carriage frame. Slide in the carriage insert and add the fourth side (see Figure 3), then attach an eye bolt to the carriage.

The Works

Turn again to the kit instructions to assemble the larger aluminum frame. As you did earlier, be sure to insert the carriage assembly before you add the fourth side. Center the completed large frame on the saw body, then secure it to the top and bottom with screws driven through the angle brackets and spacer blocks. The large frame can be squared up by slightly loosening the corner brackets, sliding one end to the right or left, then retightening.

Weights and Measures

A critical component of a panel saw is the counterweight that helps the carriage slide easier. I made this counterweight by gluing a cap and threaded coupling to a length of PVC pipe (pieces 22, 23 and 24). The result is a tube with one threaded end and one capped end. Now drill a hole in a threaded cap (piece 25) and add an eye bolt (piece 27) for the cable (piece 26). Fill the tube with sand and lightly screw the threaded cap onto the pipe. Attach the pulley (piece 29) to the pulley support, then thread the cable through the pulley and connect it to the carriage and the counterweight with cable clamps (pieces 28), as shown in Figure 4. Attach your circular saw to the mounting plate using ½" machine bolts in holes drilled through the saw's base and the Plexiglas mounting plate. Be sure the saw is mounted squarely.

Stick the self-adhesive measuring tape (piece 31) on the top edge of the low cross support and install the T-slot track (piece 30) in the dado you cut earlier. A T-bolt and star knob (pieces 32 and 33) are used to secure an adjustable L-shaped ¾" thick stop (pieces 34 and 35) to the track. This stop is machined to fit the T-slot track, as shown in the drawings on page 42. Assemble the stop with glue and nails, drill a ⅜" hole through it for the T-bolt and install the bolt and knob, as shown in the Stop Block Detail on page 43.

A separate plate can be made for the router to cut grooves and dadoes in your sheet stock. Be sure to clamp your stock in place when routing.

Finishing Up

I finished this project with Nordic Oil, both to protect the wood and to help control dust. You could also use any varnish you have on hand. With that done, you'll need to decide whether you want to mount your saw to the wall or floor. One good way to handle this is to mount a cleat to the wall between the wall braces (pieces 14), and then screw the supports to this cleat.

Once the panel saw is mounted where you want it, you'll never have to grimace at the thought of cutting sheet goods again. And you can relish in the glory of having saved a bunch of hard-earned shop dollars, too.

QuickTip

Handy Thumbnuts When Needed

Sometimes when constructing woodshop jigs, it's handy to use thumbnuts. They're especially great for tightening shop-made holding clamps. If you can't find thumbnuts at your local hardware store or woodworking supplier, you can make any size you need by using round head stove bolts and flat washers.

First grind a small flat spot on the edge of a washer.

Then epoxy the washer into the slotted head of a stove bolt.

First grind a small flat spot on the edge of the washer, then secure it to the bolt by fitting the flat spot into the bolt head slot and anchoring it with epoxy. You could also solder the washer to the bolt for a more permanent joint.

QuickTip

Hardwood

Screw and glue

Improving Your Framing Square

With the addition of two wood strips you can make that old friend the framing square even more versatile. Glue and screw two perfectly square hardwood strips, as shown, making sure that they are exactly parallel to the metal edge. You'll now find it much easier – and more accurate – to square across a board. Your new, improved square will also stand on its own when set on the wooden edges. If weight is a consideration, start with an aluminum square rather than steel.

by John English

The author's miter saw stand
features fold-down wings, casters
and integral dust collection.

MITER SAW STATION

Miter saws deserve a full-time workstation to do their best work. Unfortunately, most of us don't have six or eight feet of wall space to dedicate to one tool. This rolling cabinet with tip-up extension wings makes the perfect solution for tight space; just roll it out and flip up the wings when you need the saw, and fold them down for effective storage against a wall when you're through.

Space is at a premium in every shop I've ever been in, and yours is probably no exception. If you own a miter saw, it really should have a solid working surface with supports on either side. But it's hard to justify devoting so much space to one benchtop tool when others, such as mortising machines or benchtop drill presses, also compete for space.

The inspiration for this miter saw station actually came from a previous routing system built by contributing editor Rick White. Like this saw station, Rick's router table featured fold-down wing extensions and rolled out of the way easily. This unit also incorporates built-in dust collection and a drawer to store the rollers that are integral to the design.

This saw station is essentially a cabinet on wheels, and each side is made up of two stiles, two rails and a panel (pieces 1 through 3). Check the Material List on page 49 for dimensions, and begin construction by cutting and jointing these parts to size.

The rails are joined to the stiles by tongue-and-groove, as shown in the illustration on this page and in the Side Joinery Detail Drawing on the next page. Form tongues on the ends of the rails using either a dado head in the table saw or a router mounted in a table. Make several passes, increasing the depth of cut slightly each time until you reach the final depth.

Plow a through groove in one face of each stile. This must be done on the router because it is a stepped groove:

Side Panel Joint Exploded View

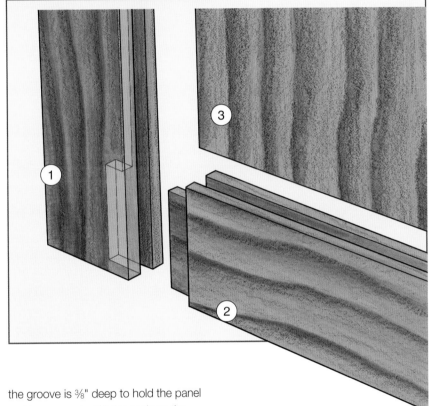

the groove is ⅜" deep to hold the panel and increases to ¾" deep where the rail tongues join the stiles. This almost doubles the glue areas and the strength of the joints.

Assemble the rails, stiles and panels with glue and clamps, but glue just the corner joints. After the glue dries, use a ¾" straight bit to plow a ¼"-deep stopped rabbet in each side for the cabinet bottom (piece 4). Glue and clamp the bottom in place, and make sure it is square to the sides.

Continuing the Carcass

The back of the cabinet (piece 5) is held in place with three U-shaped mitered moldings (pieces 6 and 7). These are ripped to size, then a groove is plowed in one edge of each, using a dado head in the table saw. Miter the moldings to fit and use glue and clamps to attach one piece to the top face of the cabinet bottom, flush against the back edge. Secure two more lengths of molding to the sides (only their bottom ends are

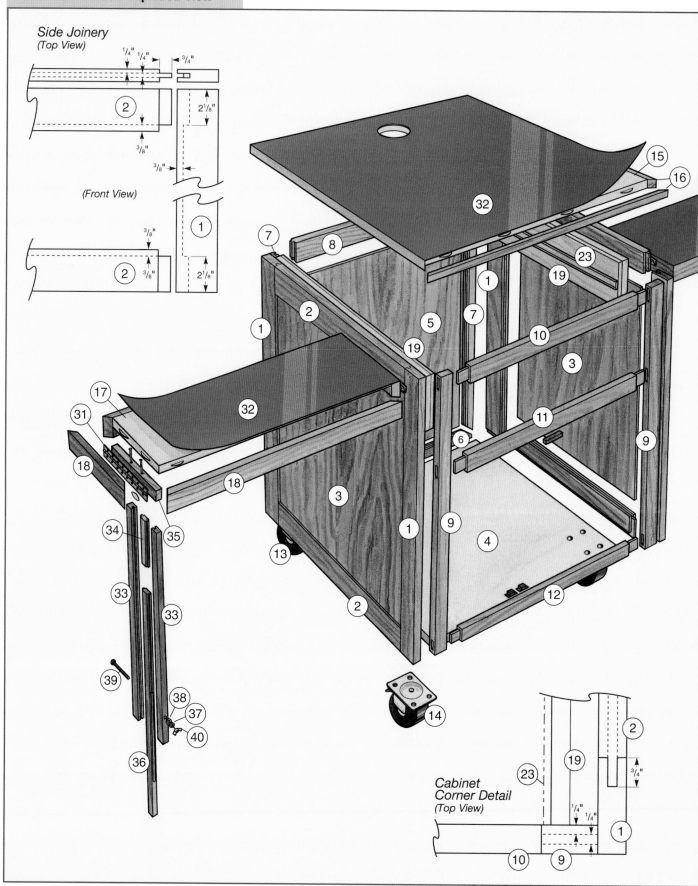

Side Joinery
(Top View)

(Front View)

Cabinet
Corner Detail
(Top View)

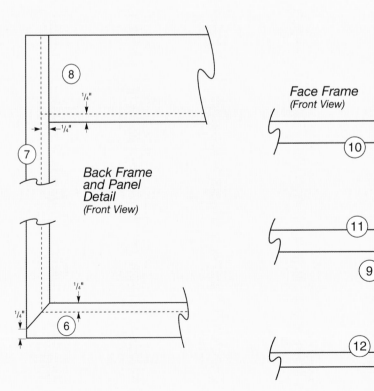

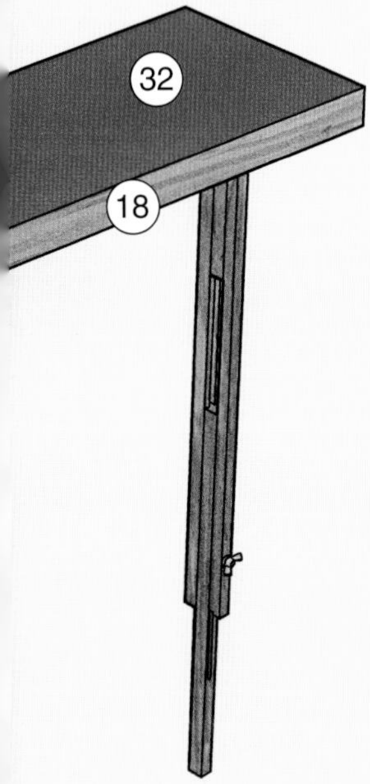

Material List - Cabinet

		T x W x L
1	Side Stiles (4)	¾" x 2½" x 30"
2	Side Rails (4)	¾" x 2½" x 26½"
3	Side Panels (2)	¾" x 25¾" x 25¾"
4	Bottom (1)	¾" x 29" x 29¼"
5	Back (1)	¼" x 27½" x 28½"
6	Back Lower Molding (1)	¾" x 1" x 27"
7	Back Side Moldings (2)	¾" x ¾" x 29"
8	Back Upper Molding (1)	¾" x 2½" x 27½"
9	Face Frame Stiles (2)	¾" x 1¼" x 30"
10	Face Frame Top Rail (1)	¾" x 1½" x 28½"
11	Face Frame Middle Rail (1)	¾" x 1½" x 28½"
12	Face Frame Bottom Rail (1)	¾" x 1" x 28½"
13	Free Casters (2)	2¼" Dia.
14	Locking Casters (2)	2¼" Dia.
15	Top (1)	¾" x 30¼" x 30¼"
16	Top Molding (1)	¾" x 1" x 130"
17	Wing Panels (2)	¾" x 9" x 26"
18	Wing Edge Molding (1)	¾" x 1⅞" x 160"
19	Drawer Slide Spacers (2)	1¼" x 6" x 28½"

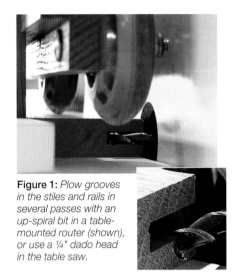

Figure 1: *Plow grooves in the stiles and rails in several passes with an up-spiral bit in a table-mounted router (shown), or use a ¼" dado head in the table saw.*

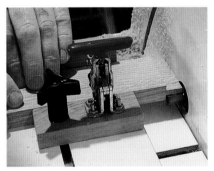

Figure 2: *Adjust the height of your spiral bit to form matching tongues on the ends of the rails. Again, make numerous passes to prevent stressing the workpiece or the tool.*

Back Frame and Panel Detail *(Front View)*

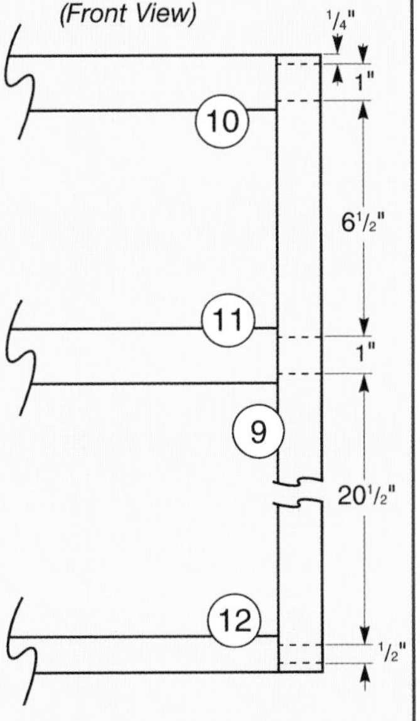

Face Frame *(Front View)*

mitered) and, after the glue dries, slide the back in place.

The top edge of the back is housed in a rail (piece 8), which has a tongue milled on each end and a groove along its bottom edge (see drawing, left). Attach the rail with glue and clamps, making sure everything is square. Leave the clamp in place while you make the face frame for the front of the cabinet.

Making the Cabinet Face Frame

The face frame accommodates both the drawer and door openings. Begin by ripping the stiles (pieces 9) to size, then chop the three through mortises in each of them (see drawings, this page).

The three face frame rails (pieces 10, 11 and 12) need to have tenons milled on their ends. Use a tenoning jig on the table saw or your miter gauge and a dado head. Glue and clamp the

Figure 3: *The drawer is built for shop use with heavy-duty, full-extension slides and screws through each of the ¾" glued finger joints.*

face frame together and, after the glue is dry, remove the clamps. Dry-fit the frame in the front of the cabinet and trim to fit. Glue and clamp the face frame in position and leave the clamps in place until the top of the cabinet is attached.

Now you can turn the station upside-down and attach the four casters (pieces 13 and 14).

Building the Cabinet Top

Cut the MDF top for the cabinet (piece 15) to the dimensions shown in the Material List on page 49, then create a hardwood molding (piece 16) to wrap its edges. This is simply ripped and jointed to size, then mitered to length.

Attach the molding with biscuits, glue and clamps and, after the glue has dried, sand the top edges absolutely flat. Dry-fit the top to the cabinet (but don't attach it yet): the top assembly should overhang the cabinet by 1⅛" all around.

The two outfeed supports (wings) add about three feet of stock support on either side of the saw. As each folds out, a hidden adjustable leg drops down to support it. Moveable rollers, clamped to the wings, support stock in a range of lengths and widths.

Each support is made up of a panel of MDF (pieces 17), trimmed with a hardwood molding (piece 18). Rip and joint the molding to size, then miter it to length and attach it to the panel with glue, biscuits and clamps. When everything is dry, sand each wing and mill a slight chamfer on the bottom edge with a bearing-guided chamfering bit.

Building the Drawer Box

It's a lot easier to build and install the drawer before you attach the cabinet top permanently. The first step is to face-glue a piece of ½" plywood to some of your ¾" MDF, to create a couple of spacers (pieces 19). These build out the edges of the drawer cavity so it's flush

with the inside edge of the face frame. Secure the spacers with glue, clamps and predrilled, countersunk screws to hold them in place while the glue dries.

I used poplar for the drawer sides, front and back (pieces 20 and 21). Use a ¾" dado head in the table saw to create the fingers, then glue and clamp the box together.

It never hurts to overbuild shop fixtures. Drive a 2" screw through each of the drawer box fingers into countersunk, predrilled holes (Figure 3).

The bottom of the drawer (piece 22) is a piece of ½" Baltic birch plywood, attached to the sides with 2" countersunk screws and no glue, so it can be replaced when necessary.

Install the drawer box with a pair of heavy-duty 24" full-extension drawer slides (pieces 23). Align the box's front face flush with the face frame's back edge to allow for the drawer face, and screw the slides to the spacers.

Making the Drawer Face

The drawer face has two stiles, two rails and a panel (pieces 24 through 26). Plow a through groove in the inside face of each stile, the bottom edge of the top rail and the top edge of the bottom rail, (see drawing, page 51). Mill matching tongues on the ends of the rails, cut the panel to size and, when everything fits, glue and clamp the drawer face together. Attach it to the drawer box with screws driven from inside the box. Complete it with walnut-stained hardwood knobs (pieces 27).

Each door calls for two stiles, two rails and a panel (pieces 28 through 30). Plow a through groove in the inside face of each stile, the bottom edge of the top rail and the top edge of the bottom rail. Then mill matching tongues on the ends of the rails, cut the panel to size and assemble the doors without glue. Check their fit in the openings.

QuickTip

Preventing Jointer Tearout

If you are getting a little tearout or feathering on boards as you run them across the jointer, try reversing the direction of the feed. Sometimes, grain hits the knives at the wrong angle. By switching the front of the board to the back, you offer a different grain angle to the cutters. If the knives are nicked, just loosen one and move it left or right, as far as it will go. Leave the others as they are and you'll get clean, sharp cuts.

Drawer Exploded View

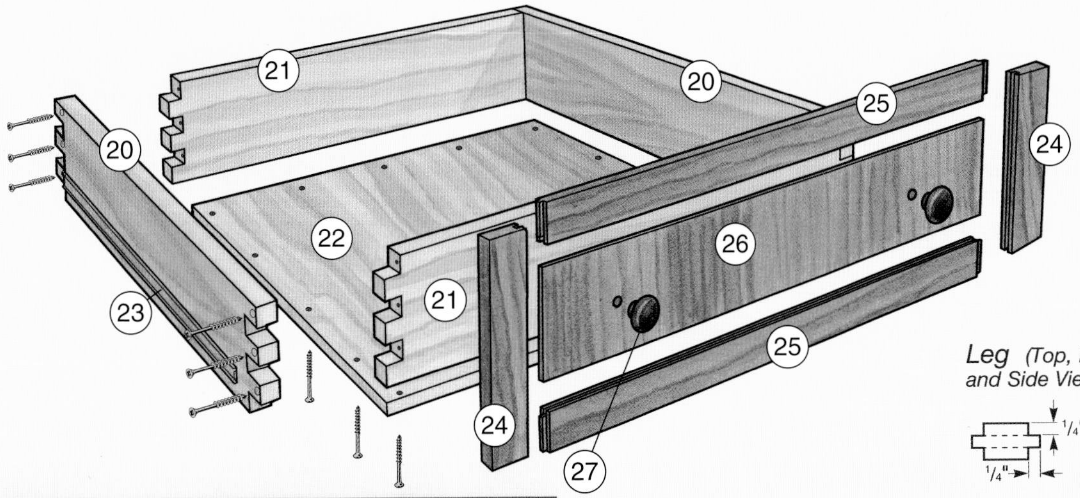

Material List

	T x W x L
20 Drawer Sides (2)	¾" x 4½" x 24"
21 Drawer Front & Back (2)	¾" x 4½" x 25"
22 Drawer Bottom (1)	½" x 24" x 25"
23 Drawer Slides (1 Pair)	24" Full-extension HD
24 Drawer Face Stiles (2)	¾" x 2" x 6"
25 Drawer Face Rails (2)	¾" x 2" x 23"
26 Drawer Face Panel (1)	¼" x 23" x 3"
27 Drawer & Door Knobs (4)	1½" Dia.
28 Door Stiles (4)	¾" x 2" x 20"
29 Door Rails (4)	¾" x 2" x 10"
30 Door Panels (2)	¼" x 10" x 17"
31 Continuous Piano Hinges (2)	1½" x 36", Brass
32 Plastic Laminate (1)	1/40" x 36" x 60"
33 Leg Housings (4)	¾" x 1" x 23⅝"
34 Leg Spacers (2)	¾" x 1½" x 5½"
35 Leg Hinge Bases (2)	¾" x 1⅜" x 8¾"
36 Legs (2)	¾" x 1 7/16" x 18"
37 Leg Lock Washers (4)	¼" I.D.
38 Leg Flat Washers (4)	¼" I.D.
39 Leg Bolts (2)	¼" x 3½" Hex head
40 Leg Wing Nuts (2)	¼" I.D.

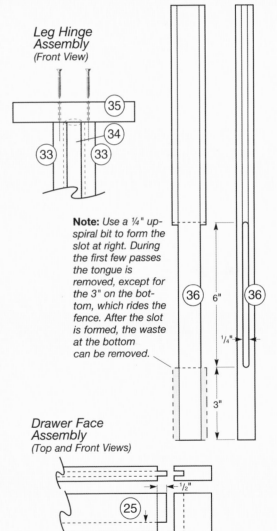

Leg (Top, Front and Side Views)

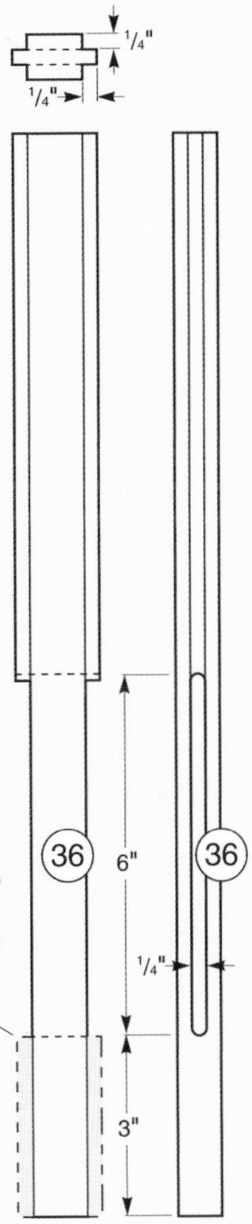

Leg Hinge Assembly (Front View)

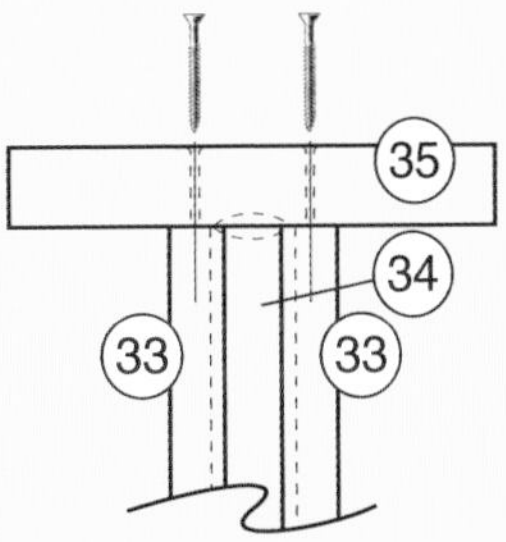

Note: *Use a ¼" up-spiral bit to form the slot at right. During the first few passes the tongue is removed, except for the 3" on the bottom, which rides the fence. After the slot is formed, the waste at the bottom can be removed.*

Drawer Side and Bottom (Side View)

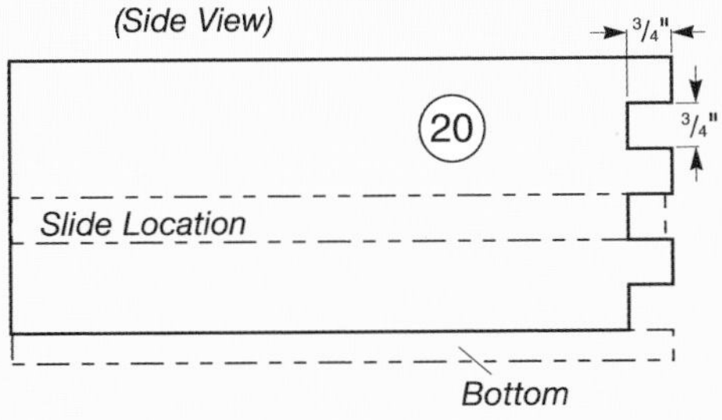

Note: *The author builds his shop fixtures to withstand a nuclear attack. The drawer bottoms can easily be removed and replaced.*

Drawer Face Assembly (Top and Front Views)

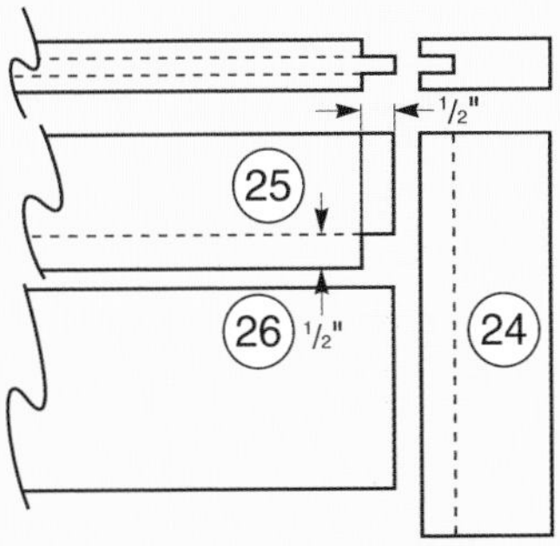

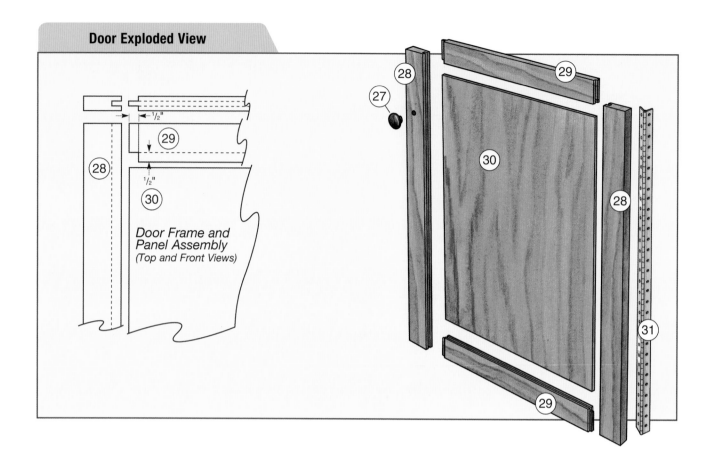

Door Exploded View

Door Frame and Panel Assembly (Top and Front Views)

When everything fits perfectly, glue and clamp each door together. After sanding, attach the doors to the cabinet with brass piano hinges (pieces 31).

Installing the Top

With the doors and drawer in place, you're ready to attach the top permanently. But first, turn it over and mill a ¼" chamfer along the bottom outside edge with a bearing-guided chamfering bit chucked in a portable router. This eliminates the sharp edge (saving slivers).

Apply glue to the top edge of the cabinet, put the top in place and drive 2" countersunk screws down through it into predrilled pilot holes in the cabinet members. Fill the holes with a wood filler that hardens completely.

After the filler dries, sand it flush. Then apply a second coat of filler and sand that flush, too, after it dries.

Applying Plastic Laminate

If you don't work with a lot of plastic laminate, you may not know that there are water-based contact adhesives for applying laminate that give off none of the volatile fumes. I advise using this formulation, especially if you are building this project during the winter in an enclosed shop.

Apply an equally thick coat to the top of each wing, the saw station top, and the bottom of each piece (cut 2" oversized for easy trimming) of plastic laminate (piece 32). Let the adhesive dry until it doesn't feel sticky, then place sticks or dowels on the wings and top. Line up the laminate (you only get one chance to get it right), remove the sticks one at a time and press the laminate in place. Use a roller to ensure complete contact, then trim the edges with a bearing-guided chamfering bit chucked in a portable router (see Figure 4). Stick some masking tape to the laminate so you can write on it, and locate the saw on the station's top.

Mark the locations of the bolt holes, remove the drawer so you don't hit it with an errant drill bit, and bore holes for appropriately sized bolts. Secure the saw to the station with bolts, washers and nuts.

Making the Legs

Before attaching the two outfeed wings to the saw, you need to install their adjustable legs. Begin by ripping and jointing the housings (pieces 33) to size then plow a ¼" square groove in the inside face of each. The spacers (pieces 34) are just cut to length, then a ¼" square tongue is milled on each of the long edges. Glue and clamp a pair of housings to each spacer and, when the glue is dry, attach a hinge base (piece 35) to each of these subassemblies. This is done with a biscuit, glue, and a pair of pre-bored, countersunk 2" screws.

The legs (piece 36) begin life as a simple molding that is just a piece of stock ripped and jointed to size, with ¼" removed from each long edge (see Figure 5). Crosscut them to length, then sand each so it slides freely in its housing.

To make the legs adjustable, each is slotted (see drawings on page 51). Cut these slots on the router table with a ¼" up-spiral bit, in several deepening passes.

On the drill press, bore a ¼" hole through each housing about 3" up from the bottom. Slide each leg into its housing, put a lock washer and a flat washer on a bolt (piece 37 through 39), and slide the bolt through the hole in the housing subassembly. Thread it through the slot in the leg and out the other side, then slide on a flat washer, a lock washer, and a wing nut (piece 40).

Wrapping Up with Dust Collection

If you have a mid-sized shop vacuum, it should fit nicely in this cabinet. Drill a 3" clearance hole in the saw station top for the vacuum hose and lightly chamfer the hole to avoid sharp edges.

Attach the wings to the cabinet with brass piano hinges. Then apply the finish of your choice. For the shop, I used a natural Danish oil finish that can easily be renewed as needed.

With that done, you're ready to start looking for a new project, preferably one that requires a whole lot of miter cuts!

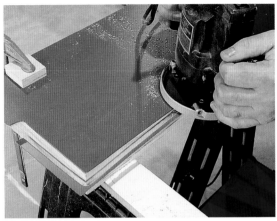

Figure 4: *After applying the laminate, trim it with a bearing-guided chamfer bit. Creating this ⅛" chamfer will eliminate sharp edges.*

Figure 5: *The two drop-down legs that support the outfeed tables are made from a simple molding milled on the table saw.*

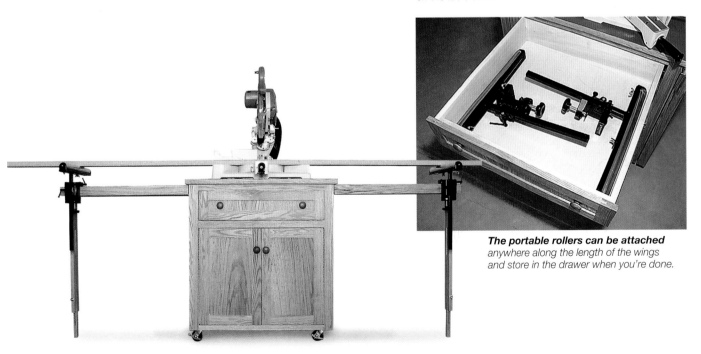

The portable rollers can be attached *anywhere along the length of the wings and store in the drawer when you're done.*

ROUTER
JIGS & FIXTURES

ROUTER BASICS REVISITED

Fess up: Is your router dusty because it's always making dust, or does it just gather dust? If you don't use this versatile machine often (or at all), maybe a few quick lessons will bolster your confidence. Once you get the basics down, a router unlocks a wealth of woodworking techniques safely and enjoyably.

By John English

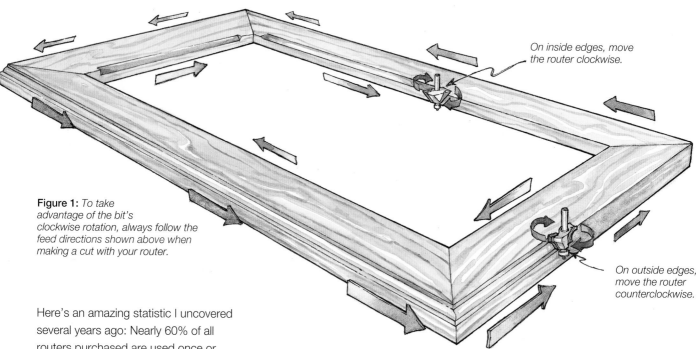

On inside edges, move the router clockwise.

On outside edges, move the router counterclockwise.

Figure 1: *To take advantage of the bit's clockwise rotation, always follow the feed directions shown above when making a cut with your router.*

Here's an amazing statistic I uncovered several years ago: Nearly 60% of all routers purchased are used once or not at all. Apparently this tool, which seems so appealing when Norm Abram uses it on his show, is scarier when you have it in your own hands. A little fear isn't such a bad thing in the woodworking shop, but a little more information is even better. Used properly, a router is quite safe.

With that in mind, I asked our own project builders to come up with some important tips that would not only instill confidence in beginners but also serve as a refresher for more experienced readers.

Tips for Successful Routing

Our crew all agreed that, for beginners, the most confusing aspect of using routers has to be figuring out the correct feed direction. The answer lies in an old shop rule that says you should always cut against the direction of the bit's rotation (see Figure 1). If you think about that for a minute, you'll realize that a portable router—with its bit facing down—should always be moved counterclockwise around the outside

of a workpiece and clockwise on an inside cut. You'll know you've got the feed direction correct if you feel the bit pushing back at you as you feed the tool along. If it pulls rather than pushes, you're going the wrong way.

The next tip addresses a very common problem. As a profiling bit travels around the corner of a board, how do you stop the wood from chipping out? The best way to avoid this is to form the edge across the end grain first, then finish up with the grain (see Figure 2). That second pass will remove any chipping that occurs on the first cut.

To a novice, machining narrow stock with a router can be both difficult and dangerous. The pros figured out a long time ago that they should machine small or narrow parts while they're still part of a wider board, then trim the piece to final width on a safer machine such as a bandsaw.

Our shop staffers are in the habit of seating the bit's shank fully into the collet, then pulling it back out about ⅛". That way, any shock the bit experiences (such as hitting an extra hard knot, or being dropped on the bench) is not transferred directly to the shaft and bearings. Also, many bits have a funnel-shaped flange below the cutter; if this gets caught in the collet, the bit won't be secure and an accident may follow.

Some routers come equipped with two wrenches. If you don't learn how to hold those wrenches when opening or closing the collet (see Figure 3), your reward will be smarting and bloodied knuckles. The key is to keep the wrench travel distance to a minimum while using only one hand to work both wrenches. Squeeze to loosen or tighten the collet nuts.

One thing everyone agrees on is that a woodworker should always buy the best tool he or she can afford. If your router has both ½" and ¼" collets, buy bits with ½" shanks if possible. Go for solid carbide cutters if your budget allows. Carbide-tipped tooling is almost as good, but standard high-speed steel simply won't hold an edge very long. The more you have to sharpen bits, the less accurate their profiles become. High-speed steel may be less expensive, but over the long term carbide is hands-down a better buy.

So far, all of these tips relate to hand-held portable routers. However, at some stage you may want to mount your router in a table. If you do so, keep in mind this one tabletop safety tip: Never feed the workpiece between the fence and the bit, because the bit will dig into the lumber, pull it through lightning fast and send it flying. Hopefully, your fingers won't follow suit.

Speaking of safety, here's some garden-variety but still sensible advice: always unplug your router before changing bits. You should also make sure the switch is turned off before plugging the tool in (routers don't have magnetic switches, so "On" is always on), and hold the tool with two hands so you're prepared for that quick jerk as the motor powers up. Above all, when you switch the router off, hold onto it until the bit stops spinning to keep the cutter out of harm's way. Now, get out there and put some hours on this supremely versatile machine. It will serve you well.

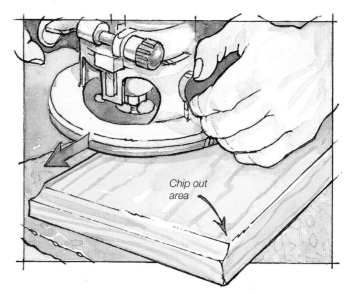

Chip out area

Figure 2: *To avoid chipping, form the edge across the grain first. The second cut, milled with the grain, removes any chipping from the first cut.*

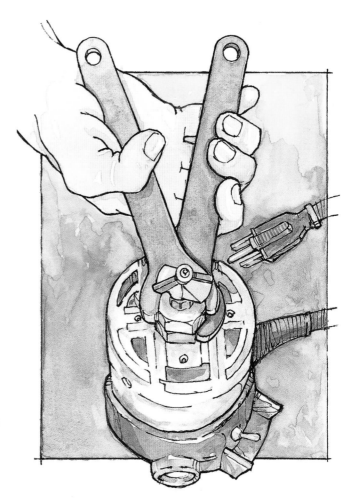

Figure 3: *Save your knuckles when changing bits on two-wrench routers. Use only one hand so your fingers don't get caught between the wrenches. Squeeze with one hand instead of pushing with two.*

ROUTER GUIDE— THE HEART OF AN ACCURATE CUT

Without a correct guide system, using a router is like steering a ship without a rudder. Master woodworker Ian Kirby shows you all the router guidance options here. If you follow his sage advice, routing will become an easier sail on calmer waters.

There are three elements to making cuts with a router: the router, the router bit and the guide system.

Routers are available from a variety of makers in a variety of models. Your choice is aided by specifications and best-buy articles. The main difference between them is whether they are fixed or plunge models.

Router bits are simple enough. What they cut is projected by their profile. How well a bit cuts is generally dependent on what you paid for it. The main difference between them is whether they are plain bits or have a pilot guide.

Guide systems are the most challenging element because they involve much more than a simple tool purchase. They

by Ian Kirby

Specialized bits, combined with the right router guide system, makes a virtually limitless variety of moldings.

Understanding Guide Systems

Understanding each guide system requires understanding the four elements that all systems have in common: fence, guide, cutting circle and offset.

Cutting circle

Guide

Fence

Offset

■ **Fences are purple.** ●⌐ **Dots indicate an object.** **Bit rotation** 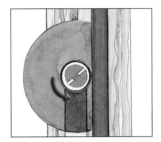 **Router bits are orange.**

◀⌐ **Arrows indicate an edge, surface or point.**

Four Router-on-top Guide Systems

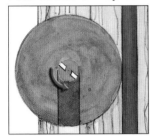 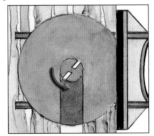 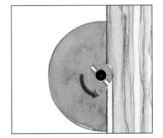

1. *Fence attached to workpiece*

2. *Base guide attached to router base*

3. *Pilot on router bit*

4. *Guide collar on router base*

require a clear understanding of the ways a cut can be made successfully.

There are a total of seven guide systems. Four are applicable when the router is passed over the top of a clamped-down workpiece; three when the workpiece is pushed past the cutter with the router mounted under a table. Each guide system allows you to make a variety of cuts, so understanding them lets you choose the best setup for your equipment and the job at hand. More than any other tool or machine, the router coupled with your creativity offers multiple solutions to most cutting problems.

Defining Terms

Understanding each guide system requires understanding the four elements that all systems have in common: fence, guide, cutting circle and offset.

The fence establishes the path—straight, curved, or complex—that the bit will follow. The fence can be a separate straightedge, it can be the edge of workpiece itself, or it can be a template. The fence is always separate from the router.

The guide is the part of the router that contacts the fence. It can be the edge of the router base plate, a base guide attached to the router base plate, a guide collar, a ball-bearing pilot mounted on the router bit or a trammel.

The cutting circle is the largest diameter of the cut a bit makes, while the offset is the distance between the fence and the router's cutting circle.

Three Workpiece-on-top Guide Systems

A one-part fence is accurate for cuts that do not remove the entire edge of the workpiece.

5. *One-part fence on router table*

A two-part fence is like a jointer turned 90°. The edge of the workpiece is guided by the infeed fence and, in turn, the stock removed by the bit is guided by the offset outfeed fence.

6. *Two-part fence on router table*

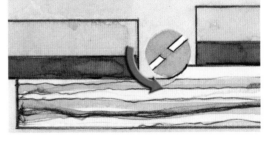

A pilot bearing on the router bit is guided by the surface of the workpiece.

7. *Pilot on router bit on router table*

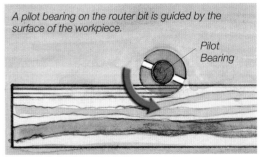

Pilot Bearing

Creating an Effective Setup

The setup is the means by which you put each guide system into practice. It includes clamps, jigs and support blocks. There are two routing setups: (1) you drive the router over a stationary workpiece; (2) you drive the workpiece over a table-mounted router.

Router-on-top Guide Systems (1 through 4): In each case you must control the travel of the router. It must be held firmly so that contact between fence and guide is constant, and the workpiece must be securely fixed.

Workpiece-on-top Guide Systems (5 through 7): In each case you must control the travel of the workpiece. It must be held firmly to the bed and fence or pilot bit on the router table. The router is securely mounted under the router table.

Controlling Chips and Dust for Greater Accuracy

Because router bits revolve at high speeds, the size of chip they make when cutting solid wood is very small. When cutting particleboard or MDF, the waste is dust that is bad to breathe and makes a greater mess than wood chips. This is a real problem because the mess gets everywhere, including the work and the jigs, and anything that comes between the guide and the fence reduces the accuracy of the cut.

You can do two things: remove as little waste as possible and exhaust it. You can often reduce the waste by removing the bulk with another machine—the router doesn't like bulk waste anyway. For example, if you are making parts with a curved edge, bandsaw the curve to 1/16" of the line. If you are making mortises, drill out the centers.

By whatever means, exhaust all the waste you can as the cut proceeds. It's worth the time and effort to rig any sort of exhaust system, even if it's considerably less than 100% effective.

Guide System 1
Fence attached to workpiece

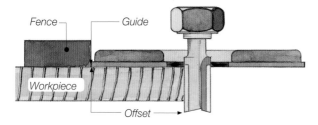

Fence — Guide — Offset — Workpiece

The fence is the wood or metal straightedge clamped to the workpiece. The **guide** is the edge of the router base. The **offset** is the distance from the guide to the router bit's **cutting circle**. This the simplest and most common guide system. With it you can:

1. Square the edge of the workpiece by taking a full cut with a straight bit.
2. Make a rabbet with a straight bit.
3. Mold all or part of the edge with a curved or complex bit.
4. Make a groove along the face of the workpiece. A fixed-base router can only make a through groove while a plunge router can make a stopped groove.
5. Make a dado or housing across the face of the workpiece. A fixed-base router makes a through housing, while a plunge router can make a housing that stops short of the edge of the wood.
6. Make a mortise using a straight bit, a plunge router and a simple jig.

Square the edge of the workpiece by taking a full cut with a straight bit. This is a quick and easy setup that will clean up a sawn or distorted edge. Using a spiral bit gives an even smoother cut and face.

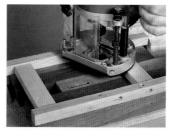

Make a mortise using a straight bit, a plunge router and a simple pocket jig. If you make the tenon on a table saw, as many people do, it's easy to chisel square the rounded ends of the mortise.

Rout a dado or housing across the workpiece. Using two fences, you can quickly and accurately make the cut any width you want. (Note the gap between the base and fence on the left.)

QuickTip

Non-stick Drawer Guide

The drawer guide shown here is non-binding and has proved very practical after several years of use. The guide (A) is a piece of wood 1⅛" square, with a concave top. The groove is ¾" wide and shallow enough that the drawer glides above the frame (B). The bottoms of the drawer sides are bullnosed to run in the groove, and the difference in the two arcs prevents binding when the wood dimensions change with surrounding humidity levels.

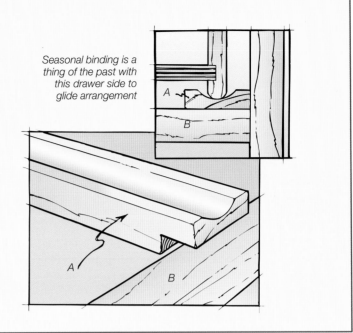

Seasonal binding is a thing of the past with this drawer side to glide arrangement

---

Guide System 2
Guide attached to router base

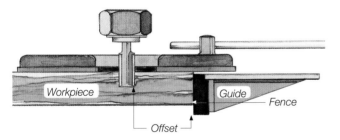

The base **guide** attached to the router base steers the router along the edge of the workpiece. The **fence** is the edge of the workpiece. The **offset** is the distance from the guide to the bit's **cutting circle**.

With this guide system you can:

1. Mold part of a square edge, though not the whole edge because part of it must remain intact to act as the fence.
2. Run grooves, flutes or decorative shapes parallel to the edge of the workpiece.
3. Mold part of the edge of a circle, using a two-point version of the base guide.
4. Flatten a surface, using an extended version of the router base.
5. Rout a circle using a trammel that attaches to the router base like the regular base guide.

Run grooves parallel *to an edge (left). Flatten a surface (above). This is a good setup to use if you want to flatten a small end grain block cutting board.*

Cutting a circle *with an extended base and a pivot is a unique router guide system. In this case the guide is a point, not an edge, so it has a foot in two camps, "Fence attached to workpiece" and "Guide attached to router base." Which camp you choose to place it in is of little matter.*

Guide System 3
Pilot on a router bit

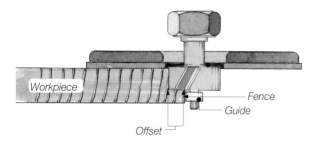

Workpiece

Fence

Guide

Offset

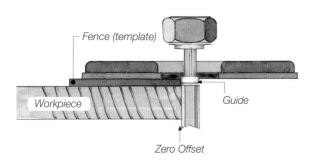

Fence (template)

Workpiece

Guide

Zero Offset

The solid pilot or ball-bearing pilot runs against the workpiece edge. The **guide** is the pilot bearing. The **fence** is the workpiece edge. The **offset** is the distance from the bearing's outer diameter to the **cutting circle**.

When the workpiece edge is the fence, the bearing can only shape part of the edge. The rest of the edge must remain untouched, or else the cut will go out of control.

With this guide method you can:

1. Make a rabbet. One way to adjust the side of the rabbet is to change the diameter of the bearing on the bit.
2. Mold part of the edge of a board.
3. Rout a groove or slot in the edge of a board.
4. Rout multi-part shapes, such as the two-part pencil mold.

When a template is the fence, (see *drawing* above) the bit can remove all or part of the workpiece edge. It's possible to construct equivalent setups with shank-mounted or tip-mounted bearings. However, when you're driving the router on top of the workpiece, you'll get the best view of what's happening with the template on top and a shank-mounted bearing. When the offset is zero, this setup reproduces the shape of the template. This is the most accurate way to reproduce a curved or complex shape. It's how most dovetail jigs work.

*Quick*Tip

Three-piece Clamp Hanger

If storing pipe clamps is a challenge for you (and you're not alone, by the way!), try the simple rack system shown here. It requires only three pieces of wood assembled with drywall screws. A top angled cleat keeps the screw end of the clamp from slipping off the rack, and the bottom wide spacer prevents the pipe from rocking.

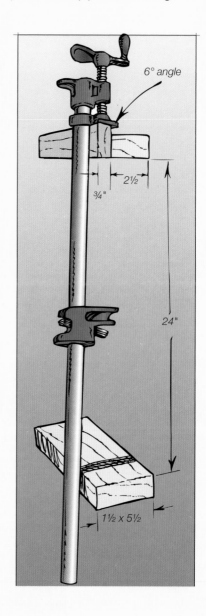

6° angle

2½

¾"

24"

1½ x 5½

Guide System 4
Guide collar on router base

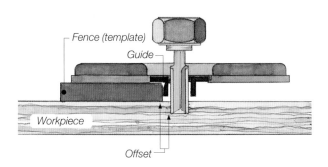

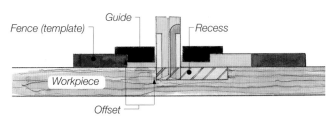

Two correctly sized guide collars following the same template can rout a recess and a matching inlay. The hatched areas of the two illustrations are equal in size. The top one is the recess. The bottom one is the inlay.

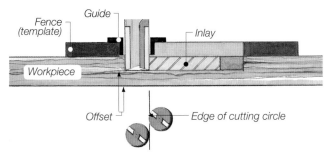

One guide collar cuts to the left and the other guide collar cuts to the right and to exactly the same line, making inlays very accurate.

The guide collar is, in effect, a much reduced router base. It runs against a template. The **guide** is the outer surface of the collar. The **fence** is the template. The **offset** is the distance from the outside of the guide collar to the bit's **cutting circle**.

With this guide system you can:

1. Make practically any shape, recess or hole in or through a board.
2. Cut the edge of a board straight.
3. Make a rabbet or a groove parallel to the edge of the template.
4. Make an inlay and a matching recess in the workpiece.

Cut the edge of a board straight.

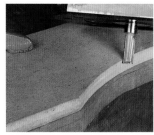

Cut a curved head rail for a raised and fielded panel. The bit can be easily adjusted to cut just beyond the depth required.

This setup works well for straight cuts. When you use guide collars with a shaped template, the template has to be adjusted to compensate for the offset. Adding and subtracting offsets from templates is a source of much confusion,

Make an inlay and a matching recess in the workpiece.

and most people have to experiment before they understand how to rout a recess that exactly fits an inlay.

Routing for Inlays

A **guide** collar can reproduce the shape of a template, reduced or enlarged by the **offset** distance between the outside of the collar and the bit's **cutting circle**. To rout an inlay and the recess it fits into, you need two different-sized guide collars. The size relationship is:

Outside Diameter (OD) of large collar minus (–) bit diameter equals (=) Outside Diameter (OD) of small collar plus (+) bit diameter.

For example, with a ½" bit, this combination works:
2" OD collar – ½" bit = 1½".
1" OD collar + ½" bit = 1½".
Similarly, with a ⅛" bit:
¾" OD collar – ⅛" bit = ⅝".
½" OD collar + ⅛" bit = ⅝".

Deciding whether to use a guide collar or a bit with a shank-mounted bearing is a tradeoff. The bearing-guided bit reproduces the exact shape of the template in the workpiece, with no need to calculate offsets. However, it doesn't allow you to control the depth of cut, making the method impractical for most inlay work. While guide collars require an offset calculation, they give you control over the depth of the cut. Don't ignore guide collars as many woodworkers do. Once you get comfortable using them, they expand the use of your bit collection considerably.

Guide System 5
One-part fence on router table

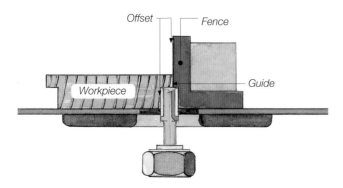

Offset *Fence* *Guide* *Workpiece*

Rabbet an edge. Router bits make very clean cuts in particleboard and MDF. But they turn the waste into a fine dust, so always use an exhaust system on a router table.

Groove the workpiece. The part is a piece of strip wall panel. The strips are connected by a center spline. One edge has been molded with a three-reed bit.

The **guide** is the edge of the workpiece. It runs against the router table **fence**. The cutter is partially buried in the fence. The **offset** is the distance from the fence to the edge of the **cutting circle**.

When it's possible to make the cut you want with a one-part fence on the router table, it is the safest and simplest method of routing.

This method is accurate for cuts that do not remove the entire edge of the workpiece. If the cutter were to remove the entire edge of the workpiece, it would also destroy the guide surface, and the setup would be thrown out of control.

Work-holding sleds with fences that run on the front edge of the router table use the same guide method.

With a one-part fence on the router table you can:
1. Rabbet an edge.
2. Mold part of edge.
3. Slot or groove the workpiece.

Note that you can use pilot-bearing bits with the router table fence, by setting the fence in line with the bearing or forward of it.

Guide System 6
Two-part fence on router table

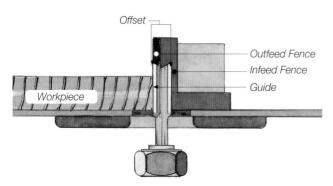

Offset *Outfeed Fence* *Infeed Fence* *Guide* *Workpiece*

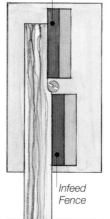

Outfeed Fence

Infeed Fence

Straightening an edge. The photo clearly shows the correct way to joint an edge by pressing the workpiece against the outfeed table after two or three inches of the cut have been completed.

This setup is like a jointer turned 90°. The **guide** is the edge of the workpiece which runs initially against the **infeed fence**. The **offset** is the distance from the infeed fence to the **cutting circle**. Once a cut of 4" to 5" is made, the workpiece must be kept in tight contact with the outfeed fence. The edge of the workpiece becomes a self-jigging fence that uses the **outfeed fence** as a guide.

With this guide system you can:
1. Remove all of an inadequate edge to make it straight and square to the face.
2. Mold all of an edge.

Running molding strips. To get consistent results, it's essential to run the molding through a "tunnel" of hold-downs to keep the workpiece tight to the table and the fence. Use a push stick to complete the cut.

Guide System 7
Pilot on router bit on router table

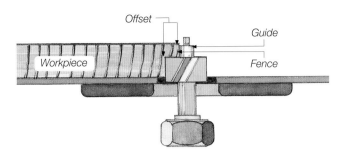

Offset — Guide — Fence

Workpiece

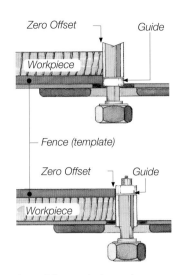

Zero Offset — Guide

Workpiece

Fence (template)

Zero Offset — Guide

Workpiece

The pilot bearing is the **guide**. The **fence** is the workpiece edge or a template attached to the workpiece. The **offset** is the distance from the outside of the pilot bearing to the **cutting circle**. This setup always requires a starting pin.

With this method you can:

1. Make a rabbet. One way to adjust the size of the rabbet is to change the bearing on the bit.
2. Mold part of the edge of a board.
3. Rout a groove or slot in the edge of a board.
4. Make cope-and-stick frames for cabinet doors.
5. Raise a panel.

To shape the full edge of the workpiece, you must use a separate template. The template can be mounted on top of the workpiece or below it.

Mounting the template below the workpiece allows the edge of a work-holding sled to act as the template. This makes a safe and stable setup for pattern-routing shaped parts, such as chair legs.

Mounting the template on top of the workpiece gives you better visibility of the contact between guide and bearing. This calls for a bit with a tip-mounted pilot. When the pilot bearing is the same size as the router bit, the offset is zero and the setup reproduces the template. When the pilot bearing is not the same size as the router bit, the offset reduces or enlarges the template profile.

---

*Quick*Tip

Pull-out Router Table
In a small shop, adding another floor-standing machine just eats up more precious floor space. One way to save space is to hang your router tabletop from a workbench using full-extension, heavy-duty drawer slides. Add a locking pin to keep the table from moving during operation. When not in use, it slips right out of sight.

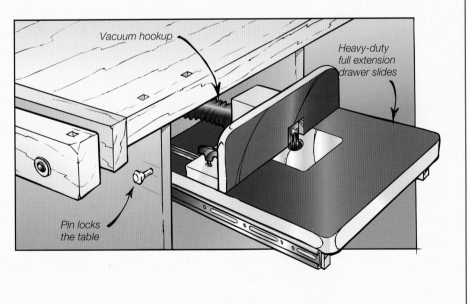

Vacuum hookup

Heavy-duty full extension drawer slides

Pin locks the table

ROUTER STRAIGHTEDGE JIG

What's the easiest way to trim the edges of a plywood panel straight? With a router, straightedge and straight bit, of course. Our version of the straightedge jig features a T-track that makes it even more versatile and hard working. This jig also breezes through rabbets, dadoes and grooves. It's a "must-build" for your shop.

by Rick White

Here's a slick jig to have handy whenever you need to straighten a rough edge or plow a groove. It's actually multi-use straightedge, designed to custom-fit to your portable router. The router runs along its fence, and that guides a straight bit along a hardboard template attached to the bottom of the fence. Whenever you need to make a cut, just line up the edge of the template with your trim line on the workpiece. You'll never have to go through the old measure-and-clamp routine again. The jig also performs a bonus task on the table saw—more on that later.

The heart of the jig is a straight, jointed plywood fence (piece 1). Seal this along its two ripped edges with strips of solid hardwood banding (pieces 2). Then plow a grove in the top to house an aluminum T-slot track (piece 2).

Cut one ¼" hardboard template blank for each straight bit you own. Each of these templates (pieces 4) should be 7" wide to begin with. Attach the first template to the bottom of the jig with bolts and nuts (pieces 5 and 6), then install your largest-diameter straight bit in your portable router. Run the router along the fence so it trims the template to size. Use a permanent marker to note the bit size on the template, then chuck the next largest bit in the router. Bolt on a new template

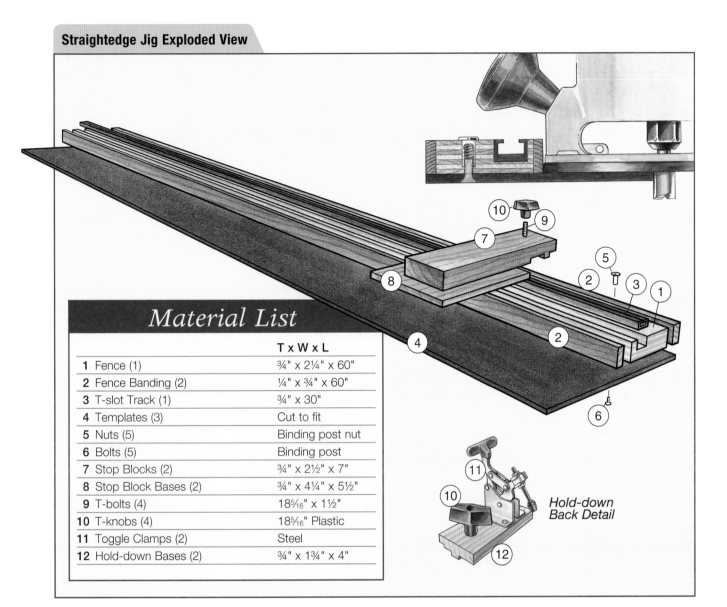

Material List

		T x W x L
1	Fence (1)	¾" x 2¼" x 60"
2	Fence Banding (2)	¼" x ¾" x 60"
3	T-slot Track (1)	¾" x 30"
4	Templates (3)	Cut to fit
5	Nuts (5)	Binding post nut
6	Bolts (5)	Binding post
7	Stop Blocks (2)	¾" x 2½" x 7"
8	Stop Block Bases (2)	¾" x 4¼" x 5½"
9	T-bolts (4)	18⁵⁄₁₆" x 1½"
10	T-knobs (4)	18⁵⁄₁₆" Plastic
11	Toggle Clamps (2)	Steel
12	Hold-down Bases (2)	¾" x 1¾" x 4"

*Hold-down
Back Detail*

piece, and repeat the process until you have individual, marked templates for each of your commonly used bits.

If you stop building this jig right now, you can make any straight trim cut, through groove, rabbet or dado you want with this jig. To tackle stopped cuts, just add a pair of adjustable stops to limit the router's travel.

The adjustable stops are simply short lengths of stock (pieces 7), each of which is attached to a base (piece 8) with glue and clamps. These bases need to be a little wider than the stops, so they won't interfere with the router's travel (otherwise, the machine's handles might hit the stops). The wide bases also keep the stops aligned at 90° to the fence.

The stops are secured to the jig with T-bolts and knobs (pieces 9 and 10), which make them adjustable along the entire fence length.

Earlier, I mentioned a bonus function of this jig, and here it is: By attaching a couple of toggle clamps (pieces 11) to a spare set of hold-down bases (pieces 12), you can use the jig to straighten the edges of rough boards. Clamp the stock to the jig and run the jig along your table saw fence to slice off the bad edge. Simple.

The hold-down option *on this jig allows you to slice straight edges on rough stock without fear of binding or kickback.*

by Carol Reed

JOINTING WITH A ROUTER

Carol Reed, alias "The Router Lady," creates a jig that makes squaring up an edge a snap. And when you're done, the whole thing stores quickly and easily on a wall. It's a convenient jig for any shop and indispensable if you don't own a jointer yet. All you need is the correct bit, a mid-sized router and a little scrap laminate and plywood.

Want a jointer in your shop? Most of us do, but not all of us have enough floor space or a big enough wallet. However, if you have a router of almost any size, you can make a jointing jig that in my opinion does some tasks better than a "real" jointer.

The secret is a spiral-flute router bit that, unlike the knives of most conventional jointers, produces tearout-free jointing on squirrely grained or bird's-eye figured wood. Even if you do have a jointer but often work in these lovely but difficult-to-machine woods—especially in smaller dimensions—a router-jointer jig will consistently create a smoother surface. The router-jointer jig also allows you to joint clean plywood edges and other composite or even plastic materials, a task that can quickly dull the knives of a regular jointer, especially if the plies are bonded with a hard glue.

A conventional jointer will perform two operations: edge jointing and face jointing. Many of us only edge-joint because we buy our wood already surfaced (face jointed). This router jointer jig will yield smooth, accurate edges— safely, comfortably, and consistently—

Offset with Laminate

When you use a traditional jointer, the two beds of the tool offset to accommodate the depth of the cut you are making. On this jig, it is the fence that has the offset built into its design.

Create that offset using the thickness of the plastic laminate on the outfeed side of the fence. This same thickness determines the depth of cut.

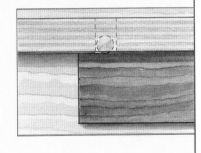

for the price of a long spiral bit and a few square feet of plywood. Obviously, this jig can't perform face jointing.

The setup has four components: a router, a spiral flute bit, the table and the fence. Ideally, the router should have a ½" collet because larger-diameter bits run smoother and make cleaner cuts than smaller diameter bits, assuming that speed of bit rotation and feed rate are the same. However, since the amount of stock removed is so small, a junior version could be made using a router with a ¼" collet. This limits the thickness of the wood to be jointed to

stock less than ¾", but if you are a box maker working in thinner woods, this may be just the ticket.

The bit of choice has spiral flutes. Because the cutting edge of the bit's flutes are in continuous contact with the wood and presented to the wood at an angle, it always produces a chatter-free, smooth edge. Just as in hand planing, presenting an angled cutting edge to wood fibers produces a cleaner edge. An additional benefit is that the bit runs cooler, thereby staying sharp longer.

Spiral-flute router bits, now widely used in woodworking, were inspired

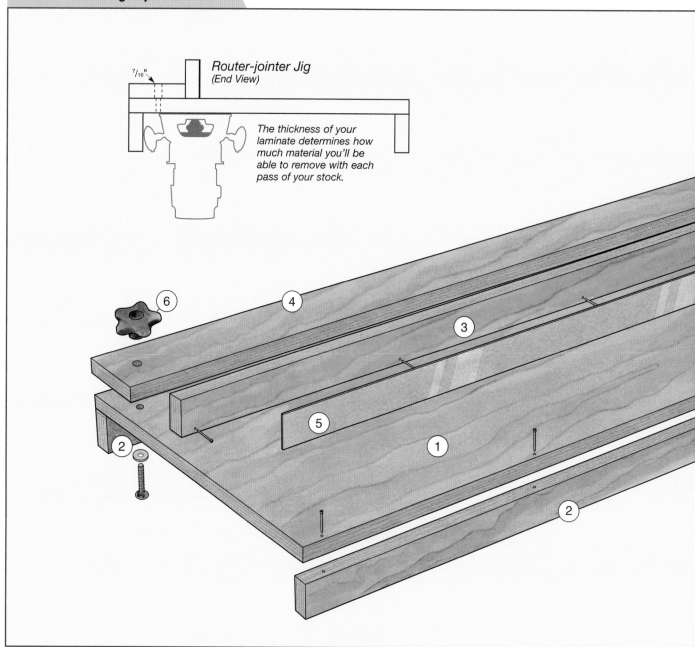

Router-jointer Jig
(End View)

7/16"

The thickness of your laminate determines how much material you'll be able to remove with each pass of your stock.

by spiral-flute bits, called end mills, long used by machinists for metal-working. The router bits come in three configurations: upcut, downcut and compression. They are available from many woodworking supply stores and web sites. I opt for an end mill because I use the same bit for mortising operations, but an upcut router bit would work just fine. Either way, a 3½" long, ½" diameter, two-flute bit is more than adequate for most edge jointing.

The jig's table and fence are made so they may be stored by hanging on the wall or shelved when not in use.

An examination of a dedicated jointer's construction shows two flat surfaces—a split table and a fence—perpendicular to one another. It's true that a jointer's fence can be tilted, but since it is most commonly used with the fence at 90°, our router-jointing jig will be constructed to produce only 90° edges. The dedicated jointer has an

infeed table and an outfeed table, separated by a cutterhead that rotates in a horizontal plane. The knives are set so they are exactly level with the outfeed table at the top of the cutting circle. The depth of cut is variable and is determined by adjusting the infeed table up or down.

The router-jointer may be seen as a modified jointer stood on its side. Its fence serves as the infeed and outfeed surfaces, and the bit rotates in a vertical

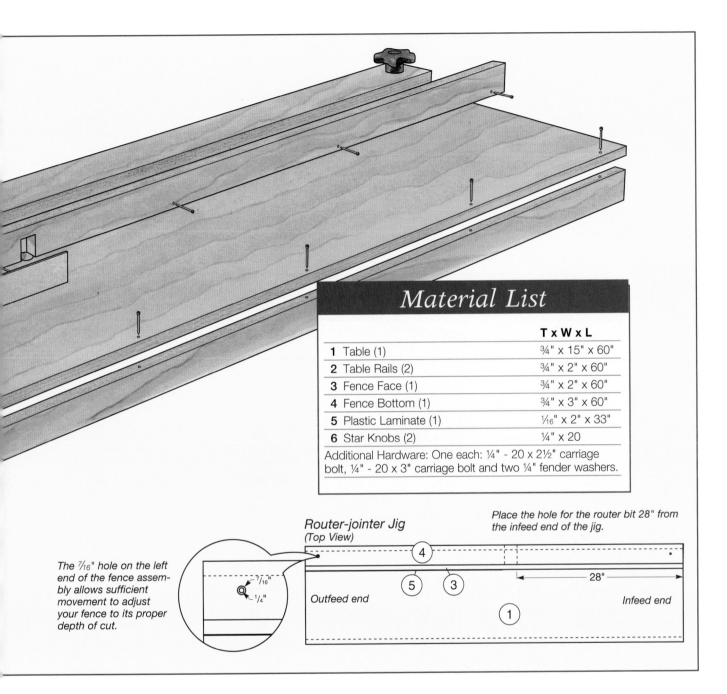

Material List

		T x W x L
1	Table (1)	¾" x 15" x 60"
2	Table Rails (2)	¾" x 2" x 60"
3	Fence Face (1)	¾" x 2" x 60"
4	Fence Bottom (1)	¾" x 3" x 60"
5	Plastic Laminate (1)	⅟₁₆" x 2" x 33"
6	Star Knobs (2)	¼" x 20

Additional Hardware: One each: ¼" - 20 x 2½" carriage bolt, ¼" - 20 x 3" carriage bolt and two ¼" fender washers.

Router-jointer Jig
(Top View)

Place the hole for the router bit 28" from the infeed end of the jig.

The ⁷⁄₁₆" hole on the left end of the fence assembly allows sufficient movement to adjust your fence to its proper depth of cut.

⁷⁄₁₆"
¼"

Outfeed end

28"

Infeed end

plane. In the case of our jig, the depth of cut is fixed. The beauty of this configuration is that wood to be edge jointed is moved past the cutter with its wide side face down on the table. This presentation is much more comfortable and controlled than standing the wood on its edge and moving it past the cutter supported only on its edge.

To create infeed and outfeed surfaces on the one-piece continuous fence, glue a piece of high-pressure plastic laminate to the outfeed side. You can find it at any home center. The thickness of the laminate determines the depth of cut. Typical countertop laminate is around ⅟₃₂" to ⅟₁₆" thick. This shallow cut removes just a small amount of stock, which is perfect for twisted or wild-grained woods.

The router is mounted on the horizontal surface, or the table, presenting the bit vertically. The upcut spiral bit or end mill exerts downward force, and actually helps to "hold" the work firmly on the table. This may sound contrary to common sense, but with the router mounted under the table, it is essentially upside-down, so an up-spiral bit or right-hand twist end mill is the proper cutter. Do not use a downcut spiral bit. It would work against you and might lift the wood off the table.

The typical length of a small conventional jointer is 48", with the knives in the middle of the table.

That presents 24" on either side of the cutterhead. Longer infeed and outfeed surfaces are better, because they provide more workpiece support. Depending on the material used for this jig, you can make the infeed and outfeed surfaces as long as you wish.

I opted for a 5'-long jig with the router positioned 28" from the infeed end. For the fence material, ¾" Baltic birch plywood (which comes in 5'-square sheets) is an ideal jig-making material. It's a high-quality lay-up, with more plies per unit of thickness than standard plywood, and it has no voids. It's also much lighter than MDF or melamine. Since this jig is intended to be stored when not in use, weight is an important consideration.

Making the Jig

Downward force on the table and sideways force on the fence is exerted when jointing, so the jig must be firmly secured while in use, to effectively oppose those forces. If the most stable item in your shop is the bench, simply clamp one end to the bench and the other end to a shop stand. For purposes of photography, I used a pair of sawhorses instead of a bench and a stand. This works well, but it may be a little low for your back. Choose the place to use your router-jointer based on a flat, sturdy surface that allows the router-jointer to be securely clamped and at a height that is comfortable for you. Remember that the router hangs down from the bottom of the table, so the jig cannot simply rest on your bench or support surface.

There are two parts to make: the table and the fence. The width of the table is determined by the amount of desired work surface, plus the diameter of the router base and the overhang for

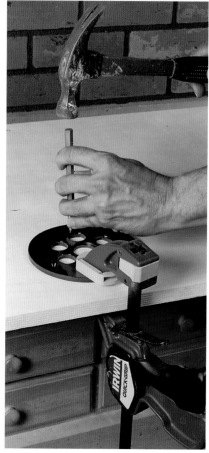

Mark the router base *mounting holes by clamping the sub-base in the desired location and tapping the properly sized transfer punch with a small hammer. This impresses a dimple in the exact center of the hole. Countersink the hole on the top side of the table.*

the clamping system. Eight inches of work space is adequate. Add this to the diameter of your router base to come up with an overall width for the table (My setup came to 15").

Rip the table to width and then measure 28" from the right end and in from back edge the same measurement as the radius of your router base to locate the router bit hole. Mark and drill the holes to mount the router base at the location of the router bit hole. Mount it so the router's motor tightening system on the base is facing the front. Drill a ½" hole for the router bit, and chamfer both sides of the hole to keep workpieces from splintering the plywood around the bit hole.

Now rip the two rails to exactly 2". Make the cuts dead straight or the router-jointer jig will be twisted when you clamp it down, and you won't be able to edge-joint at 90°.

Attach the rails to the bottom of the table with glue and brads. Be sure to countersink the brads so they can't mar the wood being jointed. Use a block plane to slightly chamfer all the edges to make the jig "splinter-free."

Rip the fence bottom and fence face. Mark the router bit recess at 28" from the right end and 1⅛" up from the bottom edge. Drill a ⅝" hole. Mark two lines tangent to the hole and perpendicular to the bottom edge. Carefully saw along the lines creating the U-shaped bit recess. Sand the sharp edges smooth.

Drill a ¼" hole 2" in from the right end of the fence bottom and a ⁷⁄₁₆" hole 2" in from the left end (for making fence adjustments). See the Drawings on pages 70 and 71 for details.

Applying Laminate

Glue the fence face to the fence bottom. Use brads to hold the two pieces while the glue dries. Again, be sure to countersink the brads. Glue a piece of high-pressure laminate to the outfeed surface, extending from the bit recess to the end. Contact cement is a good choice for adhesive here. Flush-trim the laminate so no edges extend beyond the fence edges. Freshly cut laminate can slice your fingers, so file the edges smooth to ease any sharp corners. Place the fence on the table in its proper position and use a pencil to mark the spots where you'll drill ¼" holes for installing the carriage bolts.

Using the Jig

Fasten the router base to the bottom of the table. Install the cutter in the router. Raise the cutter to extend above the thickness of the wood you'll be jointing. Flip the table over and clamp it down. Now turn the bit until a flute is presented to the widest cutter arc. Tighten the fence's right knob, then rotate the fence forward so the bit is

Spiral-Flute Bits

Spiral-flute carbide router bits produce superior cuts in a wide range of materials because their cutting edges are in continuous contact with the workpiece, slicing through the wood fibers at a shearing angle. In contrast, the cutting edge of a straight-flute bit contacts the workpiece intermittently and cuts into the entire width of the workpiece at a right angle. If the depth of cut and feed rate remain the same, more flutes will produce a better cut. That's why many woodworkers use end mills, a type of spiral-flute bit popular with machinists. They are commonly available with four flutes and longer flute lengths.

fully contained inside the recess. Place a straightedge against the outfeed surface and rotate the fence until the emerging bit just touches the straightedge. Tighten the left knob to lock the fence into final position. Because this setup guarantees that the cut equals the thickness of the laminate, the edge of the workpiece will be fully supported by the fence during the entire cut as it passes from the infeed surface to the outfeed surface, and the edge will be straight.

With the router on (use eye and ear protection), place the wood face down on the table and move the wood from the right to the left against the fence. At the start of the cut, hold the wood firmly against the infeed surface, gradually shifting pressure to the outfeed surface as the cut progresses. Repeat the operation until the edge is completely jointed. Try a test cut for straightness, and check for square as well.

Squareness is not usually a problem because it depends on the router base and its relationship to the bit. If it is a problem, check that the base is firmly attached to the table bottom. One other point: if the face of your stock is not flat or twists, the edge will not be square…it is always best to check, just to be sure.

The author checks out a tight, clean joint machined on her router-jointer jig. No muss, no fuss.

ROUTER SURFACING JIG

Thickness planers are worth their weight in gold, but adding one to your shop doesn't come cheap. If your budget won't allow for a planer just yet, we have a solution. Our surfacing jig turns a router into a serviceable planer. The moveable sled will fit virtually any make or model of fixed-base router, and a pair of holddowns keep workpieces firmly planted while you work. This jig also doubles as a handy dado and groove cutter.

by John English

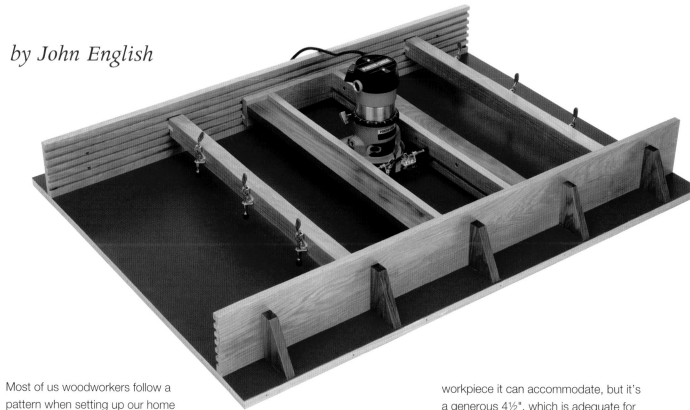

Most of us woodworkers follow a pattern when setting up our home shops. We start with a few hand tools and a drill, and pretty soon we have all the basics in place. Then we start dreaming of going to the next level—dust collection, pneumatic tools, and finally the ultimate shop machine—a thickness planer. The problem is that our skill level often grows a little more quickly than the number of tools we are able to afford. If you're ready for a thickness planer but aren't prepared for the financial outlay involved, this article presents a solution: the surfacing jig.

While this project started out with surfacing in mind, there are a number of important routing operations that it can perform (see Figures 1, 2 and 3). It will handle panels up to 19" wide, with no restrictions on length. However, there is a limit to the thickness of the workpiece it can accommodate, but it's a generous 4½", which is adequate for almost any situation.

One of the clever features of this jig has nothing to do with surfacing: Its size allows you to cut multiple dadoes across the grain of a workpiece. This means that you can build bookshelves and other cabinetry with little or no setup, and you can repeat cuts to your heart's content.

If you're intrigued by the possibilities and would like to build this surfacing jig,

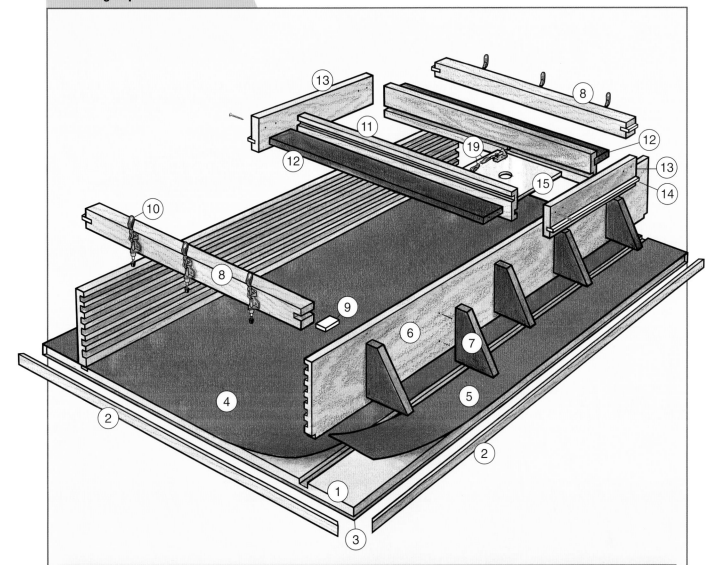

Material List - Surfacing Jig

	T x W x L			T x W x L
1 Base (1)	¾" x 35" x 47"		**12** Sled Braces (2)	¾" x 2¾" x 25⅞"
2 Hardwood Trim (1)	¼" x ¾" x 168"		**13** Sled End Caps (2)*	¾" x 2¾" x 13"
3 Laminate - Underside (1)	⅛" x 36" x 48"		**14** Sled Glides (2)*	⅜" x ¾" x 13" UHMW
4 Laminate - Top Center (1)	⅛" x 27½" x 48"		**15** Polycarbonate Sled (1)*	⅜" x 7½" x 7½"
5 Laminate - Top Sides (2)	⅛" x 3½" x 48"		**16** Router Housing Bolts (3)*	
6 Base Runners (2)	¾" x 5⅜" x 47½"		**17** Sled Clamp Bolts (6) and Nuts (6)	⅛" x 1"
7 Stabilizers (10)	¾" x 3" x 4"		**18** Sled Clamp Lock Washers (6)	⅛"
8 Holddown Beams (2)	1¾" x 1½" x 27⅜"		**19** Sled Clamps (2)	Small Push Clamps
9 Holddown Glides (4)	⅜" x 1" x 1½" UHMW		**20** Spacer Strips (2)	¾" x 5½" x 47½"
10 Holddown Clamps (6)	Small Push Clamps			
11 Sled Runners (2)	¾" x 2¾" x 25⅞"			

*Designed for a 5½" diameter router base:
Adjust to fit your router's base.*

Figure 1: *The original motivation for this jig was a means to surface uneven boards before final sanding. It became evident that the jig would also serve to plane material down to a desired thickness, as shown at left.*

Figure 2: *Cutting clean-edged dadoes across the grain of boards or plywood is easy. Just place the workpiece on the base, drop in a spacer, center the router on your cut, and the holddowns will keep both board and router sled in perfect alignment as you work.*

Figure 3: *Cutting grooves with the grain of the workpiece is just as easy as making dadoes across the grain. Use the holddowns to clamp the spacers and sled in place, and lock the router base in position on the sled. Then cut the grooves by running your workpiece between the spacers.*

the first step is to cut all the parts to size according to the dimensions given in the Material List on page 75.

Milling the Base

The base (piece 1) is a piece of MDF—medium density fiberboard—which is readily available at any lumberyard, and the first milling operation is to create two grooves in it for the hardwood runners. If you do this on your table saw, make sure that you keep the same edge against the fence for both cuts: If you just flip it, the grooves won't be absolutely parallel. Cutting them with a router and a clamped-on fence makes even more sense, and it's a more comfortable way to handle this large panel.

Trim the base with ¼"-thick strips of hardwood (pieces 2), mitering the corners. Install this trim with glue and 4d finish nails every 6", pre-drilling the hardwood so it doesn't split. Set and fill the nail holes, then sand everything flush before applying the plastic laminate.

Working with Plastic Laminate

If you haven't applied plastic laminate before, installing it is just a series of very logical steps. Following the manufacturer's instructions, apply a coat of contact cement to the underside of the MDF base and the laminate (piece 3), and let them dry to the touch. The easiest way to apply contact adhesives is with a disposable notched trowel—they're very inexpensive and you can usually just discard them when the project is completed.

When the cement is dry, place dowels or thin sticks about every 6" along the surface to keep the two parts separate while you get the laminate lined up. You'll notice that the laminate is a little oversized to allow for trimming.

Starting from the center, remove the dowels and press the plastic down

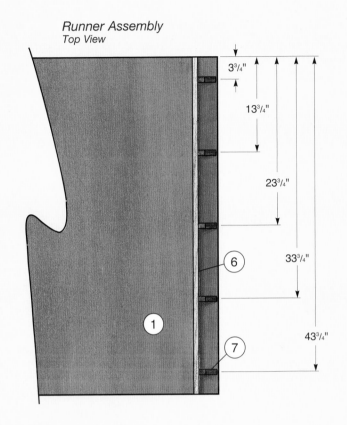

Runner Assembly
Top View

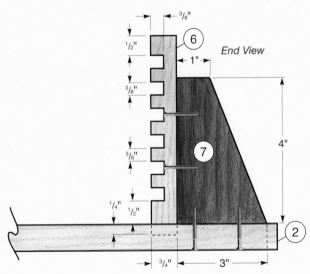

End View

Note: *The ends of the runners (pieces 6) are notched to fit over the ¼" trim*

Figure 4: *Use ¾"-thick scrap blocks to line up the laminate with the edges of the two grooves.*

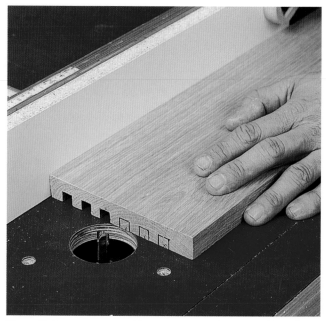

Figure 5: *Use your router table to machine the six parallel ⅜" x ⅜" grooves in the runners for the sled and holddowns.*

onto the MDF. Keep working from the center out, and when the whole sheet is in place turn to a plastic or wooden roller to ensure good adhesion. Or you can use a baker's rolling pin—it provides a large area of contact and you can really apply pressure with those widely spaced handles.

Trim the laminate with a flush-trimming bit installed in your portable router, then use some 280-grit sandpaper to break the trimmed edges. Make sure you don't scratch the laminate in the process. Then turn the base over and work on the top surface.

Begin by drilling ⅛"-diameter holes every 6" along the bottom of each groove. These are pilot holes for the screws that hold the two hardwood runners in place, and drilling them now from the top side ensures that they're lined up properly when you drive the screws in from the bottom later on.

QuickTip

Plugging Holes in Premium Wood

To shave wood plugs absolutely flush, cut five pieces of paper to fit in the opening in your router base. Stack the paper and adjust a flat bit's height so it barely touches the top paper. Now run the router across the plug. If the bit still needs to come down, remove a couple of papers and repeat the adjustment until the plug is barely above the surface. Finish with a light sanding.

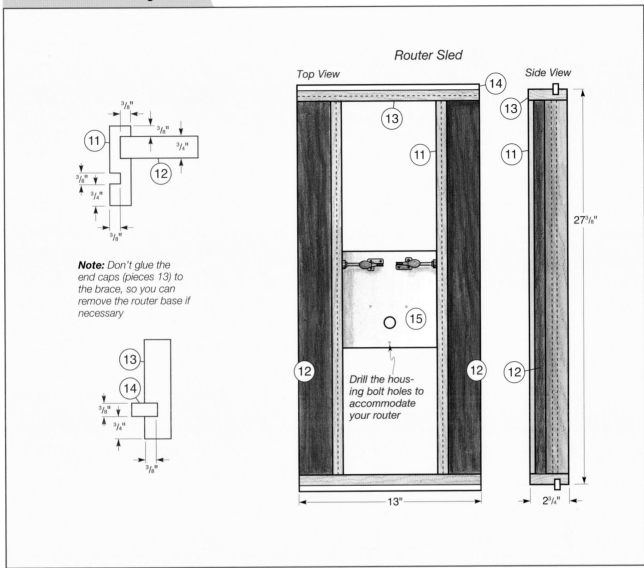

Router Sled

Top View

Side View

Note: *Don't glue the end caps (pieces 13) to the brace, so you can remove the router base if necessary*

Drill the housing bolt holes to accommodate your router

27³/₈"

13"

2³/₄"

With that done, you can apply the laminate to the top surface in the same way as the underside, with one exception: The top laminate is installed as three separate sheets (pieces 4 and 5) to fit the areas between the two top grooves. Use small blocks of ³/₄"-thick scrap (see Figure 4) to line up the edges of the laminate with the edges of the two grooves. When everything is in place, use your dowels, roller and flush-trim bit to complete the installation. Trim off any overhanging laminate with a router and piloted flush-trim bit.

Making the Hardwood Runners

These two runners (pieces 6) provide a stable parallel track for the router when making long cuts. To lay out the six grooves, refer to the Technical Drawings on page 83. Transfer this pattern to the end of your workpieces, then mill them on your router table, taking several passes (see Figure 5).

Notch the ends of the runners to fit over the ¼" trim you already installed on the base—hold the piece on edge against your table saw's miter gauge and nibble the waste away. Clamp

the runners in place and then turn the entire base upside down (you'll need a helper), to install 1¼" sheetrock screws in the pilot holes you drilled earlier to secure the runners. Countersink the screw heads and pre-drill the hardwood runners before driving the screws home. Don't glue them in as you may have to replace them if they ever start wearing out.

Reinforcing the Runners

To keep the runners perpendicular to the base, make and install the ten hardwood stabilizers (pieces 7). The

3/8" 11/16" (8)

3/8"

5/8"

(9)

Locate the UHMW white plastic glides according
to the dimensions in the elevation above.

Holddown Beam

pattern for these is included in the
Drawings. Cut the stabilizers on your
bandsaw, then clamp them in a bench
vise to belt-sand them to final size.
Mark their locations (see Technical
Drawings on page 77 or 83) on the
base, then screw them in place from
the bottom with 1⅝" sheetrock screws,
countersinking and pre-drilling as you
go. To secure them to the runners, use
1¼"-long screws. Drill countersinks in
the bottoms of the runners' grooves
with a ⅜" Forstner bit, just deep enough
to ensure that the screw heads are
below the surface. Then use a ⅛" bit to
pre-drill the runners, and continue with
a 5/64" bit to extend the pilot hole into the
stabilizers. Drive the screws home, then
move on to the holddowns.

Assembling the Holddowns
A stable workpiece is essential
for quality work, not to mention
safety. This holddown system works
wonderfully for long boards and
plywood panels.

Make the two beams for the
holddowns (pieces 8) from solid
hardwood with straight grain. With the
beams cut to size, form grooves across
each end (see the Elevation Drawings
above for dimensions) to hold the UHMW
plastic glides (pieces 9). You can cut
these grooves on your table saw with a
tenoning jig, or use a high auxiliary fence
and your miter gauge to nibble away the
waste. Epoxy the two glides in place and
when they're dry, belt-sand the plastic
flush. Then use your table saw's miter
gauge to trim the glides for a nice snug fit
in the runners' grooves.

Screw the push clamps (pieces
10) in place next—see the Technical
Drawings on page 83 for locations—and
then set the holddowns aside and work
on making the router sled.

Building the Router Sled
You've already cut all the parts for the
sled to size, so now you can go to your
router table and mill a ⅜"-wide groove
down the inside of each of the sled
runners (pieces 11) at the locations
given in the Drawings on page 79. Then
turn each piece over and cut a ¾"-wide
groove on the outside face. Glue and

screw a brace (piece 12) into each of
the wider grooves, making sure that the
ends are absolutely flush.

The sled end caps (pieces 13)
are also grooved (see Figure 6) for the
sled glides (pieces 14). Epoxy these
glides in place just like you did the ones
on the holddowns, then trim when dry.

Make the polycarbonate router
base (piece 15) next, cutting it to size
and then drilling for the bolts (pieces
16) that attach it to the router housing.
Use bolts, nuts and washers (pieces 17
and 18) to secure the two push clamps
(pieces 19) that lock the router base
in position on the sled. Screw the end
caps to the sled runners, countersinking
and pre-drilling for 2"-long screws.
Don't glue the end caps—you may have
to replace the router base one day.

If you use a fixed-base router
with this jig, I recommend purchasing
a second router base housing and
leaving it permanently and conveniently
attached to the jig. Depending on your
router model, you may have to remove
the two knobs on the base housing so
the sled won't get too wide.

Finishing and Using the Jig

Danish oil is a good finish for shop jigs, and wax is the best lubricant for the sled and base runner slots. To use the jig, clamp it to your workbench and drop in a spacer (piece 20) as needed to line up the workpiece with the router bit. See page 76 for more details on general set-up and use.

For surfacing operations, make the cuts in a series of light, skimming passes to keep from overloading the router and bit. Use a wide, carbide-tipped straight bit for this work. Since the router is captured in the jig, feed direction doesn't really matter. When you're done, hang the jig on your shop wall, using the holddowns to secure the sled in place.

Figure 6: *The router sled rides on plastic glides made from UHMW, a self-lubricating material.*

QuickTip

These plywood templates work great for setting both miter gauge and blade angles

Gauges for Setting Up Saw Angles

Rather than look for a protractor or T-bevel, or trust the arrow indicators on your miter and bevel gauges, make a set of setup gauges for quick and reliable reference. ¼" plywood works fine for this purpose. Keep them close to your table saw and miter saw for setting up angles as well as cutting pentagons, hexagons, octagons and even segmented bowls.

Base Assembly
(Top view)

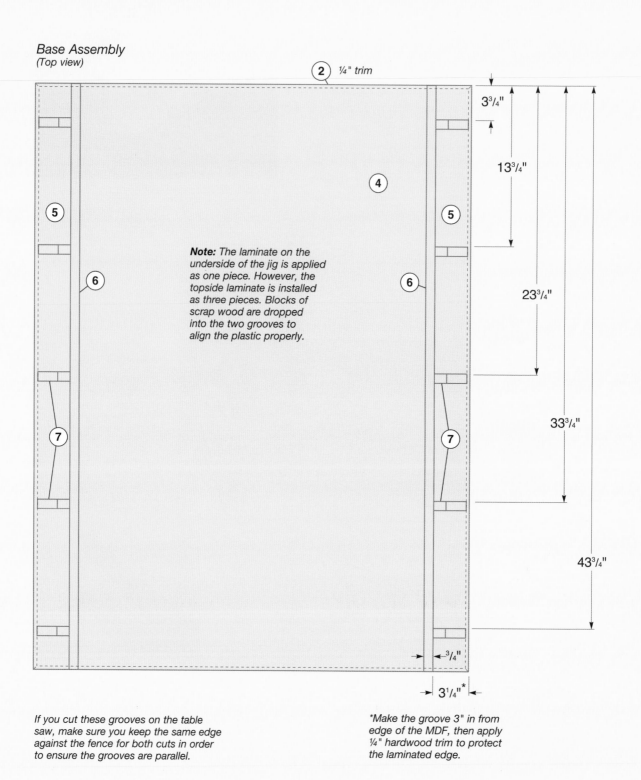

② ¼" trim

3³/₄"

13³/₄"

23³/₄"

33³/₄"

43³/₄"

³/₄"

3¹/₄"*

Note: *The laminate on the underside of the jig is applied as one piece. However, the topside laminate is installed as three pieces. Blocks of scrap wood are dropped into the two grooves to align the plastic properly.*

If you cut these grooves on the table saw, make sure you keep the same edge against the fence for both cuts in order to ensure the grooves are parallel.

*Make the groove 3" in from edge of the MDF, then apply ¼" hardwood trim to protect the laminated edge.

Base Runner
(End view)

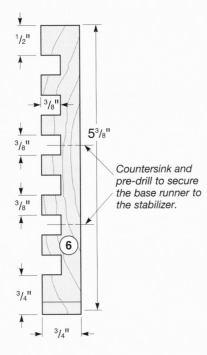

1/2"

3/8"

3/8"

3/8"

5 3/8"

Countersink and
pre-drill to secure
the base runner to
the stabilizer.

6

3/4"

3/4"

Stabilizer
(Side view)

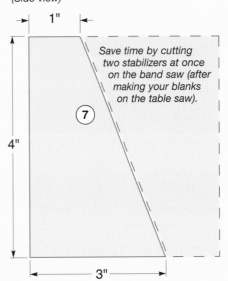

1"

Save time by cutting
two stabilizers at once
on the band saw (after
making your blanks
on the table saw).

7

4"

3"

The stabilizers are screwed to the base
from the bottom with 1⅝" sheetrock
screws, countersunk and pre-drilled.

Sled Runner & Brace
(End view)

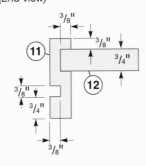

3/8"

3/8"

3/4"

11

12

3/8"

3/4"

3/8"

Sled End Cap & Guides
(End view)

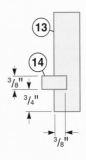

13

14

3/8"

3/4"

3/8"

Holddown Beam
(Side view)

Suggested clamp locations
(3 screws per clamp).

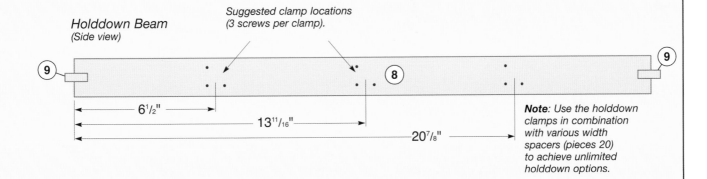

9

9

8

6 1/2"

13 11/16"

20 7/8"

Note: Use the holddown
clamps in combination
with various width
spacers (pieces 20)
to achieve unlimited
holddown options.

PATTERN ROUTING MADE EASY

Sooner or later a project will require you to make pairs of curved, complementary shapes that fit perfectly together. Before you reach for your band or scroll saw, there's a better way: use a router and guide bushings to pattern-rout them instead.

In woodworking, straight and curved cuts have one very important thing in common—you have to deal with a slight void once the cut is completed. And more often than not this kerf has a big impact on the success of your project.

If you've ever tried to cut separate curved parts that need to fit together tightly, it can be challenging with a bandsaw or scroll saw. There is, however, a technique for cutting curves that will allow them to fit back together absolutely perfectly. It's called pattern routing, and the finished cuts are made with a straight bit in the router. Saws take a back seat for this procedure.

The secret to getting this perfect fit lies in the router setup. A guide bushing, installed in the router's base plate, follows the edge of a template to create a workpiece that's the same shape, but slightly different in size. A correctly matched bushing and bit will automatically eliminate that kerf.

There are two key variations on the technique of pattern routing. The first works for projects where two edges meet in a wavy line. Here the technique is called complementary routing: the shape of one edge complements the other. The second technique is called inlay routing: one piece is completely contained by the other.

By using one of these two pattern-routing methods, a woodworker can build projects that incorporate an almost unlimited variety of shapes.

Try this simple approach to inlay and complementary routing and take the most versatile tool in your shop to a new level.

by Jim Dolan

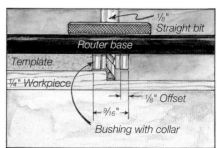

Figure 1: *When inlay routing, a removable collar follows the template while cutting the background piece, creating a ⅛" offset.*

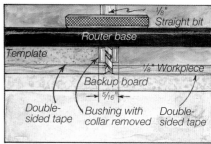

Figure 2: *Then you remove the collar to cut the inlay piece, forcing the bit ⅛" closer to the template, eliminating the offset.*

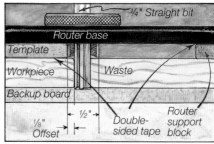

Figure 3: *When properly set up for complementary routing, the edge of the bit is ⅛" from the edge of the bushing. The two ⅛" offsets (one on the foreground template, one on the background template) combine to equal the ¼" bit diameter.*

Inlay Routing

Inlay routing is the technique that's probably used most often and is most familiar to woodworkers. During this procedure, you rout a shallow recess in a female (background) piece, then follow up by routing a contrasting inlay piece to fit the recess. Inlay routing involves just one template and a simple accessory for the router: an inlay kit that includes a bushing and a removable collar. Both are used while routing the female workpiece (background), and then the collar is removed when you're ready to rout the male (inlay) piece.

You start the process by transferring a paper pattern onto a hardboard template. Although the pattern can be any size, there is one limitation to its shape. The radius of any curve must be at least as large as the radius of the removable collar used on the router. You probably know from experience that you can't rout a female shape with perfectly pointed corners (like a star), because a router bit can't rout pointed inside corners. Well, the same principle applies to a router set up with a bushing or removable collar. There is a way to create an inlay with sharp points, but it involves chisels or carving tools.

After the template has been cut, filed and sanded to the exact shape of the pattern, the next step is to set up the router with an inlay bushing kit, as shown in the photo on the previous page. Typically, this setup consists of a ⁵⁄₁₆"-diameter bushing installed in the base plate of the router with a ⁹⁄₁₆"-diameter removable collar that fits over the bushing like a ring on your finger. Finally, a ⅛" straight bit is installed in the router and adjusted to cut a recess to the desired depth, as shown in Figure 1.

When the router has been set up, use double-sided tape to attach the template to the workpiece. The removable collar on the bushing follows the template and the bit cuts a shallow recess in the female (background) piece. You can use the same bit to remove the remaining waste or, if there is a lot to remove, a larger straight bit can be substituted. If you do decide to change to a larger bit, make a few passes on a piece of scrap wood with the ⅛" straight bit, and use this scrap to help set the depth of the second, larger bit.

To cut a matching inlay piece, use the same template but now remove the collar from the bushing, as shown in Figure 2. By removing it you effectively move the router bit ⅛" closer to the template, which compensates for the thickness of the router bit. So, in one complete circular pass you create an inlay the exact size of your recess.

Complementary Routing

The procedure for complementary routing is almost the same as for inlay routing, but no special kit is necessary. All you need is a common bushing (½" diameter for example) and a straight bit (¼" diameter). The big difference between this and inlay routing is that instead of one template there are two (or more, depending on the complexity of your design).

As with inlay routing, your first step is to transfer a paper pattern to hardboard and then cut, sand and file it to exact shape. With this technique however, you are still creating a pattern, not a template. Once this hardboard pattern is refined, use double-sided carpet tape to fix it to a second layer of hardboard, where it will guide the router to create both the foreground and background templates at the same time, as shown in the photo below.

At this point, you might wonder where the offset comes in. And how does the kerf get automatically replaced? Well, in the case of the cutting board, the edge of the router bit is ⅛" from the edge of the bushing, as shown in Figure 3. This means that when the foreground (fish) is routed, its edge will be ⅛" larger than the template edge. And when the background is routed using the complementary template, its edge will be ⅛" larger as well. In combination, these two ⅛" offsets replace the kerf left by the ¼" router bit. The result is a perfectly complementary fit.

Complementary routing allows you to achieve a perfect, kerf-free match between two parts of a pattern.

CIRCLE-CUTTING JIG

This versatile and easy-to-build jig will have you cutting circles of virtually any size in no time. It's a second-generation improvement to the original circle-cutting jig shown below. Rather than employing a pivot point, this clever design features a revolving, clear plate to guide the router.

by John English

Figure 1: *Use your regular circle-cutting jig to create the Plexiglas™ disk at the heart of the new jig. Back up the cut with scrap plywood.*

The author's original *pivot-point circle jig (above) is still useful for oversized circle-cutting, but the new design lends even more versatility.*

Many years ago, we featured my "first generation" circle-cutting jig. It was a popular project among readers, with just one glitch: it couldn't cut a circle with a diameter smaller than the radius of the router's subbase. This problem certainly isn't unique; most circle-cutting jigs have one thing in common: they cut a radius equal to the distance between the router bit and the pivot. The size of the router base limits how short that distance can be.

Being the industrious sort, I went back to the drawing board and came up with the ingenious second-generation jig you see here. It doesn't require a pivot point, which opens up the range of circle-cutting capabilities tremendously.

Creating the Plexiglas™ Disk

The basis of my jig is a large disk that revolves inside a frame. Mounting the router to this disk effectively eliminates the pivot point. To use the jig, the frame is centered on the workpiece and clamped in place. You can change the diameter of the circle simply by changing the position of the router on the disk. Clear Plexiglas™ works best for making the disk: seeing through it is essential for positioning the router bit correctly on the workpiece.

Use a regular circle-cutting jig to cut the disk (piece 1) to the dimensions given in the Material List on page 88 (see Figure 1, above). After routing the disk, gently break the top and bottom edges of the disk with sandpaper. Cut the top and bottom of the jig (pieces 2 and 3) to size from a sheet of sturdy MDF (medium-density fiberboard).

Center the disk on the jig top and mark around its edge with a pencil (see Figure 2). Then use your regular circle-cutting jig to plow the rabbet in the middle of the top that supports the disk (see Figure 3). Use the same jig to create the large hole in the center of the top. Look to the Jig Top Elevation on page 88 for key measurements.

Finish Building the Base

The safest way to secure work in this jig is to attach it to a sacrificial piece of ¼" scrap plywood, then clamp the plywood in place. That way, if you cut through

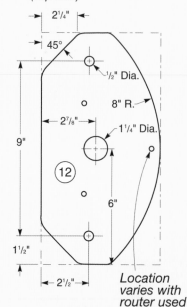

Router Mount
(Top View)

2¼"

45°

½" Dia.

8" R.

2⅞"

1¼" Dia.

9"

12

6"

1½"

2½"

Location
varies with
router used

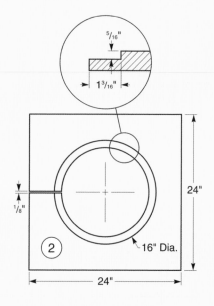

Jig Top
(Top View)

5/16"

1³/₁₆"

24"

⅛"

2

16" Dia.

24"

Material List - Circle Jig

		T x W x L
1 Plexiglas™ Disk (1)		¼" x 16" Dia.
2 Jig Top (1)		¾" x 24" x 24"
3 Jig Bottom (1)		¾" x 24" x 24"
4 Spacers (2)		¾" x 1" x 24"
5 Centering Cleats (2)		¾" x 1⅜" x 24"
6 Torque Adj. Plates (2)		¾" x 2" x 4"
7 Torque Adj. Plate Screws (4)		#8 x 2"
8 Torque Adj. Bolt (1)		5/16" - 18 x 1½" T-bolt
9 Torque Adj. Knob (1)		5/16" - 18 x 2" T-knob
10 Piano Hinge (1)		1⅛" x 24" Brass
11 Hinge Screws (20)		Brass
12 Plexiglas™ Router Mount (1)		¼" x 6½" x 12"
13 Router Mount Knobs (2)		5/16" - 18 x 2" T-knob
14 Router Mount Bolts (2)		5/16" - 18 x 1½" T-bolt
15 Router Mount Washers (4)		⅜" ID
16 Router Mount Lock Washers (2)		⅜" ID
17 Guide Knob (1)		5/16" - 18 x 2" Ball knob
18 Guide Knob Bolt (1)		5/16" - 18 x 1½" T-bolt
19 Guide Knob Washers (2)		⅜" ID
20 Guide Knob Nut (1)		5/16" - 18

Figure 2: *Center the Plexiglas disk on the sheet of MDF that will become the top of the jig, and scribe around the edge with a pencil.*

the workpiece, you won't cut into the jig, too.

With that in mind, you'll need a full inch of clearance between the jig top and bottom (¼" for the plywood and ¾" for a standard workpiece). Do it by installing two spacers (pieces 4) on the jig bottom. Secure these with glue and countersunk screws.

A pair of cleats (pieces 5) are then glued and screwed in place to add a bit of strength (see the *Exploded View* at right).

Building the Adjustable Top

The odds that the Plexiglas™ disk will fit perfectly in its rabbet (without any play) are very slim. Fortunately, there's a simple remedy: you can make the top adjustable by cutting a kerf in one of its edges, then adding a built-in clamping device. (See the Exploded View at right.) It makes the jig adjustable so the disk revolves freely, but without slop.

Before attaching the torque adjustment plates to the jig, you need to plow some grooves in the disk (see Disk Groove Elevation). Using the jig as a clamp, set the disk in its rabbet and secure it with a bar clamp. Doing this now makes sense because the torque mechanism would be in the way if it were installed first. Locate the grooves

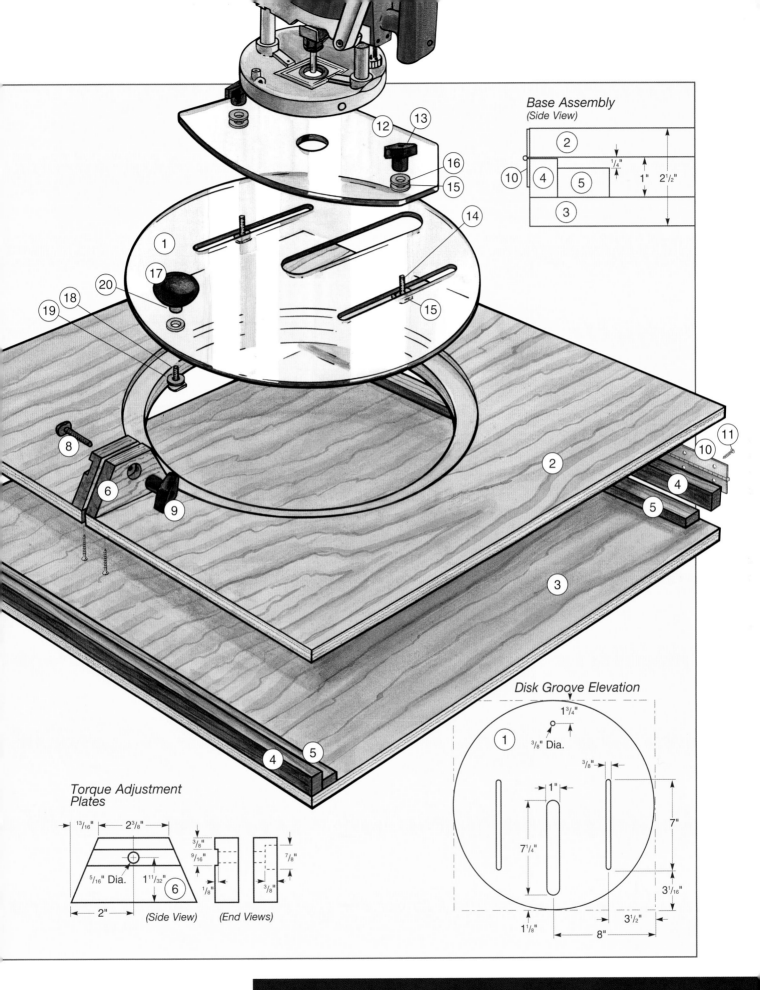

Base Assembly
(Side View)

Disk Groove Elevation

Torque Adjustment
Plates

(Side View)   (End Views)

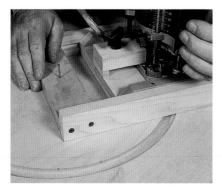

Figure 3: *Use your regular circle-cutting jig to reveal the recessed rabbet in the new jig, and to remove the waste from its center.*

Figure 4: *With a kerf cut through one edge of the jig top, clamp the disk in place and use a straightedge to mill the various grooves.*

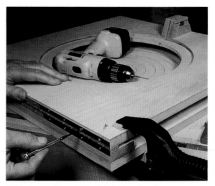

Figure 5: *Pre-drill pilot holes for the screws in the continuous hinge that keeps the top and bottom of the jig properly aligned.*

and mill them with a straight bit, guiding your plunge router with a clamped-on straightedge (as shown in Figure 4).

Begin building the torque adjustment mechanism by cutting the two plates (pieces 6) to size. Plow a dado in one face of one plate, then temporarily clamp them together and drill a hole through both (see Torque Adjustment Plates Elevation, previous page). Counterbore the hole in the second plate and band-saw both plates to their final shape. Then sand the sawn edges smooth.

Attach the plates to the jig top with glue and screws (pieces 7), driven up through the bottom of the jig top into

piloted, countersunk holes. After the glue has fully cured, insert the T-bolt and knob (pieces 8 and 9).

Attach the jig top to the bottom with a piano hinge (piece 10), securing it with screws (piece 11) driven into pre-drilled pilot holes, as shown in Figure 5. Align the top and bottom perfectly and clamp them in place as you set the hinge.

At this point, it's a good idea to sharpen your pencil and draw a series of concentric circles on the base (see Figure 6). Make them 1" apart to help you center stock under the disk. This will minimize waste as you use the jig.

Mount your Router in the Jig

Virtually any plunge router will work with this jig. Mid-sized models are perfect choices. You can use a standard machine as long as the bit height is set by screwing the motor housing into the base. Routers with a motor housing that slides freely up and down in the base until locked in position are not a safe option here.

The long edge of the router mount (piece 12) matches the diameter of the disk, while its back edge is shaped to match the router base. On a piece of Plexiglas™, lay out the basic design shown on the Router Mount Elevation, then make any necessary changes to

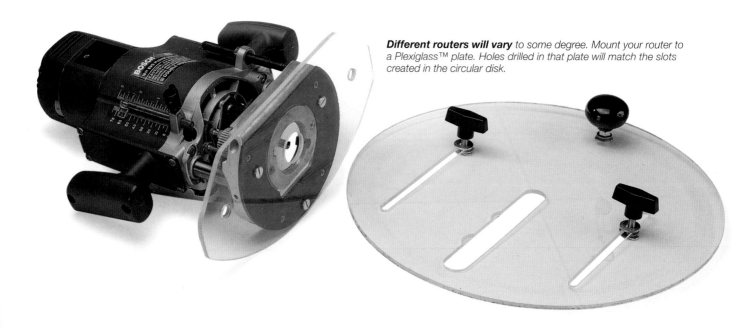

Different routers will vary *to some degree. Mount your router to a Plexiglass™ plate. Holes drilled in that plate will match the slots created in the circular disk.*

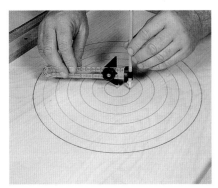

Figure 6: *Draw a series of concentric circles 1" apart on the base, to center the workpiece under the router and minimize waste.*

accommodate your specific router. Band-saw it to shape, sand the edges and drill the two large holes shown on the drawings: these house the knobs, bolts, washers and lock washers (pieces 13 through 16) that make the mount adjustable and lock it in position. Mark, drill and countersink holes in the mount for the screws that attach your router's subbase, then remove the subbase and install the router on the new Plexiglas™ mount. Attach the mount to the disk with T-knobs.

A free-turning guide knob (piece 17) makes revolving the disk a lot easier. Drill a hole for the knob and install it with a bolt, two washers and a nut (pieces 18 through 20). The knob should spin freely after the nut is tightened.

Taking the Jig for a Spin

Now it's time to fire up your router and take this jig for a spin—literally! You can use any fluted straight bit for cutting circles, and spiral carbide up-cut bits work particularly well. Cut the circles by making a series of passes, setting the bit depth a little deeper each time. Start each pass with the bit raised out of the cut, then plunge it in and turn the router slowly counterclockwise

Open up the jig as necessary to clear the chips inside or if they impede the movement of the router. For other important usage tips and a few project ideas, see the *sidebar* at right.

You can cut inside or outside circles with this jig, in stock up to ¾" thick for a through cut or 1" thick for a stopped cut. The outside diameter depends on the size of your router's base, but most routers will allow a circle up to about 12" in diameter.

The key to safe, accurate results is securing the workpiece properly. Judicious use of double-sided tape and drops of hot-melt adhesive will keep your material stationary throughout the machining process (see *photo* at right).

John also uses a piece of scrap sheet stock (secured in place with hot melt or tape) under the workpiece. This allows him to cut completely through the stock without accidentally routing into the bottom of the jig. As with many shop jigs, the creativity of the user is the only limit to its usefulness.

The jig works well *with straight bits to cut circles, but switch to a standard router table to mill decorative edges.*

Locate spots of hot-melt glue *under each of the parts you are making, so that when a part is cut free it can't drift into the spinning router bit.*

Routing perfect circles *allows you to create an unlimited number of projects and decorative motifs.*

ACCURATE DADOES... IN A HURRY

by Rob Johnstone

This jig provides quick and accurate set-ups when cutting through or stopped dadoes and sliding dovetails. The flip-up stops and hold-down clamp firmly control your workpiece. And when you're done, the jig conveniently hangs on a wall for storage.

Quick and Easy Grooves

Quick, easy and accurate ... that's what you'll get with this jig. It's quick to set up (both depth settings and dado placements), and it's quick when it comes to making repeatable cuts: the sliding hinged stops help you plow successive indexed dadoes (like those on matching bookcase sides) in a hurry.

Because you move the router across the stock—not the stock across a table saw—it's also a lot easier (especially on your back). And if you do any type of cabinetry, from bookcases to entertainment centers, you'll find this jig indispensible for plowing three styles of common dadoes: stopped, through and sliding dovetail.

Through dadoes are the easiest to make, although not as attractive if they remain in plain view.

Stopped dadoes allow you to hide the forward aspect of the joint, but they also force you to accommodate the stopped portion of the joint with a matching notch or rebate.

Sliding dovetails are a more challenging variation of a dado. The familiar wedge-like shape creates a strong and attractive mechanical joint.

Scrap wood and a little know-how are all you need sometimes. For example, a bare-bones version of this jig hung in my father and uncle's woodworking shop from the day I set foot in it. It was made from fir plywood and nondescript scrap lumber, but it was constantly in demand as people worked through their various projects. As a matter of fact, the first bookcase I made for my wife was machined on that jig more than 20 years ago. Of course my version is a Mercedes when compared to that basic Volkswagen bug, but if you're looking for a valuable tool for your shop, feel free to use whatever hardwood scrap you have on hand to create your own version.

Start by cutting the deck (piece 1) from a sheet of melamine and the rails (pieces 2) from hardwood stock. Go ahead and cut the front and rear rail returns (pieces 3 and 4) at the same time. Move to your table saw, and with a dado head in place, plow the long grooves in the rails and the shallow rabbets on the front and rear rail returns. Look to the Exploded Drawings on the opposite page and Technical Drawings on pages 98 and 99 for the machining details. Remember most sheet stock these days is just a bit under a true ¾" thickness. Check your grooves in scrap lumber to be sure they fit properly. Now take a few moments to find out how large an opening you will need to create for your router.

For this jig to be accurate, your router must fit snugly between the guide rails. And to ensure smooth sliding action, these rails are lined with plastic laminate. This also means they'll wear better for you. If the liners do begin to show wear, you can just peel them off and replace them with fresh laminate. (Voila!, good as new!)

Measure the width of your router base plus the two pieces of the plastic laminate you will be using. This is the only way to arrive at the opening you'll need for your router, as shown in Figure 1, above.

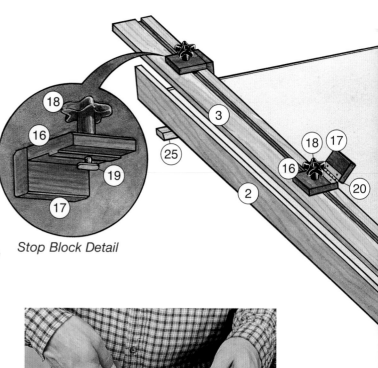

Stop Block Detail

Figure 1: *Determining the space required for your router is critical to the success of this jig. Measure your router and the two pieces of laminate to get the exact dimension.*

Custom Measurements

Take the measurement you found for the router opening and transfer it to the top edges of the rails, 24" from one end (see the Technical Drawings). Form a notch on each rail to accommodate

the router rest and receiver. I left the dado head in the saw to nibble out these notches with the help of a miter gauge.

Measure from the end of the rails to the edges of your notch and cut your front and rear rail returns into properly sized segments. Then look to the Technical Drawings for the location of the track groove in the face of the left front rail return segment. While you're at it, find the locations of the quick depth-setting aids in the face of the right front rail return. Use a Forstner bit to bore these four 1" diameter stopped holes at exactly ⅛", ¼", ⅜" and ½" depths. These holes serve as instant depth setters.

Now you're ready to start the first assembly phase. Predrill and counterbore pilot holes, then attach the rails to the deck with #8 x 1¼" screws and glue (see Figure 2). Cap the screw holes with walnut plugs (pieces 5). Next, join the front and rear rail return segments to the deck/rail subassembly, again using

Melamine, an easy to find sheet stock, is a good choice for this shop jig, due to its hard plastic surface and dimensional stability. It is sized in sheets measuring 49" x 97" to allow for trimming. The factory edge is often damaged during shipping.

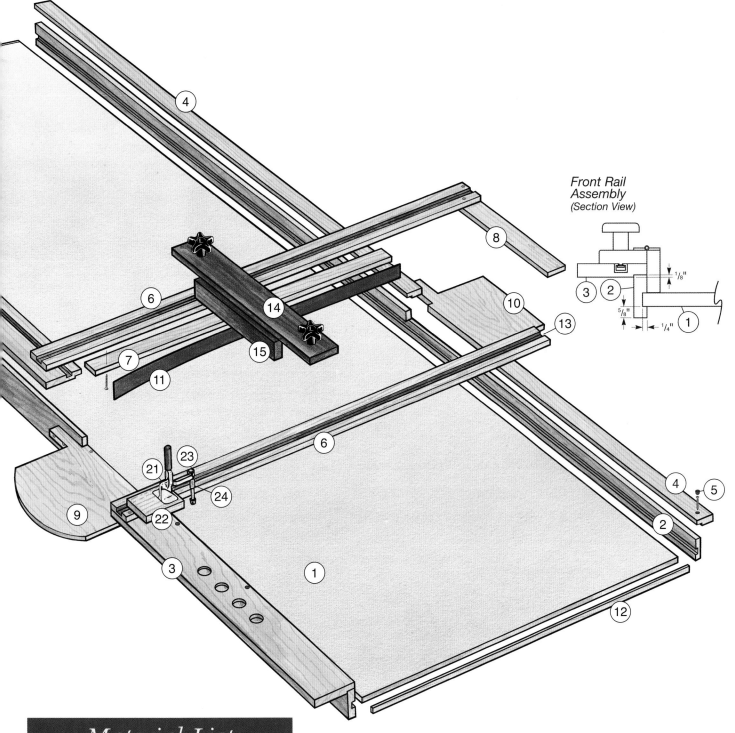

Front Rail Assembly (Section View)

Material List

	T x W x L		T x W x L
1 Deck (1)	¾" x 26½" x 72"	**14** Centering Stop (1)	¾" x 2½" x (*)
2 Rails (2)	¾" x 2⅜" x 72"	**15** Center Stop Return (1)	¾" x 1½" x (*)
3 Front Rail Return (1)	¾" x 4" x 72"	**16** Side Stop Tops (3)	¾"" x 2¾" x 2⅞"
4 Rear Rail Return (1)	¾" x 2½" x 72"	**17** Side Stops (3)	¾" x 2⅜" x 2⅞"
5 Walnut Plugs (bag)	⅜" Dia. flat	**18** Stop Knobs (5)	Plastic, 5⁄16" thread
6 Guide Rails (2)	¾" x 2½" x 39"	**19** T-Bolts (5)	Steel
7 Under Rails (2)	¾" x 2¼" x 25⅞"	**20** Stop Hinge (1)	1½" x 36" (Piano)
8 End Spacer (1)	¾" x 2½" x (*)	**21** Hold Down Clamp (1)	Steel
9 Router Rest (1)	¾" x 8¾" x 12"	**22** Clamp Spacer (1)	¾" x 2½" x 4"
10 Router Receiver (1)	¾" x 6¼" x 12"	**23** Hex Bolt (1)	5⁄16" x 1" Steel
11 Laminate liners (2)	1⁄16" x 1¼" x 25⅞"	**24** Connector Nut (1)	5⁄16 ID
12 Deck Trim (2)	⅛" x ¾" x 26½"	**25** Hanger Cleats (2)	¾" x 1¾" x 24"
13 Aluminum T-Tracks (3)	48"		

(*) Adjust these pieces' lengths to accommodate your router.

Four holes drilled *to specific depths become a feature that lets you quickly set your router to predetermined settings. Use a Forstner bit to bore these holes to ⅛", ¼", ⅜" and ½". It's quicker and safer than flipping the router over to measure from the base plate.*

The center stop *not only allows you to stop your dadoes accurately, but it also lines up your dado cuts to the path of the router bit. Use contrasting paint colors in shallow saw kerfs to identify where the center of the dado is, as well as where a full ¾" dado will fall.*

Flip-up sliding stops *allow you to register multiple identical dadoes on matching pieces. Bookcases, display shelves and cabinets of all sorts are easier to make with this basic shop jig.*

glue and screws capped with the walnut plugs. Check to be sure the rail segments are square as you proceed.

Cut the guide rails and under rails (pieces 6 and 7) to size. Move back to the table saw and plow grooves for more aluminum track down the length of each guide rail, then attach the under rails to the guide rails with glue and screws driven up through the bottom. Clamp the guide rail subassemblies onto the deck subassembly exactly flush to the edges of the notches. Measure edge to edge across the guide rails to determine the exact length of the end spacer (piece 8). Cut this piece to length and secure it to the guide rails with countersunk screws and glue. Finally, go ahead and attach the guide rail subassembly to the deck subassembly with countersunk screws, but no glue.

Special Seating

The router rest and the router receiver (pieces 9 and 10) are made from hardwood and are mounted into the notched openings that you created earlier in the rails. Both of these pieces must be

Figure 2: *Attach the rails to the melamine deck with screws and glue. Cover the exposed screw holes with walnut plugs.*

surface-sanded or planed down to the nominal thickness of manufactured sheet stock (about ¹¹⁄₁₆"). This will keep your router from "stepping down" as it enters sheet stock clamped to the deck.

On the bandsaw, shape both pieces to fit into the notched opening and form the rounded rest's back edge. Predrill

Keep your jig out of harm's way by machining matching beveled hanger cleats. One goes on the back of the jig, the other on the wall.

for countersunk screws as shown on the Exploded View, page 95, and mount them to the jig with screws only. On your table saw, slice the laminate liners (pieces 11) from high-pressure plastic laminate. Then, using contact cement, glue the liners to the inside faces of the guide rail subassembly. Use a file to smooth the edges of the plastic laminate.

Slice the deck trim (pieces 12) from a piece of hardwood, cut two pieces to length and glue them to both ends of the deck. I used masking tape to "clamp" the trim in place until the glue cured.

Bells and Whistles

Now you've come to the features that really add to this jig's versatility. Start by mounting the aluminum tracks (pieces 13). Cut the pieces to length with a hack saw, and be sure to file or sand the ends smooth to remove any sharp edges. Next cut the centering stop (piece 14) to the same length as the end spacer and the center stop return (piece 15) so it's ¹⁄₁₆" less than the distance between the laminate liners. Glue these pieces

together (as shown in the Technical Drawings). After the glue has cured, place the stop on the guide rails and drill ⁵⁄₁₆" diameter holes to align with the aluminum track. Next, cut the side stop tops and side stops (pieces 16 and 17) to size. Reveal the top's raised tenon, which slides in the aluminum track, in two passes on your table saw. Drill the ⁵⁄₁₆" holes to mount the knobs and T-bolts (pieces 18 and 19) and cut sections of piano hinge (piece 20) to join the tops and sides, forming two flip-up sliding stops. Glue up the third side and top for the end stop, which does not flip up.

To hold your work in place as you are routing, mount a hold-down clamp (piece 21) just to the right of the guide rail. I found that to get the proper reach and clearance when operating the clamp, I needed to glue a clamp spacer (piece 22) to the front rail and add a hex head bolt and connector nut (pieces 23 and 24) to the clamp, as shown in Figure 3.

One quick note: This jig is designed to plow dadoes into ¾" stock. If you need

Figure 3: The hold-down clamp is mounted on a spacer block and modified with a 1"-long hex head bolt and a connector nut.

to work in ½" or ⅜" material, all you need to do is slide the appropriate thickness spacer on top of the deck. (Double-stick tape will help keep the spacer from sliding.)

Final Details

When properly marked, the center stop can help you line up one-off dadoes. To find your registration lines, use your router to plow a ¾" dado in a scrap of plywood that is clamped in place. Slide the center

stop over the dado and use a combination square to transfer the edges of the dado onto the stop. Find the halfway point and mark it. Take the center stop to the table saw and, with the blade just barely above the tabletop, scribe the three lines into the face of the center stop. Once you clean up the kerfs, you can paint them contrasting colors.

Now would be a good time to mount the hanger cleats (pieces 25) to the back of the jig and on a convenient spot on your shop's wall. Apply a couple of coats of an oil finish to it to keep the dust from sticking.

Technical Drawings
Router Dadoing Jig

Hold Down Clamp Subassembly
(Side View)

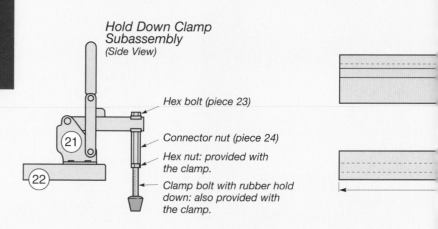

Hex bolt (piece 23)

Connector nut (piece 24)

Hex nut: provided with the clamp.

Clamp bolt with rubber hold down: also provided with the clamp.

Front and Back Rail Subassembly Detail

Track on left side

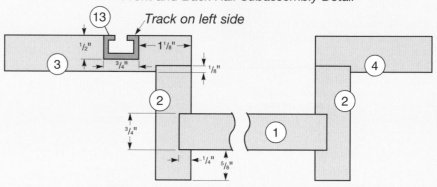

Flip-up Sliding Stop
(End View)

45° chamfer

The fixed stop is identical to the flip-up stops: simply glue piece 17 to piece 16 in the exact orientation shown at left.

45° chamfer

Sliding Stop Machining Detail

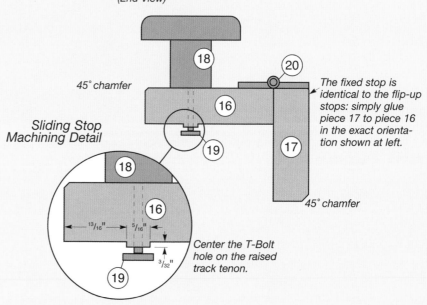

Center the T-Bolt hole on the raised track tenon.

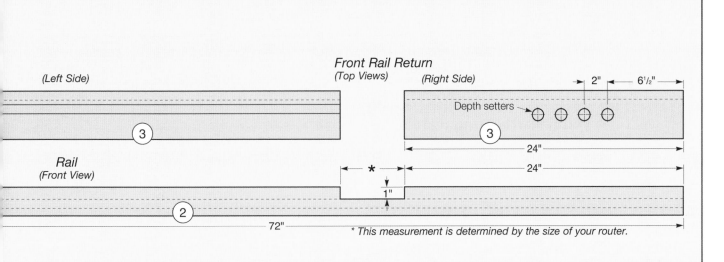

Front Rail Return
(Top Views)

(Left Side)

(3)

(Right Side)

Depth setters

2"   6½"

(3)

24"

Rail
(Front View)

*

24"

1"

(2)

72"

* This measurement is determined by the size of your router.

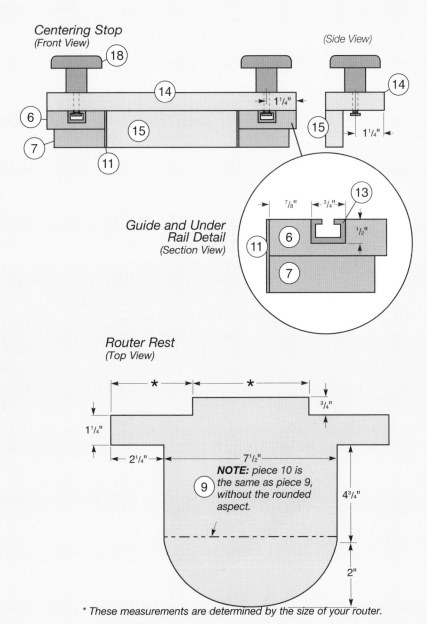

Centering Stop
(Front View)

(Side View)

(18)

(14)

(14)

(6)

1¼"

(15)

(15)

1¼"

(7)

(11)

(13)

**Guide and Under
Rail Detail**
(Section View)

⅞"   ¾"

(11)   (6)

½"

(7)

Router Rest
(Top View)

*   *

¾"

1¼"

2¼"   7½"

NOTE: piece 10 is
the same as piece 9,
without the rounded
aspect.

(9)

4¾"

2"

* These measurements are determined by the size of your router.

SLIDING DOVETAIL SYSTEM

During his years spent in a busy furniture shop, our author created a pair of sliding dovetail jigs that are as stone simple as they are rock-solid. Build a set for yourself, and we'll bet you'll start adding more sliding dovetails to your projects.

by Jack Gray

Working in the sample shop of a high-end furniture manufacturer was a challenge. Designers would come in with a blueprint of a new piece of case goods (where all the cross rails had sliding dovetails) and say: "I need this built by the end of the week." Early on I devised a two-jig system for sliding dovetails that would handle the tails and grooves without calculations. I relied on this system for the next 11 years. Sometimes I even made the groove jig long enough to be used for fixed shelves. Our rails and shelves were always 13/16" thick, so my preferred bit

was a ¾" dovetail on a ½" shank. I needed this heavy bit since all the cuts were made in one pass.

Making the First Jig

To use these jigs, you'll need to replace your router's base plate with a 6"-square piece of ¼" Lexan® or other sheet plastic. The hole in the center should be ¾" diameter to minimize the throat. For the groove jig itself, use a piece of stock ¾"-thick, about 4" wide, and at least a foot long for the base (piece 1). Lap join one arm (piece 2) perpendicular to the base, as shown

below. Place your router (with its new plate) on the base, position the second arm parallel to the first and clamp it in position. Slide the router back and forth in an even, smooth action and adjust the arm as needed. Secure the second arm the same as the first.

Chuck a V-groove bit in the router to project ever so slightly from its base. Score the base with this setup to create a centerline on the jig. Transfer the scoreline onto the front edge of the jig with a square and knife. Now chuck your dovetail bit into the router and set the depth of cut to ⅜". Rout fully across

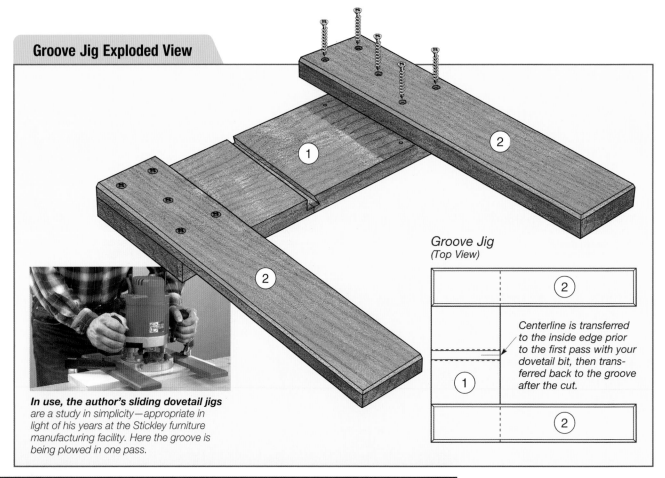

Groove Jig Exploded View

Groove Jig
(Top View)

Centerline is transferred to the inside edge prior to the first pass with your dovetail bit, then transferred back to the groove after the cut.

In use, the author's sliding dovetail jigs are a study in simplicity—appropriate in light of his years at the Stickley furniture manufacturing facility. Here the groove is being plowed in one pass.

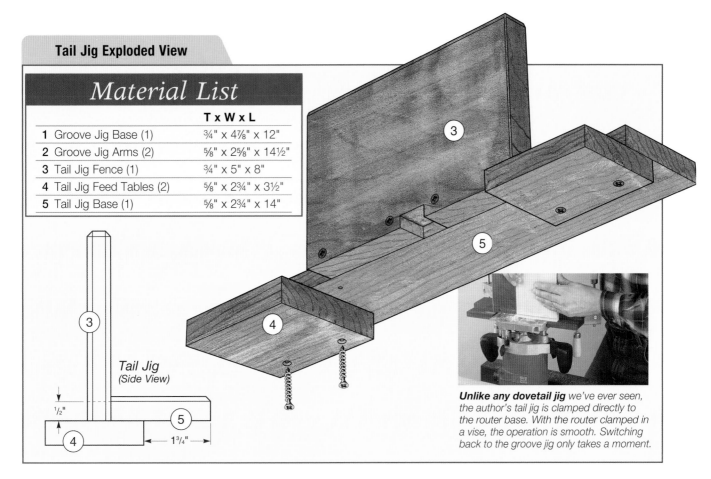

Material List		
	T x W x L	
1 Groove Jig Base (1)	¾" x 4⅞" x 12"	
2 Groove Jig Arms (2)	⅝" x 2⅝" x 14½"	
3 Tail Jig Fence (1)	¾" x 5" x 8"	
4 Tail Jig Feed Tables (2)	⅝" x 2¾" x 3½"	
5 Tail Jig Base (1)	⅝" x 2¾" x 14"	

Tail Jig
(Side View)

½"

1¾"

Unlike any dovetail jig we've ever seen, the author's tail jig is clamped directly to the router base. With the router clamped in a vise, the operation is smooth. Switching back to the groove jig only takes a moment.

the base of your jig and extend the centerline with a knife inside this cut. That's it…the first jig is ready.

Using the Groove Jig

Position your jig so its centerline is perfectly lined up with the layout line of your desired dovetail. Clamp the jig, stock and bench together and you're ready to plow your first groove. You can use this jig when you're forming rails, fixed shelves, toeboards and shelf supports.

Making the Second Jig

Don't change that dial!

The beauty of this sliding dovetail system is that by using the same router, setting and base plate to form both the groove and tail, you can virtually eliminate errors. As you can see from the *Drawings* above, the tail jig is equally simple to make: just a tall fence (piece 3) with small infeed and outfeed tables (pieces 4) all screwed to a base (piece 5). Cut a small notch into the center of the fence to fit the bit, then

assemble the pieces with glue and screws. It's all clamped to the router's new 6"-square plastic base plate. Rail stock will be run vertically across the face of this jig, another advantage of the new base plate—you get a nice smooth surface with a small throat.

Using the Tail Jig

Clamp your router in the inverted position. I used to just clamp mine in the tail vise of my bench, but now I use another jig to hold it more efficiently. Clamp the jig to the router base with the bit projecting just past the fence edge.

The only trial-and-error adjustment in this whole system is arriving at the width of your dovetail. By using a few pieces of scrap stock, you can easily establish the proper size by adjusting the position of the jig and testing the fit in the groove. Once you get it right, all your cuts will be correct because you have not changed the depth of the cut.

While this system will guarantee perfect sliding dovetails when used correctly, it also demands control and

organization on your part. All your pieces must be cut to length and sized before you start. And remember, once you set your router depth it cannot be changed until all the routing is completed.

Case Good Tips From an Old Pro

When assembling case goods, it's helpful to use clamps to hold the sides and pull them together, in case there is any bow in them. Also, it doesn't hurt to clamp the sides at each rail until the glue dries. And speaking of glue—polyurethane glue in a sliding dovetail works like grease. It doesn't swell the wood like carpenter's glue, and it's not tacky either. Sliding a fixed shelf into position with any other glue is an absolute nightmare. Just trust me on that.

ROUTER MORTISING MADE EASY

Plunge routers cut mortises cleanly and easily, but centering the router over the work can be finicky and time-consuming. This mortising jig takes the effort out of the centering process without sacrificing precision. A pair of bearings on the baseplate straddle the workpiece, which automatically centers the bit on the wood.

by Rick White

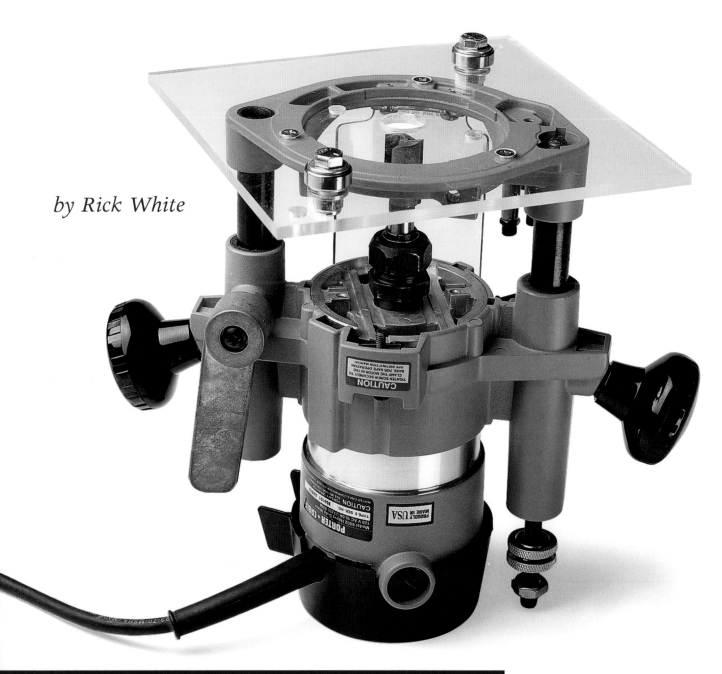

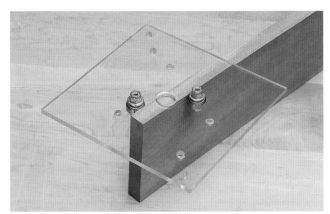

Drill extra bearing guide holes *closer together for mortising narrower stock. This allows you to get closer to the ends of a board.*

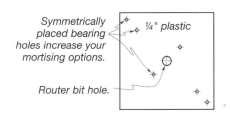

Symmetrically placed bearing holes increase your mortising options.

¼" plastic

Router bit hole.

Drill countersunk holes to match your router base mounting pattern.

There isn't much to this jig, but it's been one of my favorites for years. It's a mortising guide that automatically centers itself on the edge of just about any board. With it, you'll cut perfect mortises every time, right down the center of your workpiece. All you need is a plunge router and a straight bit with a diameter that matches your intended mortise. Clamp a ¼" piece of plywood to one side of your stock, and you can even form an off-center mortise. Like most of the jigs that earn a spot in my shop, simplicity, flexibility and ease of use are key.

The jig is just a simple, ⅜"-thick Plexiglas™ router base, with ten holes drilled in it. Two of these holes are occupied by 5⁄16" bolts that hold 5⁄16" ID bearings in place with the help of a washer and aircraft nuts. (Contact Eagle America, 800-872-2511 or www.eagleamerica.com, for supplies.) The bearings can be moved to any set of mated holes to accommodate various board thicknesses. Three holes mount the base to the router, and the last hole is for the bit.

To change the width of a mortise, just change the bit to one of a different diameter. You can even leave this base on the router permanently as a replacement for the original baseplate. In that case, just remove the bearings when you're performing other tasks.

by Ralph Bagnall

ULTIMATE FLUTING JIG

Make multiple, parallel flute cuts spaced any way you like using this jig. Our author cleverly designed it with a pair of fences and a moveable base so you can set it for different stock widths and bit positions while keeping the router tracking straight.

Transfer your router's mounting hole pattern to the jig, using its own plastic base. The jig's router base is made from ¼" plywood.

Over the years, I have made many a decorative flute cut by simply using a router and an edge guide. But a recent job, which required me to make a number of fluted newel posts (with varied spacings between the flutes), inspired me to create a dedicated jig. Because edge guides can allow the router to waver during the cut, spoiling the flute, I needed a jig that would keep the router on track.

But how do you hold the jig snug to both sides of the stock and still allow it to slide easily while routing? My solution was an adjustable and flexible second fence. It keeps the fixed fence firmly against the edge of the stock as you rout, while allowing for small variations in the stock's width. The jig also has a moveable base for the router so you can adjust the bit position easily on the workpiece.

The body of the jig is made from good-quality ½" plywood, while ¼"

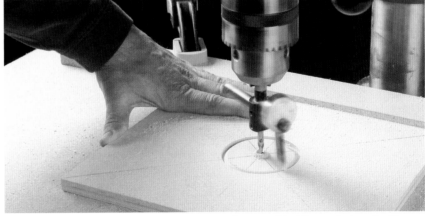

The author used an adjustable circle-cutting attachment on his drill press to form the 3" openings on the jig and router bases. He removed the rest of the waste on the table saw.

plywood is used for the router base. For strength and durability, choose straight-grained hardwood for the guides and fences. Go ahead and cut all the parts to size using the Material List on page

107 as a reference. Lay out the grooves and holes on the jig and router base (pieces 1 and 2), using the Elevation Drawings on the next page. Everything is symmetrical, so start with an accurate

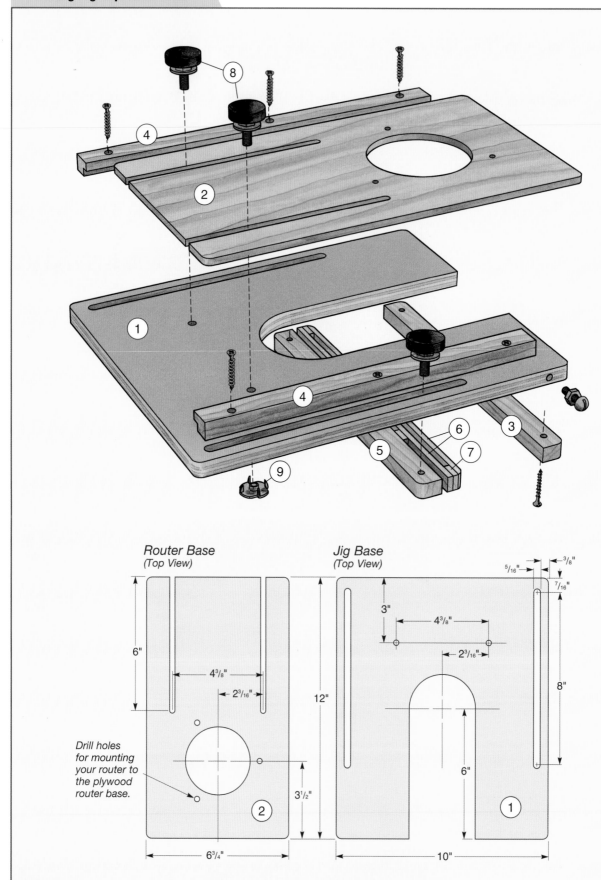

Router Base
(Top View)

Jig Base
(Top View)

Drill holes
for mounting
your router to
the plywood
router base.

Fixed and Spring Fence
(Bottom Views)

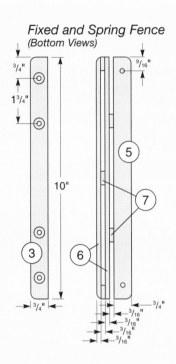

3/4"
1 3/4"
10"
3/4"
9/16"
3/4"
3/16"
3/16"
3/16"
3/16"

(5)
(7)
(3)
(6)

Guide
(End View)

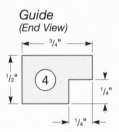

3/4"
1/2"
(4)
1/4"
1/4"

Making the slots *in the jig base is a three-step process. After you've marked where the slots belong on the base, set up your router table with a ¼" straight bit. Pivot the jig base slowly down onto the bit with the base pressed against the router fence. After the bit protrudes through the plywood, push the piece forward to complete the slot cut.*

centerline and work outward toward each side. Remove the sub-base from your router and center it on the router plate center hole so you can mark and drill the mounting holes, as shown in the top photo on page 105.

Use a drill press circle cutter (see bottom photo, page 105) to bore the 3" openings in both bases. Use a table saw or band saw to remove the rest of the waste in the jig base and follow up by milling the slots in both bases (see photo sequence, upper right). If you don't have a router table, cut the slots with a jigsaw.

Milling Solid Stock

The fixed fence (piece 3) is a straight piece of stock, rounded at the ends, glued and screwed to the edge of the jig base. The guides (pieces 4) receive a small rabbet and are affixed to the face of the base. Mount them by attaching one of the guides to the jig

base, slide in the router base, then add the second guide. The fit must be snug enough to guide the router base without binding.

Now that you have the guides properly in place, check the accuracy of the T-nut hole locations, drill the holes and counterbore for the T-nuts.

Next, the spring fence (piece 5) needs to be built. It's the flexible fence that makes the whole jig work well. Thin strips of hardwood held together with small blocks (pieces 6 and 7) provide a spring effect that presses the workpiece firmly against the fixed fence.

Mill up the fence parts a little wide so you can sand the assembly to a uniform thickness after glue-up. Check the spring fence against the outer slots in the base, then drill and tap ¼" -20 holes in the body of the guide for the knobs. Install the knobs and T-nuts (pieces 8 and 9) and you have the lion's share of this jig project behind you.

The final step is to create additional accuracy and adjustability by installing adjustable stops. These are just a couple of stove bolts that thread into the front and back edges of the jig. The addition of a nut (see the Exploded View on page 106) turns them into "micro-adjustable" stops. Simply drill and tap a ¼"-20 hole in each edge of the base, or use a threaded insert. Mount your stove bolt and nut combination and you are ready to rout. Once the stop is set, tighten the nut against the base to lock it in place.

Using the Jig

Putting this jig to work is easy as pie (and I mean apple…not the transcendental number). Mount the router, then slide the router plate onto the base, and set the center of the bit at the desired distance from the fixed fence. Then, set the depth of cut. Don't be afraid to make more than one pass if needed, to keep from overloading the bit and router. The jig allows this level of accurate repeatability. For stopped flutes, you'll have to clamp stop blocks at each end of the workpiece to limit the path of the jig. The stops on the base sides can be set to stop the jig correctly on the ends of the cut.

After you rout the first flute, flip the jig around and set it back in place. This creates two evenly spaced flutes along the edges of the workpiece face. With the two outer flutes made, you can loosen the jig knobs and reposition the router and bit on the workpiece to cut another pair of flutes or a centered flute, if applicable.

After you get used to using this jig, you'll probably find all sorts of other tasks to use it for, some of which are described at right. The two-fence system makes slotting and grooving long narrow parts easy and accurate. So, next time you need to make a mantle or reed, flute a table leg or make wooden slides, grab this jig. It will definitely keep your router on the straight and narrow!

The jig's moveable fence, with its "spring" construction, is one of the main reasons it is so effective. It has just the right amount of give to accommodate minor variations in the width of the stock you are fluting.

As often happens in the world of woodworking, this jig, which was designed for one task, easily lent itself to other related operations. Although necessity is the mother of invention, creativity might be the stepfather of flexibility.

Because this jig accurately guides a router in lineal cuts, any of a variety of routing operations can be preformed with it, including rabbets, grooves or mortises. Its one limitation is the distance from the edge to the router bit. This offset must be accounted for in any setup as you expand the uses of this versatile fluting jig.

Rabbets are easily formed with this jig. To accommodate the offset of the jig base, you can first make the rabbet and then cut the stock to width.

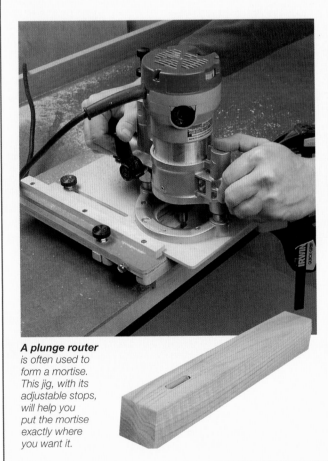

A plunge router is often used to form a mortise. This jig, with its adjustable stops, will help you put the mortise exactly where you want it.

A groove is just a rabbet moved to the middle of the board (or vice versa!). Be creative and get the most from your fluting jig.

MULTI-FUNCTIONAL ROUTING SYSTEM

Here's a router table—complete with its own dust collection system—that can be used with or without its base.

by Rick White

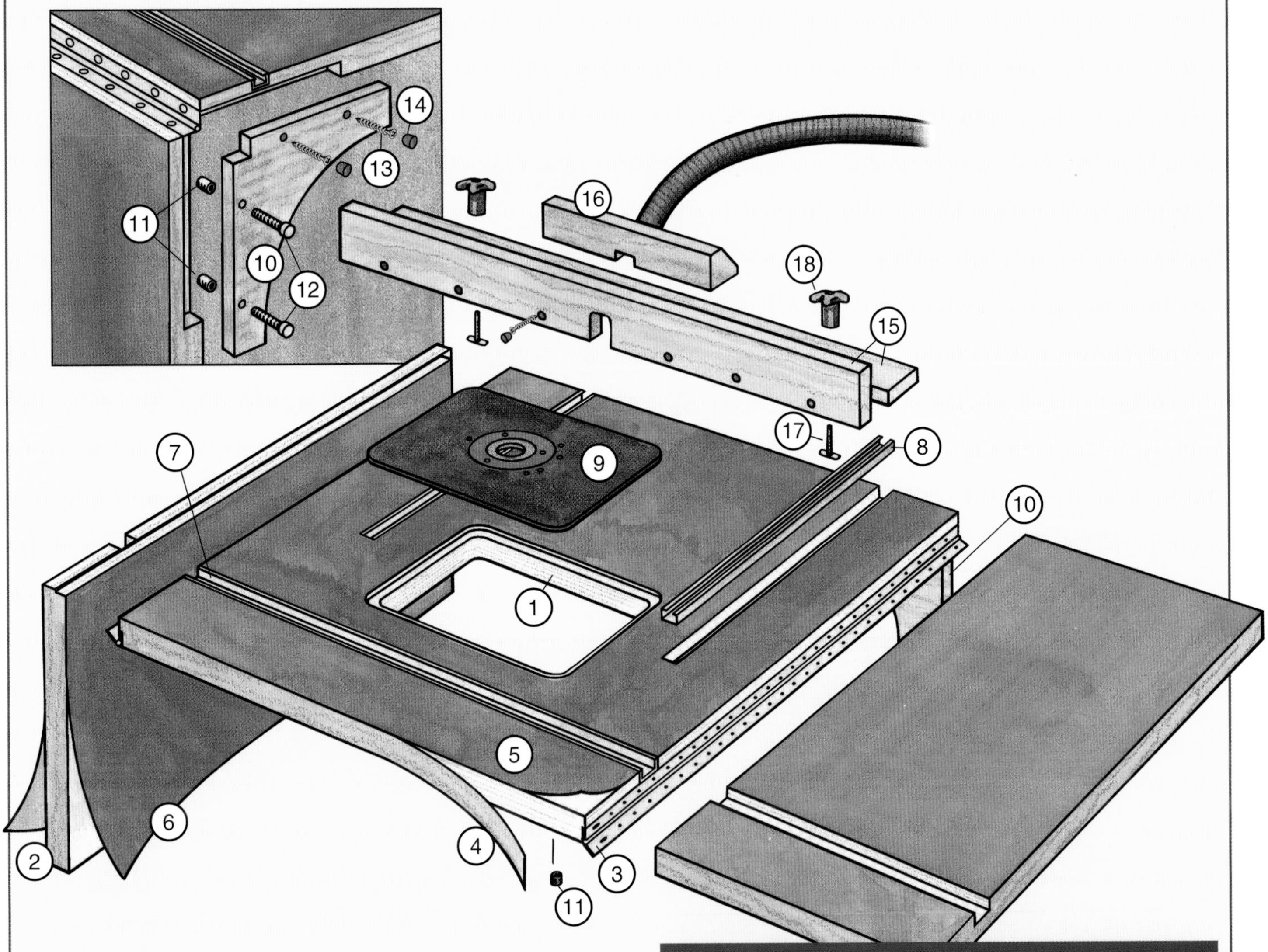

If your shop has neither loads of floor space nor a central dust collection system, this multi-functional router table is for you. With its wings up, it provides plenty of support for long stock. Flip the wings down, and it rolls up against a wall for ordinary-sized routing tasks or doubles as an extra table for storage. In this mode, it only occupies a little over 4 square feet of floor space. I've designed the fence with a port to hook up to your shop vac, which should help keep your lungs cleaner. Best of all, the top comes off and becomes a stand-alone benchtop unit that you can take with you for those routing jobs outside the shop.

Material List

	T x W x L
1 Tabletop (1)	1½" x 26" x 26¼"
2 Wings (2)	1½" x 26" x 12"
3 Piano Hinges (2)	1½" x 26"
4 Edging (2)	1½" x 8' Plyedge
5 Tabletop Laminate (2)	1/40" x 26¼" x 26½"
6 Wing Laminate (4)	1/40" x 26¼" x 12¼"
7 Miter Gauge Track (1)	½" x 1" x 26¼"
8 Fence T-track (2)	½" x 13/16" x 15½"
9 Router Base Insert (1)	¼" x 9" x 12"
10 Gussets (2)	¾" x 8" x 8"
11 Threaded Inserts (8)	¼"-20
12 Brass Knurled Knobs (4)	¼"-20
13 Screws (36)	#8 x 1½"
14 Plugs (36)	⅜" Diameter
15 Fence Face and Brace (2)	¾" x 3" x 26¼"
16 Dust Collection Port (1)	2" x 2" x 9"
17 T-slot bolts (2)	5/16"-18 x 1½"
18 Star Knobs (2)	5/16"-18

Template Key for Sliding Dovetails on your Router Table

Sliding dovetails are a great joint. There's lots of surface area available for glue, they look great and hold forever. But they can be fussy to set up on a router table.

Generally we find the easier something is to do, the more likely we are to do it. An example is making this simple guide block for setting up sliding dovetails. Using a scrap of hardwood, carefully cut and fit both the groove and tail of a dovetail joint. Now, instead of starting from scratch each time, use the guide block to establish your bit height and fence setting. Mark the bit size on the guide block as well. Save the block, and you'll probably build more sliding dovetails than ever. Make similar blocks each time you set up a different joint size.

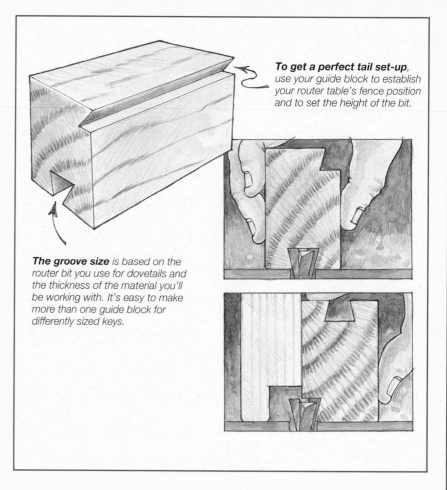

To get a perfect tail set-up, use your guide block to establish your router table's fence position and to set the height of the bit.

The groove size is based on the router bit you use for dovetails and the thickness of the material you'll be working with. It's easy to make more than one guide block for differently sized keys.

Tabletop Core

The tabletop is the most critical element of any router table. If it doesn't stay flat, sturdy and stable, your milling suffers. So building the tabletop is the first order of business.

To ensure that this table stays flat, I built the core from two layers of Finnish birch plywood. However, a less expensive high density fiberboard (the same material used by cabinet shops for countertops) would also work, and so would ordinary ¾" MDF.

Begin by gluing and clamping two sheets of ¾" thick core stock (26" x 50½" — large enough to make pieces 1 and 2) together, exerting enough pressure on the center of the panel to ensure good adhesion. To do that, you can use special clamps with long jaws, or you can weigh down the center with sand bags or cinder blocks. Another good idea is to screw the two panels together. If you go this latter route, screw from the bottom up with 1¼" screws after drilling clearance holes through the bottom sheet. The screws will pull the two plates together. Use a straightedge to check that the assembly is flat. After the glue has dried, cut the top and wings to size on your table saw. Then reset your fence and blade height to create the rabbets for the hinges (pieces 3) on the four inside edges (see the drawings on pages 114 and 115).

Glue and clamp hardwood tape (piece 4) to all the edges of the three panels except the ones to which the hinges will be screwed, using long straight pieces of scrap between the clamps and the tape to ensure even pressure. Sand the tape flush with the top and bottom and move on to laminating the tabletop and the wings.

Laminating the Tabletop

Each piece of laminate in the Material List on page 111 (pieces 5 and 6) is deliberately oversized by ¼". This is because you'll be using your router to trim it to the correct size after it has been applied to the top and wings.

If you used screws to glue up the tabletop, fill any depressions and sand the filler flush. Then spread a coat of contact adhesive on the bottom surface of each wing and the tabletop, following the adhesive manufacturer's directions. (Note: Laminating the bottom surfaces will ensure that the tabletop will stay flat.) Apply a similar coat to the relevant pieces of laminate. When the cement is dry to the touch, lay dowels or thin sticks every six inches along the plywood, then position the laminate on top of these spacers. Remember, you'll only get one shot at lining up the laminate—contact adhesive is unforgiving.

When you're happy with the positioning, begin removing the spacers from the center. Work your way toward the ends, pressing the laminate down firmly as each spacer is removed. Use a roller to roll the entire surface once all the spacers are removed, then use a laminate trimming bit in your router to cut the laminate flush with the edges of the tabletop and wings. When the bottoms of all three panels have been laminated, repeat the process on the top surfaces. This time, set the router bit height so the bearing doesn't ride into the hinge rabbets.

Tabletop Hardware

Now that your tabletop and wings are laminated, you can start machining for the hardware that guides the fence and miter gauge. The first step is to install the piano hinges that hold the wings, then lay the entire assembly on a flat workbench. Secure it to the bench with clamps, then install a 1" straight bit in your router (if you

don't own a 1" bit, make several passes with a smaller one). Refer to the Technical Drawings for the location of the miter gauge groove, then clamp a fence in place and rout this groove across all three panels at the same time. That way, you'll be sure they line up.

Install the miter gauge track (piece 7) in the tabletop next, but don't install track in the wing grooves or the gauge will get stuck. Predrill and countersink for screws to hold the track in place, then slip the miter gauge from your table saw into the track and tighten the screws until it slides easily with no play.

The T-tracks for the fence (pieces 8) are installed in a similar fashion. Cut the grooves according to the locations given in the Technical Drawings, then screw the tracks in place. The last hardware element in the top is the table insert (piece 9). Follow the instructions that come with your insert plate for cutting the rabbet (shown in Figure 1) that holds it in the tabletop.

Adding Portability

To use the tabletop as a stand-alone unit, the wings serve as legs. They are secured in position with a pair of gussets (pieces 10) that are mortised into the back of the tabletop like hinges are mortised into doors. These mortises (see the Technical Drawings) are cut with a router equipped with a straight bit (after removing the piano hinges), then cleaned up with a chisel. A matching mortise is then cut in the back of each wing.

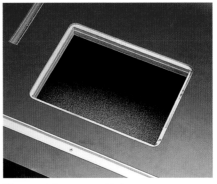

Figure 1: *The router table insert rests on a rabbet that holds it flush with the tabletop. Follow the instructions that come with your plate for cutting this opening and rabbet.*

Bore holes in each wing for the threaded inserts (pieces 11), and in each gusset (see Figure 2, at left) for the knurled knobs (pieces 12). The Technical Drawings locate the holes for the inserts plus the screws and plugs (pieces 13 and 14) that anchor the gussets to the tabletop. To secure the wings in the down position, pass the brass knobs through the holes in the gussets and screw them into the inserts.

The Fence

Use straight hardwood stock to make the fence face and brace (pieces 15); then, cut a hole in the middle of the face (see Technical Drawings) for router bits before screwing and gluing the two pieces together. Counterbore the screw heads (they'll be plugged later), then make the dust collection port (piece 16), a block of wood (see Technical Drawings for profile) with a hole drilled in it at an angle: Use a hole saw or Forstner bit that matches the diameter of your shop vac hose fitting. Screw, but don't glue, the port to the back of the fence behind the hole: You may need to replace the fence face sometime in the future.

The fence is secured to the tabletop with two T-slot bolts (pieces 17) and a couple of star knobs (pieces 18). This hardware also allows you to easily move and set the fence.

Figure 2: *Gussets that are mortised into the back of the tabletop allow the top to be converted into a portable benchtop unit.*

Tabletop
(Top View)

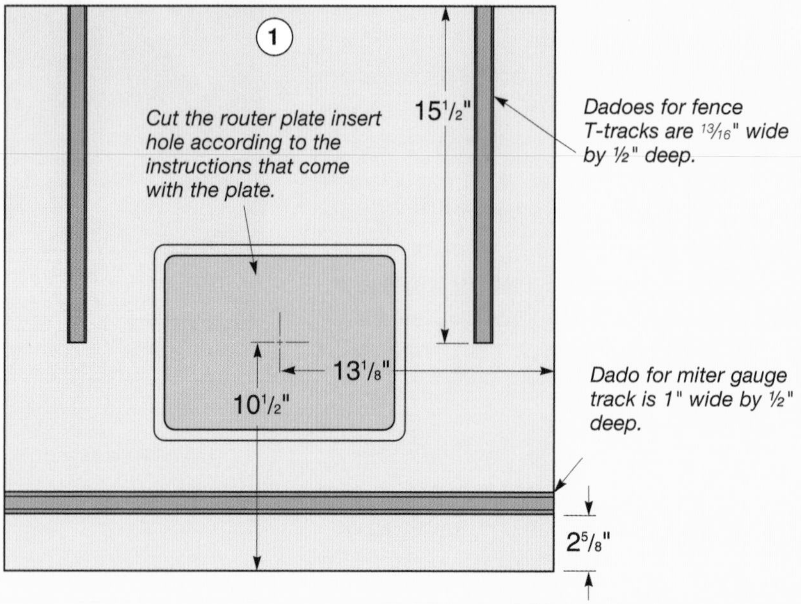
1
Cut the router plate insert hole according to the instructions that come with the plate.
15 1/2"
Dadoes for fence T-tracks are 13/16" wide by 1/2" deep.
13 1/8"
10 1/2"
Dado for miter gauge track is 1" wide by 1/2" deep.
2 5/8"

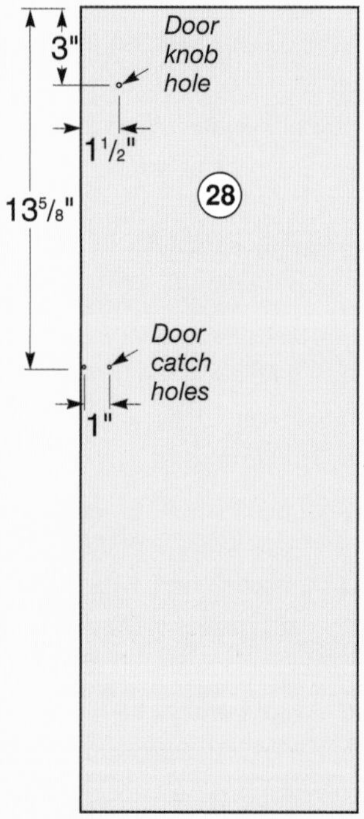
3"
Door knob hole
1 1/2"
13 5/8"
28
Door catch holes
1"

Door
(Back View)

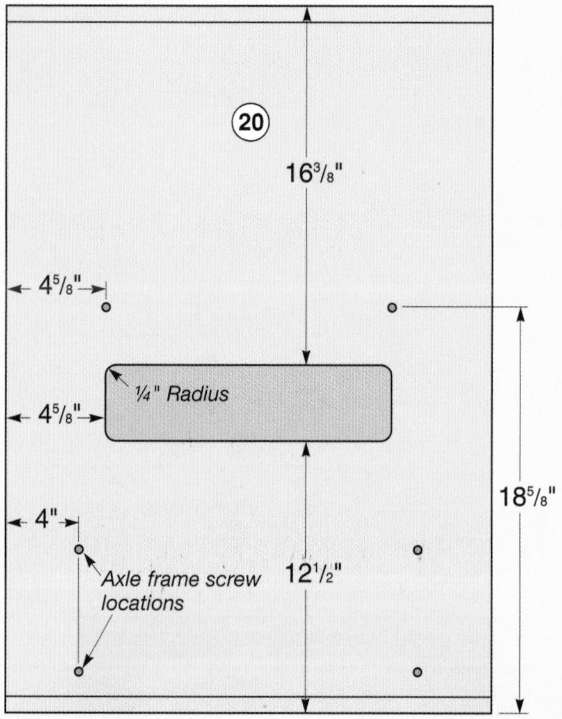
20
16 3/8"
4 5/8"
1/4" Radius
4 5/8"
18 5/8"
4"
Axle frame screw locations
12 1/2"

Base Back
(Front View)

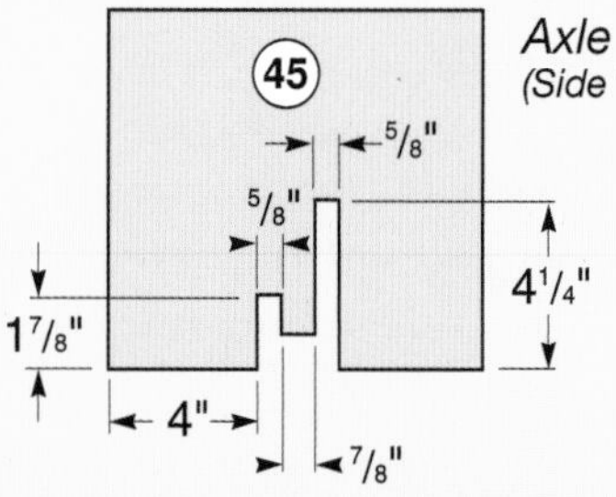
45
5/8"
5/8"
4 1/4"
1 7/8"
4"
7/8"

Axle Frame
(Side View)

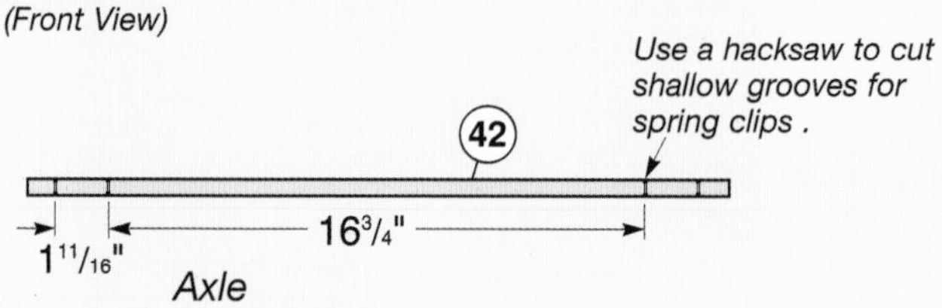
Use a hacksaw to cut shallow grooves for spring clips .
42
1 11/16"
16 3/4"

Axle
(Front View)

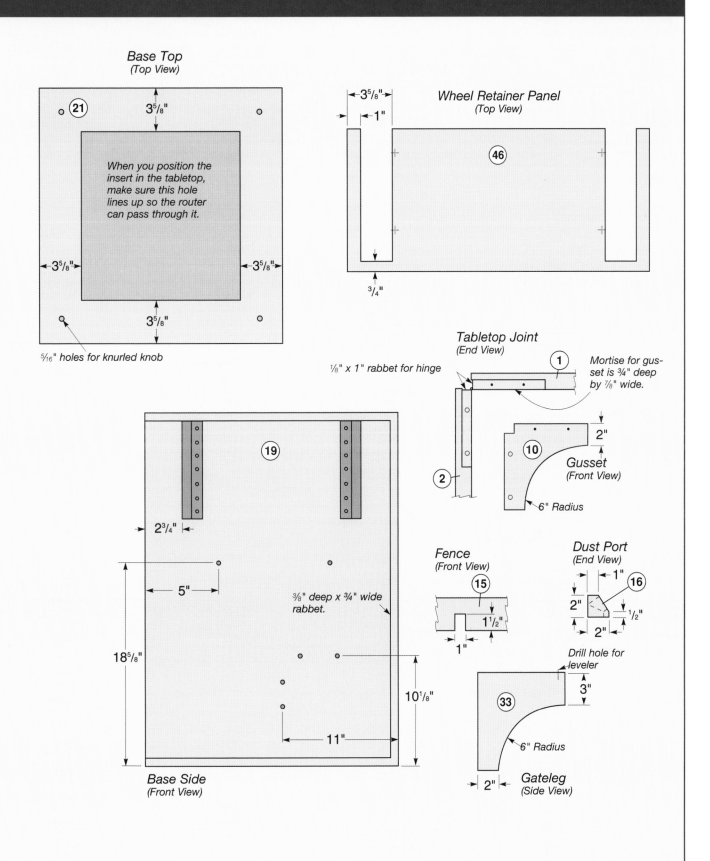

Base Top
(Top View)

21

3⁵/₈"

When you position the insert in the tabletop, make sure this hole lines up so the router can pass through it.

3⁵/₈"

3⁵/₈"

3⁵/₈"

⁵/₁₆" holes for knurled knob

Wheel Retainer Panel
(Top View)

3⁵/₈"

1"

46

³/₄"

Tabletop Joint
(End View)

1

Mortise for gusset is ¾" deep by ⅞" wide.

⅛" x 1 " rabbet for hinge

2

2

10

Gusset
(Front View)

6" Radius

19

2³/₄"

5"

³/₈" deep x ¾" wide rabbet.

18⁵/₈"

10¹/₈"

11"

Base Side
(Front View)

Fence
(Front View)

15

1¹/₂"

1"

Dust Port
(End View)

1"

16

2"

½"

2"

Drill hole for leveler

33

3"

6" Radius

2"

Gateleg
(Side View)

Mylar™ templates

Router Bit Templates

An easy way to create complex profiles with your router bits is to simply trace the profile of each onto Mylar (a stiff, opaque, thin sheet of plastic film that's available in blueprint and artist supply stores). Note the profile of the bearing as well, then carefully cut out each profile with scissors. Punch holes in the templates and store them on a key chain. When designing a stacked shape, create a paper storyboard by using the various profiles to lay out the final shape. The slightly opaque Mylar allows you to see profiles already traced. While designing in this manner, you can easily determine if the bit will have a bearing surface to ride on. If it doesn't, just use the fence on your router table as your guide.

The Base Cabinet is Next

Even though it becomes a portable, self-contained unit, the tabletop subassembly is designed so it can rest on a mobile base cabinet. This base's two sides (pieces 19) are rabbeted on their top, bottom and back (see the Technical Drawings for locations and dimensions), and these are easy cuts to make on your table saw.

The cabinet back (piece 20) is milled next. The only machining here is a rabbet along the top edge and a large hole (see the Technical Drawings) that will allow air to reach your shop vac if you stow it in the cabinet and the router cord to exit the cabinet. If you already have a dust collection system, all you'll need is a hole large enough to accept your cord's plug. If not, the hole can be cut with a jigsaw after first drilling out the four corners. Finish up by sanding any jagged edges left by the saw.

After you have cut the top, shelf and bottom (pieces 21, 22 and 23) to size, return to your jigsaw to cut the hole in the top (see Technical Drawings) for your router. You also need to drill a hole in the back of the shelf for your router's power cord. Note: If you decide not to install wheels on your cabinet, the bottom should be the same size as the top.

You can now assemble the top, bottom and shelf to the sides and back, using glue and 1½" screws. The screw heads should be sunk ¼" below the surface in ⅜" diameter counterbores that are drilled with a Forstner bit (for clean edges and a flat bottom).

Figure 3: *Apply pressure sensitive hardwood tape to all four edges of the base unit's plywood doors, then sand the tape flush. Sand carefully to keep from sanding off the plywood surface veneer.*

Add Some Trim

There's something about a well-built shop fixture (a fine European workbench, for example) that brings pleasure to the most mundane woodworking tasks — even sanding! That's why I suggest you trim out the router table's base cabinet, giving it a frame-and-panel look. The trim pieces are simply cut and jointed to size, then applied to the cabinet with glue and clamps.

The trim pieces must be applied in a specific order so that everything fits perfectly. Begin by attaching the side stiles (pieces 24), followed by the front and back stiles (pieces 25), the side rails (pieces 26) and the edging (pieces 27).

Making the Doors

Flush doors (pieces 28) are simple to make and have a low profile. To build them, cut plywood panels to the correct dimensions and apply pressure sensitive hardwood tape (piece 29) to all four edges (see Figure 3). Sand the tape flush, then dry fit the hinges (pieces 30), the catches (pieces 31) and the door knobs (pieces 32). Locations for all of these can be found on the Technical Drawings. Once all the screw holes have been started, you can remove the hardware until after the cabinet has been finished.

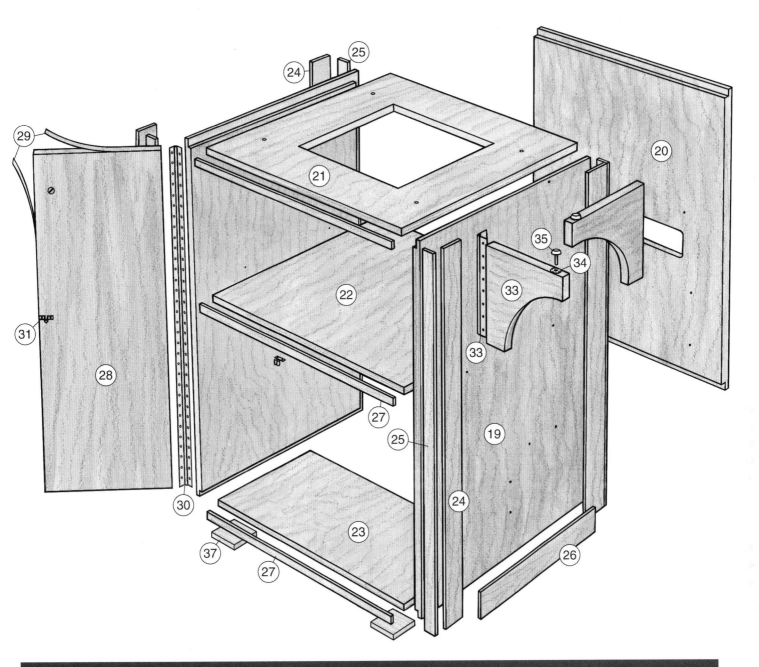

Material List - Base

		T x W x L			T x W x L
19	Base Sides (2)	¾" x 23⅞" x 32½"	**29**	Door Edging (2)	¾" x 96" Tape
20	Base Back (1)	¾" x 23" x 32½"	**30**	Door Hinges (2)	1½" x 30¾" Piano
21	Base Top (1)	¾" x 23" x 23½"	**31**	Door Catches (2)	Double Roller
22	Base Shelf (1)	¾" x 22¼" x 21¹⁵⁄₁₆"	**32**	Door Knobs (2)	1½" Diameter
23	Base Bottom (1)*	¾" x 23" x 13"	**33**	Gatelegs (4)	¾" x 9" x 8⅜"
24	Side Stiles (4)	⅜" x 2¾" x 32½"	**34**	Threaded Inserts (4)	⁵⁄₁₆"-18
25	Front & Back Stiles (4)	¼" x 1" x 32½"	**35**	Gateleg Levelers (4)	⅜" x 1⅛"
26	Side Rails (2)	⅜" x 2¾" x 18⅜"	**36**	Gateleg Hinges (4)	1½" x 9" Piano
27	Edging (3)	¼" x ¾" x 22¼"	**37**	Cabinet Feet (4)	¼" x 2" x 2"
28	Doors (2)	¾" x 11" x 30¾"			

If you decide not to install the wheel system, the bottom should measure 23" x 23½".

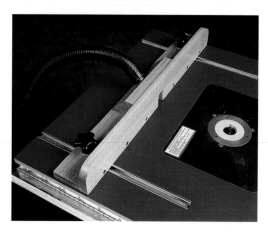

Figure 4: *The router table's fence incorporates a dust collection port. Your shop vac hose should friction-fit to this hole.*

Gatelegs Support the Top

When working with long stock, this router table's two extension wings are invaluable. However, it's essential that the wings are lined up in the same plane as the tabletop. To ensure that they are, two pairs of gatelegs (pieces 33) support them when they're in use.

To make these gatelegs, begin by transferring their shape from the Technical Drawings onto your plywood stock, then move to your drill press. Bore a hole in the top of each blank for a threaded insert (pieces 34). These inserts will house plastic leveler glides (pieces 35) that will allow you to make fine adjustments to the height of the wings. Boring holes for them is a lot easier to do now, before the gateleg profile is cut. That's the next step, and it's done on your bandsaw. Then use a drum sander in your drill press to refine the bandsaw cuts.

Install the gatelegs with 9" lengths of piano hinge (pieces 36). The locations for these hinges can be found on the Technical Drawings. Once they're in place, attach ¼"-thick feet (pieces 37) to the four corners to keep the bottom of your cabinet off the floor.

Wrap up the base by gluing plugs in the screw counterbores. Trim these with a chisel and sand them flush.

The same four brass knurled knobs that hold the wings in position when the router system is being used on a benchtop are also used to secure the top to the base. Drill holes through the top of the base, then bore four corresponding holes in the underside of the top for the threaded inserts (pieces 11). This ensures that you'll get a steady, safe and non-moving surface.

Building the Wheel Assembly

To make the table mobile (so it can be pushed against a wall and moved out when needed), I added a pair of wheels (pieces 38). However, if you decide that you don't need this option, just skip the rest of this section and move on to "Wrapping Up".

The wheel system I devised lets you tip the router table away from you to engage the wheels, then toward you to disengage, using the stepped slots cut in the axle frames (pieces 45). It's enclosed by the lower shelf (piece 39) and a support (piece 40). These are cut to size, then the leading edge of the shelf is trimmed with an oak strip (piece 41). Cut and build the wheel assembly using the Technical and Exploded Drawings as guides. Assemble the axle, wheels, washers and clips, then build the wooden assembly. You'll need to hacksaw a pair of grooves into the axle at both ends for locking the pair of clips that hold each wheel in place. To mount the assembly in the cabinet, position it so the bottoms of the wheels are even with the cabinet feet when the axle is resting in the shorter stepped slots in the axle frames. Drive countersunk screws through the cabinet sides into the lower shelf and lower shelf support. Plug these screw holes in the base.

Wrapping Up

After all the assembly is accomplished, you're ready to finish the cabinet. I sprayed the base and tabletop edging with four coats of lacquer, sanding between coats.

Mount your router to the insert plate you've selected for your project. It probably comes either predrilled to fit your router or with instructions for drilling the holes yourself. If not, remove the baseplate from your router and use it as a template for locating the countersunk screw holes in the insert plate. Attach the router to the insert plate with screws and drop it into place.

Note: Wheel assembly is shown here from the back view.

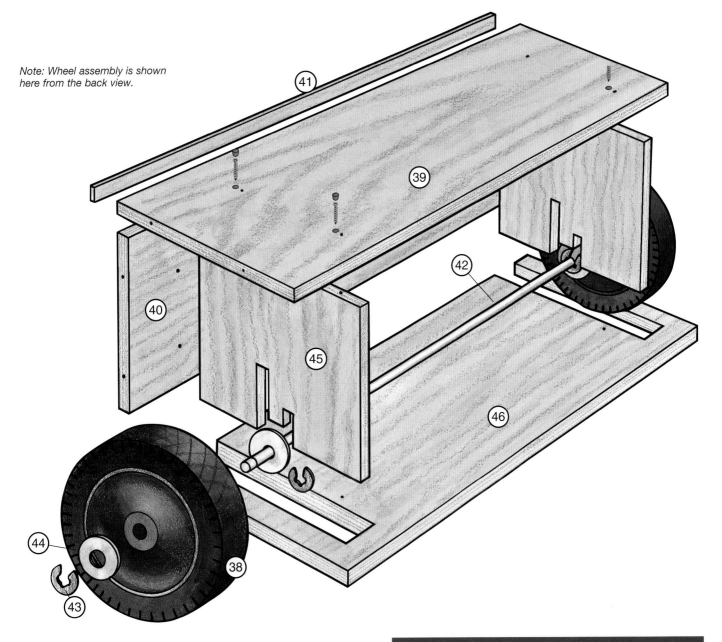

Material List - Wheels

		T x W x L
38	Wheels (2)	8" Diameter
39	Lower Shelf (1)	¾" x 22¼" x 10¼"
40	Lower Shelf Support (1)	¾" x 22¼" x 9"
41	Lower Shelf Edging (1)	¼" x ¾" x 22¼"
42	Axle (1)	½" x 22" Steel Rod
43	Axle Clips (4)	½" ID Spring Clips
44	Axle Washers (4)	½" ID x 2" OD Fender
45	Axle Frames (2)	½" x 9¾" x 9"
46	Wheel Retainer Panel (1)	¾" x 23" x 10½"

DUST-COLLECTING ROUTER TABLE FENCE

Routing particleboard or MDF without dust collection is like standing in the desert during a sand storm. The air becomes a hazy mess, your router table and floor are covered with fine dust and—worst of all—what's in the air ends up all over you. This fence provides shelter from the storm by drawing dust and chips away at the source.

Over time you've probably inhaled and swallowed enough wood dust to qualify it as a fifth food group. Dust is not only a nuisance, but recent findings indicate that it's also a suspected carcinogen. Thank goodness this dust-collecting router table fence with replaceable bit inserts can finally put you on a dust-free diet.

The genesis for the idea came when I was searching for plumbing fittings. I found a PVC reducing fitting that fits perfectly inside a 4" dust

collector hose. It inspired me to design this router fence. If you don't own a dust collector, experiment with other fittings to find one that connects to your shop vac hose instead.

Making the Base Parts

Start by cutting the base, braces, divider and back (pieces 1 through 4) to size and shape. I made the back from particleboard and the rest from yellow poplar. You'll find dimensions for all the parts in the Material List on page 123.

The Exploded View Drawing as well as the Elevation Drawings on pages 122 and 123 provide machining details and assembly relationships. Note: You may need to adjust the overall length of the fence to suit your router table or table saw size (I designed my fence to fit a table saw-mounted router table).

A great project that will enhance your woodworking and your health, this handy fixture helps clear the air in your shop while it makes your router table more accurate.

by Chris Marshall

With the first pieces cut to size, it's time to start machining. Begin by milling round openings to accept the PVC tubing in two of the braces. Plow dadoes across the inside face of the two center braces for the lid to slide in. Build the dust chamber by assembling the center braces, divider and back with screws. Screw the dust chamber and the other two braces to the base.

Making the Built-Up Fence

The fence is a sandwich composed of doubled-up particleboard with a plastic laminate face. Particleboard provides dimensional stability and flatness in this application. Cut the subfence and fence parts (pieces 5 and 6) to size, and then cut the router bit opening in both pieces. Mount an oversized piece of plastic laminate (piece 7) to the fence next with contact adhesive. Use a flush-trim bit and router to trim the laminate neatly to size. Finish the fence piece by routing the rabbet around the bit opening that will house the replaceable hardboard inserts. Square up the rabbet's corners with a sharp chisel.

Finishing Up

Screw the subfence to the braces and base, then attach the subfence to the fence with glue and more screws driven in from the back. Make sure the edges of the fence parts align exactly. Cut the three poplar edging strips (pieces 8 and 9) to length, rounding the corners of the top piece (see the Elevation Drawings on the next two pages). Join the edging to the fence assembly with glue and #20 biscuits. Ease the front edges of the poplar strips with a ¼" roundover bit.

Make the dust chamber lid by fitting and screwing a piece of ¼" Plexiglas™ into a matching slit cut in the lid pull (pieces 10 and 11). Bevel-cut

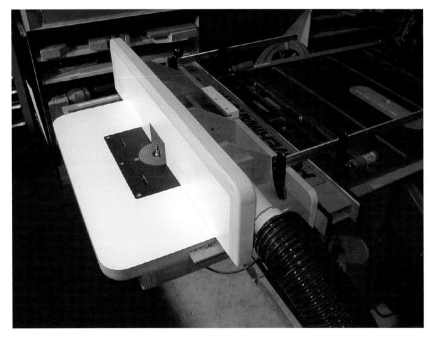

The author made the prototype of this router fence for use on his table saw/router table combo setup. In that version, he added a back stretcher for clamping to his table saw fence. This way, the rip fence locked the router fence as well. Useful and clever.

the pull's bottom edge before attaching it to the lid so it fits against the angled edges of the braces.

Now turn to the dust collection apparatus. Join the PVC tubing and reducing coupling (pieces 12 and 13) with solvent-weld glue and make the collar (piece 14). Slip the collar over the tubing and slide the tubing through the braces. Secure the collar to both the end brace and tubing with a few short screws. If you have a grounded dust collection system, the screws driven through the collar provide a perfect place to attach your grounding wire.

Cut a bunch of hardboard blanks for the replaceable inserts (pieces 15) while you have your saw settings dialed in. The storage compartment behind the dust collection chamber should hold 10 inserts. Drill countersunk holes in the inserts for attachment screws, and use an insert as a template for drilling holes through the fence assembly. Mount the inserts with flathead machine screws and locknuts. I use nuts fitted with nylon to keep them from vibrating loose. To prepare an insert for use, hold a router bit against the insert and trace

a slightly oversized profile and cut out the shape on a scroll saw.

Up and Running

Using the router fence is a snap. Set the fence on the router table so the profile on the insert straddles the bit. Clamp the base to the table. Slide your dust collector hose over the reducing fitting and you're ready to go. Now indulge in all the routing you like—you won't even miss the chips.

Apply contact cement to both the fence and plastic. After it dries tacky, press the parts together. Use small sticks or dowels to help line up the parts; you only get one shot.

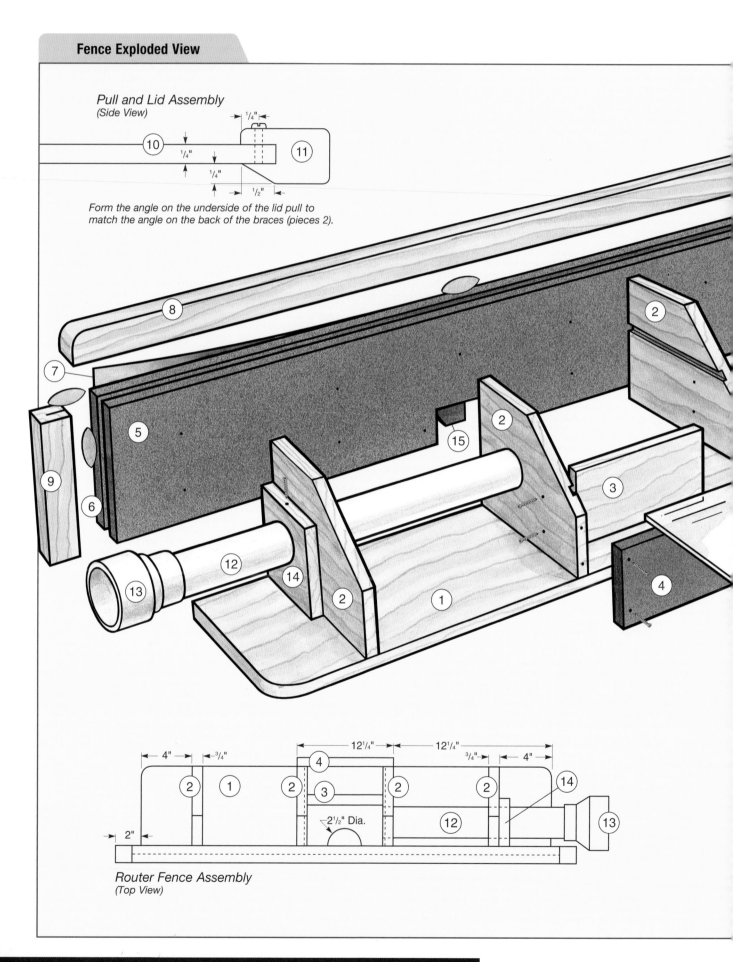

Pull and Lid Assembly
(Side View)

Form the angle on the underside of the lid pull to
match the angle on the back of the braces (pieces 2).

Router Fence Assembly
(Top View)

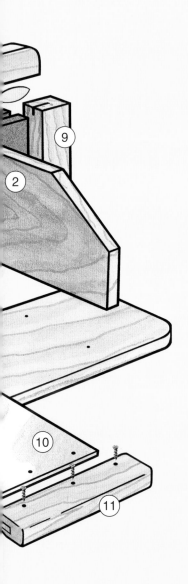

Material List

	T x W x L
1 Base (1)	¾" x 6" x 32"
2 Braces (4)	¾" x 5¼" x 6"
3 Divider (1)	¾" x 3⅜" x 6"
4 Back (1)	⅝" x 3¾" x 7½"
5 Subfence (1)	⅝" x 6" x 33⅜"
6 Fence (1)	⅝" x 6" x 33⅜"
7 Plastic Laminate	¹⁄₁₆" x 6" x 33⅜"
8 Top Edging (1)	¹⁵⁄₁₆" x ¹⁵⁄₁₆" x 36"
9 End Edging (2)	¹⁵⁄₁₆" x ¹⁵⁄₁₆" x 6"
10 Lid (1)	¼" x 6¼" x 5⁷⁄₁₆"
11 Lid Pull (1)	¾" x 1¼" x 6¼"
12 PVC Tubing (1)	2 Dia. x 16"
13 Reducing Coupling (1)	3" Dia. x 2" Dia.
14 Collar (1)	¾" x 3⅝" x 3⅝"
15 Replaceable Inserts (10)	¼" x 2⅜" x 4¾"

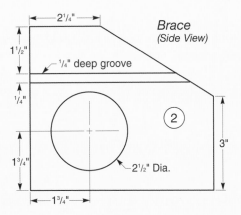

Brace
(Side View)

2¼"

1½"

¼" deep groove

¼"

2

1¾"

3"

2½" Dia.

1¾"

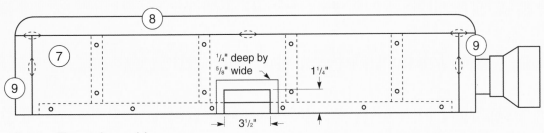

Router Fence Assembly
(Front View)

8

7

9

9

¼" deep by
⅝" wide

1¼"

3½"

9

by John English

TRAVELING ROUTER TABLE

This handsome dovetailed cabinet slips off your shop wall to serve as a carrying case for a router and good selection of bits. Flip it over and it becomes an instant router table, complete with an adjustable fence. Truly, a router table made for the road.

It had already been one of those days when I took off in a hurry to visit a woodworking friend in need of some routing help. So it wasn't a surprise that I remembered my router bits 14 miles down the road. That little oversight cost me 45 minutes and several degrees of stress—but it did give me time to come up with the design for this combination router storage case and work site router table.

Two days later, this beauty was hanging on the wall in my shop. Obviously, such a fixture will be just as handy and useful if you make it out of plywood, but I was also looking for a workout on my dovetail jig, and a pile of scrap walnut seemed like just the thing. Aside from keeping everything together, this fixture shelters the router from excessive dust. I can check out my bit selection through the Plexiglas™ window, so I always have the right bits when I take the case to a job. It easily lifts off the wall and the heavy-duty handle lets me carry everything I need to the truck.

For set-up, just place the carrying case upside down on a table or bench (the truck's tailgate works well, too), and you'll have an instant router table,

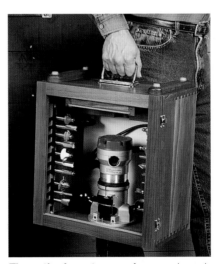

The author's router carrying case is ready to move to the job site on a moment's notice.

Turn the case over and you have an instant router table, with an adjustable fence.

Door Stile
(Front and End Views)

1/4"
1"
1/4"

⑥

⑰

⑯

⑱

①

⑤

②

②

㉘

③

⑨

⑳

⑱

⑥

⑲

④

㉑

⑫

⑩

⑨

㉗

㉔

⑩

①

⑭

⑪

⑮

Door Rail
(Front and End Views)

⑦

1/4"
1/4"
1/4"
1 1/4"

㉕

⑬

㉓

㉖

Fence Board (Top View)

Front Edge   1 1/8" Dia.
               1/8" Deep
⑲

2"

1 9/16"   10 7/8"

Fence (Top View)

7/16"
1 7/8"
⑯   2" Dia.
              1/2"

1 1/2"   10 7/8"   2 3/4" Dia.

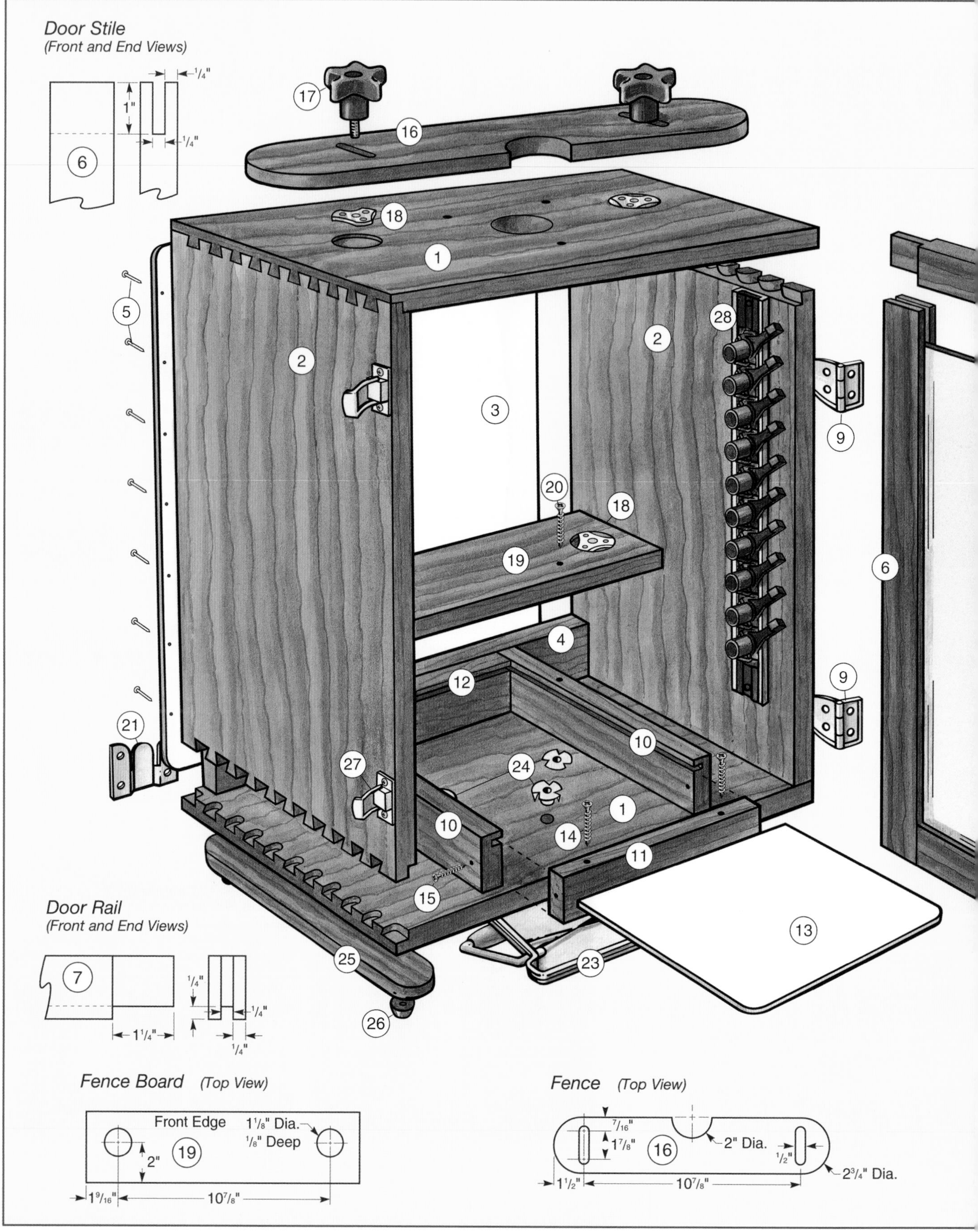

Case Top (Top View)

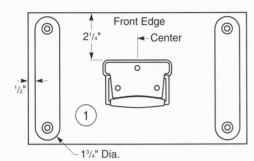

Front Edge

$2\frac{1}{4}$"

Center

$\frac{1}{2}$"

1

$1\frac{3}{4}$" Dia.

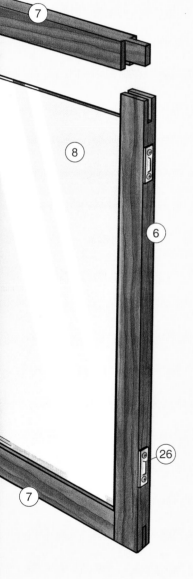

7

8

6

26

7

Material List

		T x W x L
1	Top and Bottom (2)	$\frac{3}{4}$" x $9\frac{1}{16}$" x $15\frac{1}{2}$"
2	Sides (2)	$\frac{3}{4}$" x $9\frac{1}{16}$" x $16\frac{1}{4}$"
3	Back Panel (1)	$\frac{1}{8}$" x $14\frac{3}{4}$" x $15\frac{11}{16}$"
4	Hanging Cleat (1)	$\frac{3}{4}$" x $1\frac{3}{4}$" x 14"
5	Brads (28)	1"
6	Door Stiles (2)	$\frac{3}{4}$" x $1\frac{1}{4}$" x $16\frac{3}{16}$"
7	Door Rails (2)	$\frac{3}{4}$" x $1\frac{1}{4}$" x $15\frac{1}{2}$"
8	Plexiglas™ Door Panel (1)	$\frac{1}{4}$" x $13\frac{3}{8}$" x 14"
9	Door Hinges (1 Pair)	90° Stop hinges
10	Compartment Sides (2)	$\frac{3}{4}$" x $1\frac{3}{4}$" x 8"
11	Compartment Front (1)	$\frac{3}{4}$" x $1\frac{7}{16}$" x $7\frac{5}{16}$"
12	Compartment Back (1)	$\frac{3}{4}$" x $1\frac{3}{8}$" x $7\frac{5}{16}$"
13	Compartment Top (1)	$\frac{1}{8}$" x 8" x 8"
14	Screws (4)	2" x #10
15	Screws (6)	$1\frac{1}{4}$" x #8
16	Fence (1)	$\frac{3}{4}$" x $2\frac{3}{4}$" x 137/8"
17	5-Star Fence Knobs (2)	$\frac{5}{16}$" - 18 1" Stubs
18	T-Nuts (4)	$\frac{5}{16}$" - 18 Screw-on
19	Fence Board (1)	$\frac{3}{4}$" x $3\frac{1}{2}$" x 14"
20	Fence Board Screws (2)	$1\frac{1}{2}$" x #8
21	Flush Mount Brackets (1 Pair)	Extra thin
22	Bracket Small Screws (8)	$\frac{3}{4}$" x #8
23	Carrying Handle (1)	5" x $3\frac{11}{16}$" Chrome
24	T-Nuts (3)	Supplied with handle
25	Feet (2)	$\frac{3}{4}$" x $1\frac{3}{4}$" x $8\frac{1}{2}$"
26	Bumpers (4)	$\frac{5}{16}$" x $\frac{3}{4}$" Dia.
27	Door Catches (2)	Plated steel
28	$\frac{1}{4}$" Router-Loc™ Bit Holder (1)	$\frac{3}{8}$" x $1\frac{1}{4}$" x 13"
29	$\frac{1}{2}$" Router-Loc™ Bit Holder (1)	$\frac{3}{8}$" x $1\frac{1}{4}$" x 13"

Case Bottom Layout (Top View)

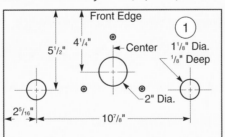

Front Edge

$5\frac{1}{2}$"

$4\frac{1}{4}$"

Center

1

$1\frac{1}{8}$" Dia.
$\frac{1}{8}$" Deep

2" Dia.

$2\frac{5}{16}$"

$10\frac{7}{8}$"

The bit access hole and mounting holes will vary. Use your base plate as a template.

Compartment Groove
(End View)

$\frac{3}{16}$"

$\frac{5}{32}$"

$\frac{3}{8}$"

10

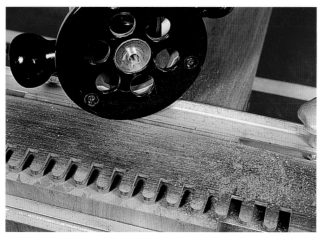

Mill half-blind dovetails to join the carcass parts with a dovetail jig and a hand-held router equipped with a guide collar.

Form the ¼" deep back panel rabbet with a bearing-guided rabbeting bit. A router table makes this machining step more stable.

complete with a moveable fence. Four rubber feet stop it from slipping, so you'll only need to clamp it down when routing large workpieces.

If you need to make a hand-held cut, removing the router is just a matter of reversing out three machine screws and attaching the base plate. And the plate, along with two wrenches and a spare collet, all stow away in a special built-in compartment.

Making the Dovetailed Carcass

Routers weigh a lot, and this case is designed to travel. Those two facts mandate that the joinery for this case should be strong, so interlocking dovetails are a natural choice. My dovetail jig only cuts half-blind dovetails, but that's actually an advantage; it means the bottom of the case (which becomes the router table) remains smooth.

Get started by edge jointing and gluing up several boards to create stock for the top, bottom and sides (pieces 1 and 2). If you're new to dovetailing, you can cheat a little by making the parts ½" too wide and trimming them to size after all the milling is done. Set up your jig according to the manufacturer's instructions and remove any excess glue from the boards. Install a dovetail

bit and guide collar (see your jig instructions for sizes) in your router and make practice cuts on some scrap lumber exactly the same dimensions as the actual workpieces. When you're satisfied with the setup, mill the boards.

Dry-fit the carcass parts together. The joints should be snug but not so tight that you need a hammer to close them. If your setup was slightly off, trim a little from the edges to achieve perfect alignment of pins and tails.

Glue and clamp the top and bottom to the sides, making sure that the assembly is square and flat as you apply clamping pressure.

Milling Rabbets for the Back

I chose bright white ¼" hardboard paneling for the back of my case (piece 3). This sets off the bits nicely, so it's easy to see their profiles through the Plexiglas™ door. Remove the clamps from the carcass and install a bearing-guided rabbeting bit in your router. A table-mounted router works well here, since the thin walls of the carcass don't provide a stable base for a portable router. Set the bit height to exactly the thickness of the back panel, so the panel will sit flush in its rabbet.

Mill the rabbet for the back in a single pass (see photo, above). Next,

glue and clamp the hanging cleat (piece 4) in place, flush with the edge of the newly milled rabbet (see Exploded View on page 126). When the glue dries, trim the back panel to size and sand a radius on each corner to match the corners left by the rabbeting bit. Wrap up by gluing and tacking the back in place with 1" brads (pieces 5), spaced every 3".

Building a Frame-and-panel Door

The door is built with an open saddle mortise on each end of the stiles (pieces 6) and matching tenons on the rails (pieces 7). The clear Plexiglas™ panel (piece 8) is 1/4" thick to stand up to use and abuse.

Rip, crosscut and joint the stiles and rails to size, then install a ¼"-wide dado head in your table saw. Plow a groove in one edge of each stile and rail for the clear panel, using the Elevation Drawings on page 126 for dimensions.

Use a tenoning jig on the table saw to hold the door stiles vertically for cutting the saddle mortises (see photo, next page). Note that these mortises are not as deep as the rails are wide, because the door panel grooves you just machined have the effect of reducing the width of the tenons (check the drawings on page 126 for all the appropriate measurements).

You can reset the tenoning jig and dado head to mill the tenons, or they can be cut even more quickly with a wider dado head and a miter gauge, as shown in the photo on the next page.

Dry-fit the stiles and rails, sliding the panel in place as you do. Note that the door is flush with the top of the case, but it remains 1/16" shy at the bottom. This prevents the door from expanding into the working area if the wood swells.

When you're happy with the way things fit, glue and clamp the door together. Let the panel float freely and make sure the door is flat and square as you apply clamping pressure. After the glue cures, remove the clamps and install the door with a pair of surface-mounted hinges (pieces 9).

Making the Small Parts Compartment

Every router comes with a handful of small parts—wrenches, different sized collets, a manual, extra base plate and so on. You'll need to size your case's compartment to fit everything you'll need on the job.

If the compartment shown with this fixture is the right size for your router accessories, rip the sides, front and back (pieces 10, 11 and 12) to 1¾" in width. Now, mill a groove (see drawing) for the compartment top (piece 13) in one face

A tenoning jig works great for cutting the mortises on the door stiles, but measure twice when setting the depth—the panel grooves on the rails have the effect of reducing the tenon width.

of this stock. Crosscut all four parts to length, then rip the front to final width (eliminating the groove and thin section of material above it). Predrill and countersink for 2" screws (pieces 14), apply a little glue and assemble the compartment with simple butt joints.

After the glue dries, drill pilot holes for 2" screws in the front of the compartment and 1¼" screws (pieces 15) in the rear, and secure the compartment subassembly within the case. See the Exploded View Drawing for screw locations. Note that the front of the compartment ends up ¼" shy of the front of the case.

QuickTip

Shop-built Router Stand

For safety reasons, it's not a good idea to lay a router on its side after turning it off and while the bit spins down. This stand provides a safe parking place. You can make it from ¾" plywood and just glue the parts together. Make the stand about ½" wider than your router's base so it's easy to set the router in place. Put pieces of low-nap carpet or non-slip router pad on the top to keep the router from shifting. Stack the platform with plywood spacers so it's high enough to provide plenty of clearance in the bit area to suit a variety of bit lengths.

Cut the door rail tenon cheeks on your table saw *using both the miter gauge and a wide dado head.*

Use your router's base plate *as a template when you're ready to drill both the bit access hole and the router base's mounting holes.*

Cut the compartment top to size from the same material you used for the back panel of the case. Test-fit it, then sand a slight radius on each front corner. Size the lid so it's flush with the Plexiglas™ panel when the door is closed; this secures it in transit, and it leaves you about ½" of material to use as a handle.

Creating the Hidden Router Table

It doesn't take much more work to create the "secret" router table for this storage case. By drilling a few holes in the bottom, you can mount your router there. When you get to the job site, turn the case upside-down and you have a small but functional router table. This also serves to secure the router in transit. Refer to the Elevation Drawings for the locations of the mounting holes and the bit access hole. Use your machine's base plate as the template for drilling the router mounting holes.

Band-saw the fence (piece 16) to the shape shown in the drawing on page 126; then use a drum sander in the drill press to clean up the edges. The fence is secured by means of a couple of large plastic knobs with threaded stubs (pieces 17). These pass through slots in the fence and are screwed into a pair of T-nuts (pieces 18) that are recessed into the case's bottom. Plow the slots in the fence on your router table, using a straight bit and a pair of clamped-on stops to establish the beginning and end of each cut. Check the drawings for the slot dimensions. Make the cuts in several passes, raising the bit about ⅛" each time and using a miter gauge to guide the workpiece.

A large Forstner bit is ideal for setting the T-nuts flush. Just drill about ⅛" deep with a 35mm bit, then bore a ½" hole in the center of this depression all the way through the case's bottom (see drawing for locations). Tap the T-nuts in place, and drill pilot holes for the supplied screws.

In order to stand the case up, you'll have to store the fence inside the case. To do this, install a second pair of T-nuts in a short board (piece 19) that is attached to the small parts compartment with screws (pieces 20). Space these T-nuts like the first pair.

Adding Hangers and Handles

One nice feature of this case is that it can be hung on the wall just like a regular cabinet. This is done with some extraordinarily simple hardware that allows for quick and easy removal when it's time to hit the road. Two pairs of ⅛"-thick flush-mount brackets (pieces 21) are all that are required. Simply screw one half of each bracket to the back of the cabinet and the other half to the wall. Use 1¼" screws (pieces 15) in the top two screw holes and the bottom outside hole, but switch to ¾" screws (pieces 22) for each of the last two holes, as you're only screwing through the back into the ¾"-thick hanging cleat.

Because of the router's weight and value, choose a strong handle (piece 23) for your case. The one shown here is fastened to the top of the cabinet with three T-nuts (pieces 24), supplied by the handle manufacturer. This handle is spring-loaded and very comfortable. To install it, center the handle (not the mounting plate) on the top of the case, locate the three screw holes and drill them. Tap the T-nuts home from inside the case, then screw the handle in place.

Now attach two feet (pieces 25) to the top of the case. These are simply band-sawn to shape and sanded. Predrill for screws (pieces 15), then run the screws through four small rubber bumpers (pieces 26) as you drive them home. These bumpers give the case sure footing when it's being used as a router table.

Completing the Final Details

After removing all the hardware and masking the Plexiglas™, spray three coats of clear finish on all the wooden parts, sanding lightly between coats.

Once the finish dries, reinstall the hardware and add two flush-mounted catches (pieces 27) to secure the door.

Complete the project by screwing a couple of Router-Loc™ bit holders (pieces 28 and 29) to the inside of your carrying case. They come in two styles: one holds ten ¼"-shank bits, while the other holds ten ½" shanks. If your case is large and you're lucky enough to own a generous selection of bits, there's no reason you couldn't add a couple more of these strips. After all, you don't want to be 14 miles down the road when you realize you forgot to pack the right bits!

The router case shown here was designed to house a Makita RF1101 router. You'll need to adjust the project dimensions to fit your model.

CUSTOM ROUTER TABLE

There's no better fixture you can build or buy for your router than a router table. It turns your handheld router into a makeshift shaper and expands the range of joints and moldings you can make. There are easier paths to a router table than this one, but our design provides maximum versatility, convenience and storage space—all on wheels.

by Rick White

After reviewing numerous router table designs, *we took the best features from each to create our customized version. Key concerns were accuracy, easy access, and tool and bit storage.*

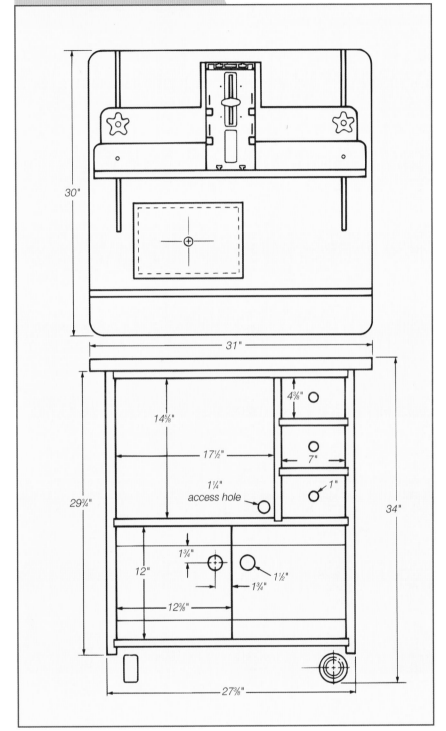

Next to a table saw, I consider a quality router table to be the next most important piece of shop equipment a woodworker can own. Aside from its joint-making and profiling capabilities, a router table can serve as a jointer if you don't have one. It also makes a handheld router safer to use for milling small, narrow or odd-shaped workpieces.

Designing a router table involves two challenging requirements, and our group of woodworking experts has come up with very good solutions. The first challenge is making the router easily accessible for exchanging bits or adjusting their height. On our cabinet the router can be removed through the table top for major alterations or adjusted from the front for raising and lowering the bits. The second hurdle is designing a fence that works for every possible routing operation. Our system begins with a conventional fence that adjusts quickly for general routing. With the addition of an Incra jig attachment, the fence system offers precise, incremental adjustments for routing perfect dovetail joints, finger joints or flutes.

Several other minor considerations must also be met. In our shop, tools need to be mobile, so I put wheels on the router cabinet to get it out of the way when it's not needed. The drawers provide storage space for router bits and accessories, and the lower cupboard shelters power tools from all the dust in the shop. The addition of an electrical strip on the right side of the cabinet is a handy feature that provides easy access to the on/off switch.

I built this router cabinet from white oak, using a half sheet of ¾" plywood, 11 board feet of ¹¹⁄₁₆"-thick solid stock and 4 board feet of ¾"-thick material. Making the top requires a half sheet of ½"-thick baltic birch plywood and another half sheet of ¾" baltic birch plywood. In addition to the lumber and plywood, I used a piece of plastic laminate to cover the router table surface for improved durability and a roll of oak iron-on edgebanding to cover the exposed plywood edges.

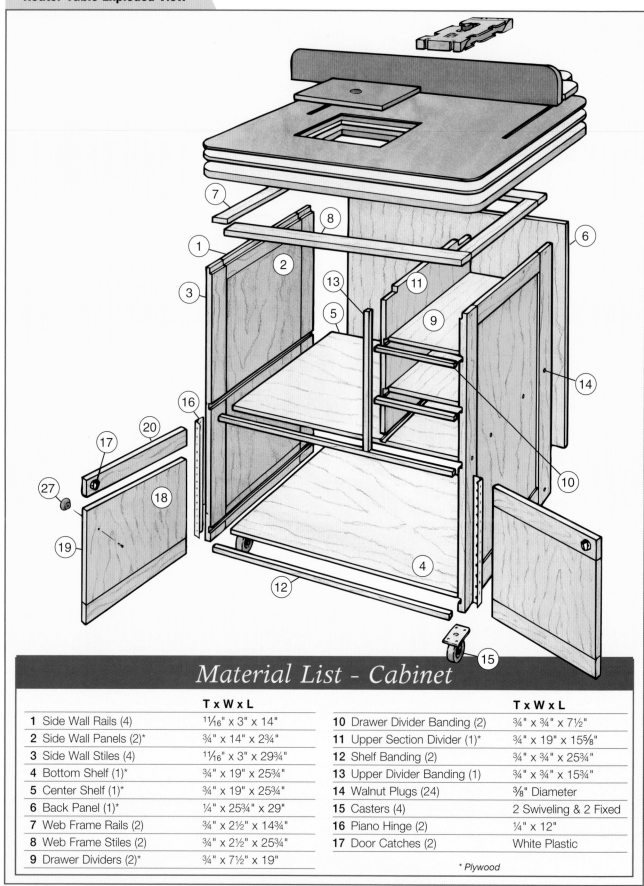

Material List - Cabinet

	T x W x L			T x W x L
1 Side Wall Rails (4)	11⁄16" x 3" x 14"		**10** Drawer Divider Banding (2)	¾" x ¾" x 7½"
2 Side Wall Panels (2)*	¾" x 14" x 2¾"		**11** Upper Section Divider (1)*	¾" x 19" x 15⅝"
3 Side Wall Stiles (4)	11⁄16" x 3" x 29¾"		**12** Shelf Banding (2)	¾" x ¾" x 25¾"
4 Bottom Shelf (1)*	¾" x 19" x 25¾"		**13** Upper Divider Banding (1)	¾" x ¾" x 15¾"
5 Center Shelf (1)*	¾" x 19" x 25¾"		**14** Walnut Plugs (24)	⅜" Diameter
6 Back Panel (1)*	¼" x 25¾" x 29"		**15** Casters (4)	2 Swiveling & 2 Fixed
7 Web Frame Rails (2)	¾" x 2½" x 14¾"		**16** Piano Hinge (2)	¼" x 12"
8 Web Frame Stiles (2)	¾" x 2½" x 25¾"		**17** Door Catches (2)	White Plastic
9 Drawer Dividers (2)*	¾" x 7½" x 19"			

* Plywood

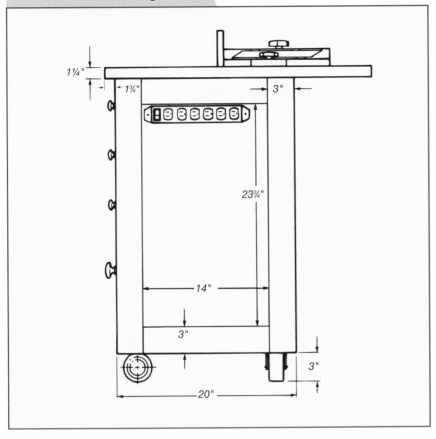

1¼"
1¾"
3"
23¾"
14"
3"
3"
20"

Building the Cabinet

Begin constructing the router table by making the frame and panel sides. You'll want to continually refer to the Drawings while building the router cabinet, as they detail all the parts and joint locations. The two side walls are made of ³/₄" plywood surrounded by ¹¹/₁₆"-thick solid-oak frames. Cut the frame rails (pieces 1) and plywood panels (pieces 2) to size and rout one edge of the rails with a ¹/₄" roundover bit. Join the rails to the plywood with biscuits as shown in the Figure 1, next page. Now cut the stiles (pieces 3) to match the overall length of the panels. Hold the stiles up to the panels and mark the points where the frame pieces intersect, then rout the length of the edge between the marks with the roundover bit. Join the stiles to the panels with biscuits.

After the two side walls are constructed, lay them on their faces

and mark the dado and rabbet locations shown on page 136. The dadoes and rabbets are all ¾" wide and ¼" deep. In the left side wall, rout two dadoes—one for the bottom shelf (piece 4) joint and one for the center shelf (piece 5) joint—and rout a rabbet along the top inside edge for securing the web frame (pieces 7 and 8). The right side wall requires dadoes for the bottom shelf joint, the center shelf joint and the two drawer dividers (pieces 9) as well as the top rabbet. Use a straightedge jig such as the one shown in Figure 2 to guide the router while cutting the dadoes and rabbets. Also, while the panels are still laying face down, rout a ³/₈"-deep by ¼"-wide rabbet along the back edge of each side wall for the back (piece 6).

The web frame, which secures the router table to the cabinet, is made of four pieces. Rip and crosscut the two rails (pieces 7) and the two stiles (pieces

8) to size, then join the frame together using the biscuit joiner and your smallest size biscuits.

Rip ¾"-thick plywood for the bottom shelf, the center shelf and the upper section divider (piece 11) all at the same time, then crosscut the pieces to length. Glue on the solid-wood banding (pieces 12 and 13). Now cut the two drawer dividers (pieces 9) to size and band their front edges with solid wood (pieces 10).

Next, rout the ¾"-wide by ¼"-deep dado in the center shelf for securing the upper section divider. The same size dadoes must also be routed into the upper section divider for the drawer dividers, as shown in Figure 1. Finish up on this piece by cutting notches out of the upper corners so that it fits around the web frame stiles.

All the shelf dado joints in the side walls are reinforced with screws. To accurately drill the pilot holes for these #8-2" wood screws, first dry-assemble the cabinet, then draw the three lines on the outside face of each side wall to indicate the center of each dado or rabbet. One hole is centered on each stile and two more are spaced on the panel. Drill ³/₈"-diameter by ⁵/₁₆"-deep counterbores for the plugs and follow the counterbores with a ⁵/₃₂"-diameter bit for drilling the 2"-deep pilot holes.

One operation that you definitely should perform now rather than after the cabinet is assembled is drilling the pilot holes for the Blum drawer slides (pieces 28). Set the Blum slides ¹³/₁₆" back from the front edge of the right side wall and the upper section divider to allow for the inset drawer fronts, and position the slides directly above each drawer divider dado. Use an awl to mark the screw locations and then drill the pilot holes with a ¹/₈"-diameter bit.

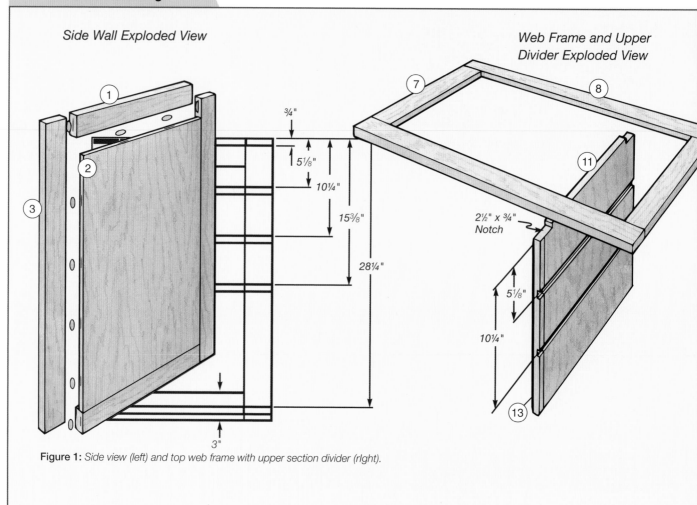

Side Wall Exploded View

Web Frame and Upper
Divider Exploded View

Figure 1: *Side view (left) and top web frame with upper section divider (right).*

Disassemble the cabinet and spread glue in the side wall dadoes for the bottom shelf and the center shelf. Pull these four pieces together once again and drive the sixteen screws into place. Now spread more glue in the center shelf dado, the two dadoes in the upper section divider and in the two remaining dadoes in the right side wall. Slip the upper section divider into the center shelf dado, then set the lower drawer divider in place, followed by the upper drawer divider, and slowly pull the assembly together.

Wrap up the carcass assembly by applying glue to the rabbets on the side walls and drop in the web frame, slipping it over the upper section divider. Fasten the walls to the web frame with #8-2" screws, and drill countersunk 5/32" pilot holes through the web frame into the upper section divider. Secure the joints with #8-2" screws. Lastly, glue walnut plugs (pieces 14) into the counterbored holes in the side walls; sand them flush when the glue dries.

Making Drawers and Doors

The cabinet doors are made from ¾" plywood (pieces 18) banded on their vertical edges with ¾" by ½" banding (pieces 19) and trimmed on the top and bottom edges with rails (pieces 20). Regularly refer to the Exploded Views of the doors and drawers throughout this section of the project. Cut the plywood pieces to size, then glue on the banding strips. Now cut the rails and join them to the plywood with biscuits.

The drawers are made with a simple, durable joint. Cut the ½"-thick plywood drawer sides (pieces 21), fronts (pieces 22) and backs (pieces 23) to the sizes shown in the Material List. Next, install a dado blade in the table saw and set it to cut ¼"-wide by ¼"-deep grooves. Clamp a spacer block onto the tablesaw's rip fence and, using a miter gauge, pass the drawer sides over the blade to cut dadoes ¼" from each end.

Move the rip fence to align the edge of the spacer block with the dado blade and make the ¼"-wide by ¼"-thick tongues at the ends of the front and back pieces to fit into the

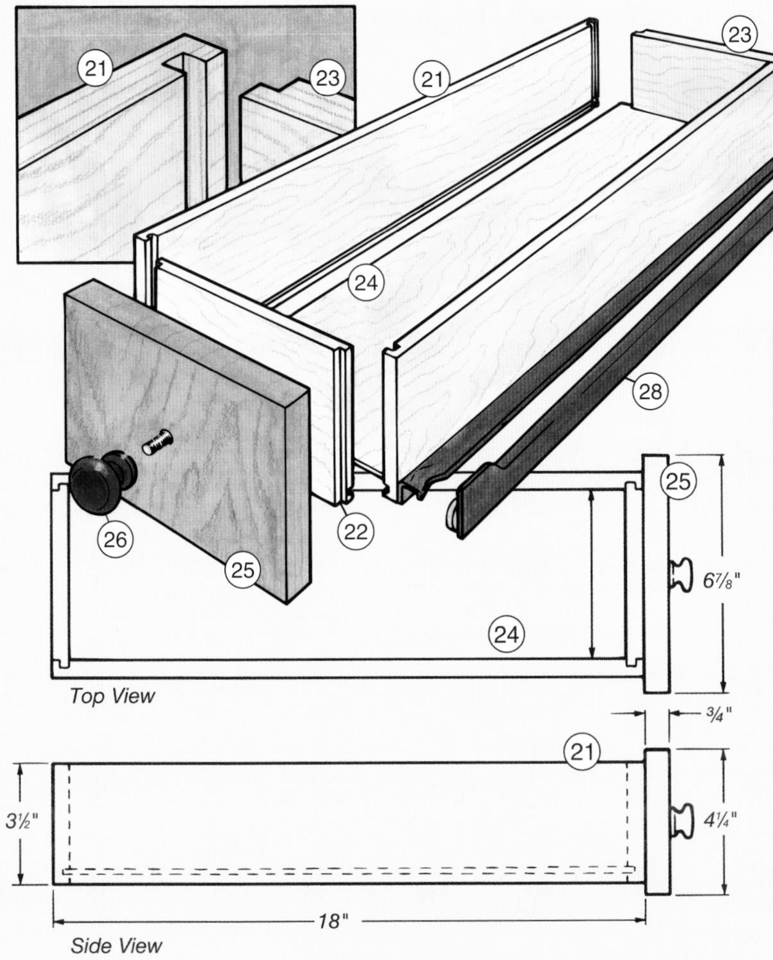

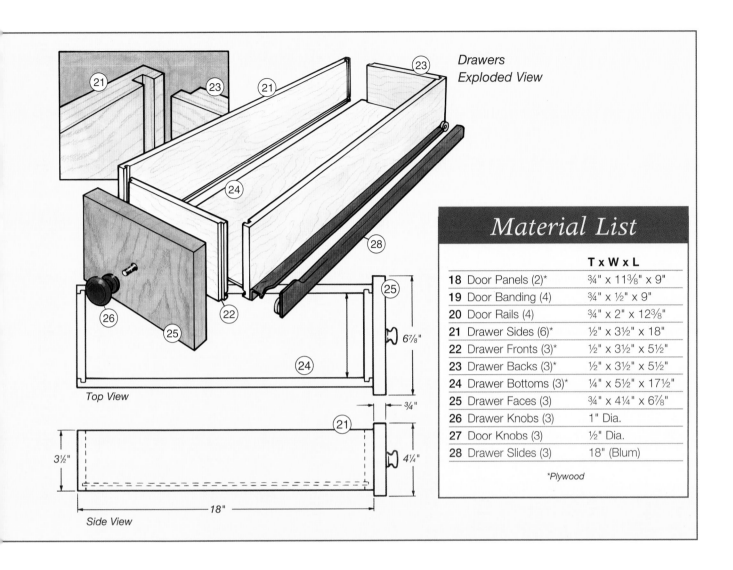

Drawers
Exploded View
21
23
21
23
24
28
25
22
26
25
24
6⅞"
Top View
¾"
21
3½"
4¼"
18"
Side View

Material List

		T x W x L
18	Door Panels (2)*	¾" x 11⅜" x 9"
19	Door Banding (4)	¾" x ½" x 9"
20	Door Rails (4)	¾" x 2" x 12⅜"
21	Drawer Sides (6)*	½" x 3½" x 18"
22	Drawer Fronts (3)*	½" x 3½" x 5½"
23	Drawer Backs (3)*	½" x 3½" x 5½"
24	Drawer Bottoms (3)*	¼" x 5½" x 17½"
25	Drawer Faces (3)	¾" x 4¼" x 6⅞"
26	Drawer Knobs (3)	1" Dia.
27	Door Knobs (3)	½" Dia.
28	Drawer Slides (3)	18" (Blum)

*Plywood

dadoes in the drawer sides. Readjust the blade to cut a 7⁄32" dado and move the rip fence ¼" away from the blade (remove the spacer block). Cut a dado on the inside face of all the drawer pieces for holding the bottoms in place. Cut the drawer bottoms (pieces 24) to size and dry-assemble the three units. Once the fit is satisfactory, glue the drawer parts together and sand them thoroughly.

The drawer faces (pieces 25) are made from solid oak and are cut to fit the drawer openings with a 1⁄16" gap all around. Cut this stock and attach it to the drawer fronts from the inside with a couple of #8-1" screws. With the drawers and the doors completed, drill the holes for attaching the knobs (pieces 26 and 27). You'll need to counterbore the drawer fronts to allow the knob screws to bridge the combined thickness of the front and face. Mount the doors to the cabinet with surface-mounted piano hinges (piece 16) and screw the door's roller catches (pieces 17) in place. As usual, the back panel (piece 6) is the last piece to make for the cabinet.

Figure 2: *To make this straightedge jig, fasten a straight, narrow board to an oversized piece of hardboard, then rout the edge of the jig with the router and bit you intend to use for the dado. Next, align and clamp the edge of the jig with the layout line and rout the dado.*

Cut this out of ¼" plywood, but don't nail it onto the cabinet until after the top is attached.

Building the Table Top

The table top is made with two layers of plywood, which accommodate the two tracks for the fence system and give the table as much vibration resistance and stiffness as possible. The top of the table is covered in plastic laminate, providing a slick surface to slide the stock over and making it easy to clear off wood chips and dust. While building the table top, continually refer to the Exploded View Drawing on the next page, as it lays out all the details for constructing the top and the fence.

The first step in constructing the table is to cut a piece for the top (piece 29) to the shape shown in the Top View from ½"-thick baltic birch plywood, and make another piece in the same shape from ¾" baltic birch plywood for the sub-top (piece 30). Clamp the two pieces together and sand all the edges smooth. Use a jigsaw to cut 1½" corner radiuses, and sand the four corners smooth.

Take the clamps off the plywood and set the top aside for the moment. Chuck a ¾" mortising bit in the router and attach an edge guide. Now, rout $\frac{7}{16}$"-deep fence adjustment tracks in the sub-top, following the positions shown in the Drawing. Once the grooves are routed, lay out the rectangular insert area as shown in the Drawing and drill a ½"-diameter hole at the inside of each corner. Use a jigsaw to cut out the insert area, then sand the edge of the hole smooth. Drill the pilot holes for the ¼" threaded inserts at both ends of the opening, as in Figure 3.

Before gluing the two top pieces together, cut the rectangular insert area out of the top piece of baltic birch

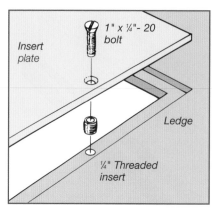

Figure 3: *Use ¼"-20 threaded inserts and 1"-long bolts to hold the interchangeable insert plates in place.*

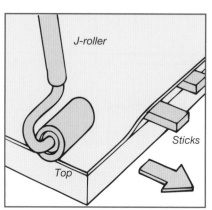

Figure 4: *Position the laminate, then remove the sticks one at a time, rolling the laminate down as you go.*

plywood. You'll notice that the hole in the top is larger than the hole in the sub-top. The difference in the two holes creates a sturdy ledge to support the insert plates and the router.

Liberally spread glue over the sub-top, keeping it at least ½" back from the fence adjustment track dadoes, and lay the top onto the sub-top. Clamp the two pieces together, making sure the edges line up perfectly, and let the glue dry overnight. The next day, clean up any glue squeeze-out and apply iron-on veneer edging to the table's edges.

Cover the surface of the top with plastic laminate, which is easy material to work with if you take your time and

position it carefully. Cut a piece of laminate (piece 31) about one inch larger than the top all the way around and lay it upside down on your workbench. Clean the plywood and the bottom of the laminate thoroughly, removing sawdust or particles of any kind. Apply an even coat of non-flammable contact cement to both surfaces and let it dry, which usually takes about 20 minutes. After the first coat is dry, apply a second coat and let it dry. Now lay about eight narrow sticks across the table top and set the laminate on top of the sticks (see Figure 4). The sticks enable you to situate the laminate on the table before the two pieces meet and permanently bond.

Begin removing the stickers at one end of the top and press the laminate against the surface of the plywood. Use a J-roller to press the laminate down once the surfaces are making contact, but avoid rolling the unsupported insert plate area to prevent cracking the laminate. Once you've applied pressure to all points on the table's surface, trim any laminate overhanging the top with your router and a piloted flush-cutting bit. Also, drill a ½" starter hole through the laminate near one inside corner of the insert plate area, then run the router around the rectangular opening to uncover the hole.

The insert plates are laminated on both sides, making them thicker than the top by $\frac{1}{16}$". As a result, the insert area's ledge must be lowered for the top surface to be even. Chuck a piloted straight bit in your router and, following the upper edge of the insert area, lower the ledge on the sub-top by $\frac{1}{16}$". Square up each corner of the insert area where the router bit couldn't reach and ease all the laminate edges on the top with a mill file. Install the threaded inserts in the pilot holes at both ends of the insert plate area.

Table Top Exploded View

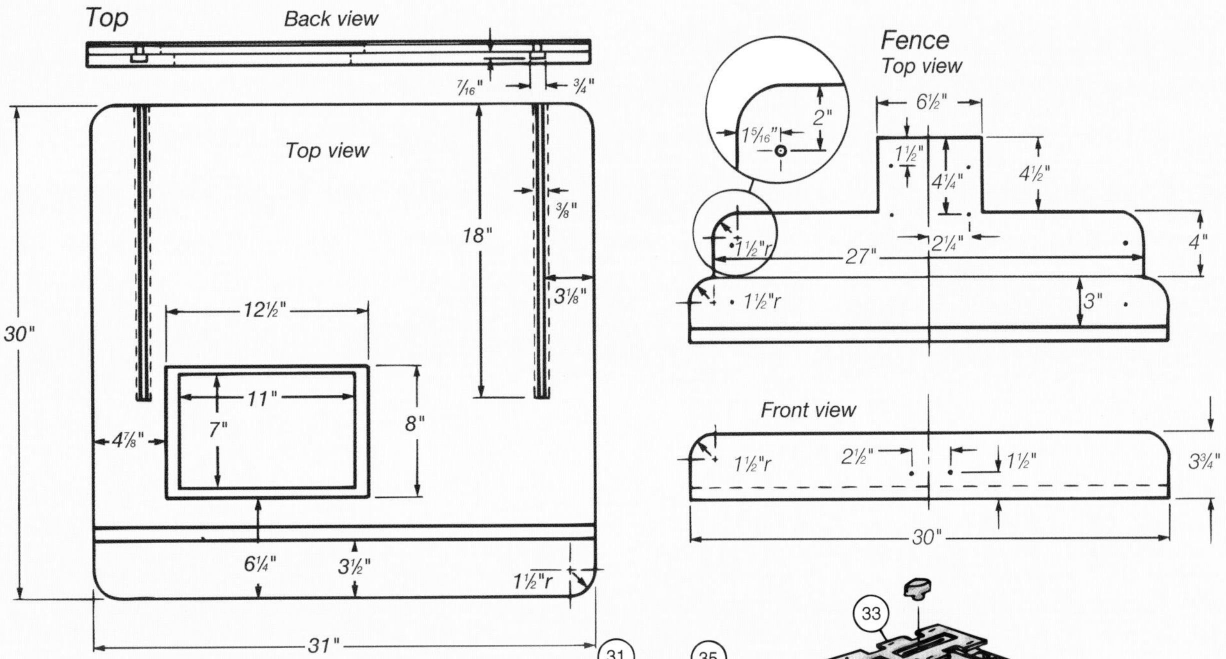

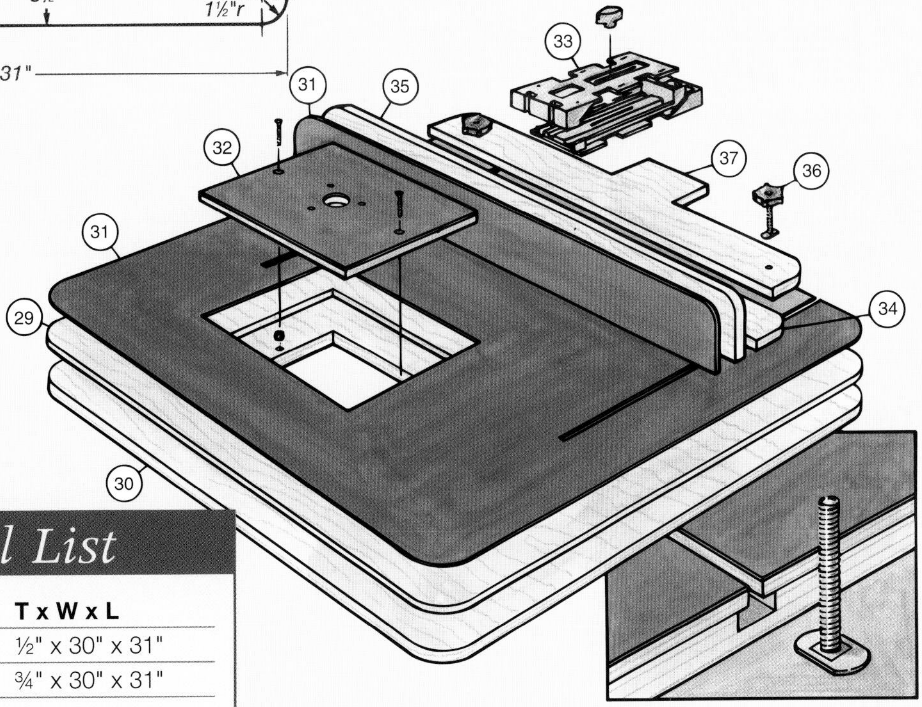

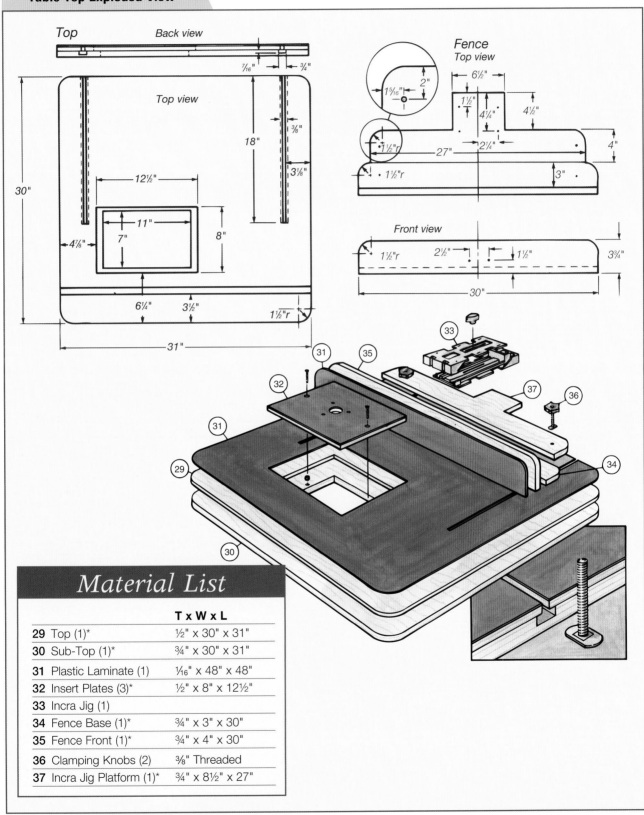

Material List

	T x W x L
29 Top (1)*	½" x 30" x 31"
30 Sub-Top (1)*	¾" x 30" x 31"
31 Plastic Laminate (1)	1⁄16" x 48" x 48"
32 Insert Plates (3)*	½" x 8" x 12½"
33 Incra Jig (1)	
34 Fence Base (1)*	¾" x 3" x 30"
35 Fence Front (1)*	¾" x 4" x 30"
36 Clamping Knobs (2)	⅜" Threaded
37 Incra Jig Platform (1)*	¾" x 8½" x 27"

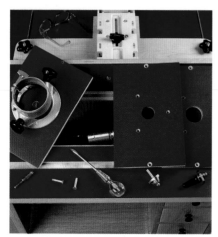

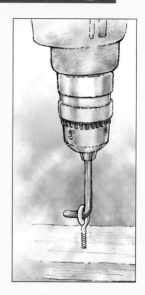

Our router table *is full of convenient features that make it a more efficient shop tool. Ample storage space in the drawers and cupboard provides room for routers, bits and other accessories; the interchangeable insert plates accommodate a wide range of router bit sizes; and the fence system adjusts mechanically or the old-fashioned way—with a quick tap of the hand at one end.*

Now put a ⅜" straight bit in your router and rout the fence adjustment tracks into the top (see Top View Drawing, page 139). Use an edge guide attachment on your router base to follow the top's side edges, routing the slot through the entire ½"-thick plywood, centered on the ¾" adjustment track in the sub-top.

Rout the miter gauge slot, using a straightedge guide as you did for the dadoes on the side walls. We use our Delta Unisaw's miter gauge for the router table, so we cut the slot to match. You should likewise size your miter gauge slot to fit your tablesaw's equipment.

Before moving on to construct the fence, laminate both sides of some extra ½" plywood to make three insert plates (pieces 32). Don't try to get by with laminating only one side of the plywood, as this will cause an unbalanced moisture exchange between the laminated side and the uncovered surface, resulting in warped insert plates.

Cut the laminated plywood to fit the insert hole snugly, then mark the center

of each insert, at which point you should drill a one-inch hole in the first insert, a 1½" hole in the second, and a 2" hole in the third. Be sure to ease all laminate edges with a mill file, otherwise it easily cuts up your hands.

When operating the router table, choose the most appropriate insert for the bit you intend to use, and make more inserts with different hole sizes if you need them. Drill ¼" pilot holes at either end of the inserts for securing the plates to the table. Countersink the holes so the head of the bolt sits below the laminate surface and screw one of the plates into place with 1", ¼"-20 bolts.

Building the Fence

The heart of the fence system is an Incra jig (piece 33), which excels at making incremental adjustments for repetitive cuts. This is a great device, but it isn't always needed for general router work, so we made it easy to remove. When the jig is disconnected the fence can move freely over greater distances.

Begin constructing the fence by making the main L-bracket from ¾"

plywood, first cutting the base (piece 34) and then the fence front (piece 35). Cut the back corners of the base to a 3" diameter as shown in the Fence Drawing on page 139. Laminate the fence front and drill the series of countersunk holes for screwing the front to the base. There's no need to laminate the back side of the fence front as it is restrained from warping by the base connection.

Also, drill the counterbored bolt holes to secure the Incra jig to the front. Screw the front to the base and drill a hole at each end of the base to install the clamping knobs (pieces 36) and T-bolts.

QuickTip

Power-Driving Screw Eyes
Instead of twisting screw eyes in by hand, drill a pilot hole, insert the short leg of an Allen wrench in the eye of the screw, and chuck the other end in your drill. Set the clutch at its lowest torque and use a slow speed to drive the screw eye home.

I made the two adjustment track T-bolts from standard hardware store stock. Take two ⅜" inside diameter fender washers and file the hole to fit around the square nut area of a ⅜"-diameter by 2½"-long carriage bolt. Use five-minute epoxy to permanently glue the washers onto the bolt. Now use a hacksaw to cut two sides of the washers flush with the head of the carriage bolt and file or grind these edges smooth. Insert the T-bolts into the fence adjustment tracks, set the fence assembly onto the bolts and thread the clamping knobs into place.

The Incra jig platform (piece 37) is made from ¾" plywood and has two ⅜"-diameter holes for securing the platform to the router table tracks. The other four holes shown in the Drawing hold the jig to the platform and need to be countersunk. Drill the ¼"-diameter holes and countersink each one on the underside of the platform. Insert ¼"-diameter flathead bolts through the platform, and set the Incra jig onto the bolts. Secure the assembly with four hex nuts.

To mount the Incra jig, first undo the clamping knobs from the T-bolts and remove the fence. Now set the Incra jig platform onto the T-bolts and thread on the clamping knobs. Butt the fence into the front of the Incra jig and insert two ¼"-diameter by 1½"-long flathead bolts through the fence front's holes and into the Incra jigs' mounting slots. Thread the hex nuts on firmly. Move the fence into position and tighten the clamping knobs. Now release the Incra jig knob to position the fence.

Completing the Final Details

Set the router table top on the cabinet and square the two pieces to each other. Now drill a number of ⁵⁄₃₂" holes up through the web frame into the top

for #8-1½" screws, making sure to stay clear of the tracks. Countersink these pilot holes and secure the cabinet to the top.

Disassemble all the parts of the router cabinet and the table and apply a durable finish to all the wood surfaces. Once the finishing is dry, drill four ¼" holes in each corner of the bottom shelf for the carriage bolts that mount the casters (pieces 15) under the cabinet. Install the swiveling casters near the back edge of the cabinet and the stationary casters along the front edge. I mounted an electrical outlet strip to the outside right wall and drilled a 1" access hole in the back panel for the router's cord. Put all the doors and drawers into the cabinet and nail on the back panel. Mount your router housing to an insert plate, then install the router

motor in the housing. Now set the assembly into the insert hole in the table and secure the plate.

Constructing the router table takes thirty hours and costs about $350 in materials, depending on the wood you choose. There really isn't a particularly difficult technique or assembly involved in building this project, but pay close attention to the layout measurements. Following the small details will make your router table more accurate and result in greater returns for your time and investment.

by Barry Chattell

ULTIMATE ROUTER TABLE

Want to bump your routing up to production levels? Ever get tired of constantly changing bits and depth settings on a router table with just one router? This ample, fully appointed router table could be a dream come true. It sports twin routers, dust-collecting fences with micro-adjusters and a horizontal routing attachment. All that's missing from this hot rod is a hood ornament.

Sometimes for the projects we all build, one router just isn't enough. In fact, sometimes even two aren't. Need a solution? Here's a router table big enough to support two routers, complete with a horizontal routing attachment. I designed it to feature many of the best details of conventional router tables, plus more. It's made from economical and reliable medium-density fiberboard (MDF) and hardwood, and the addition of a second router will cut your bit changes in half.

Loaded with Design Features

The basic table design includes a separate fence for each router that pivots on a bolt and tightens down with just one clamp. I've added micro-adjusters so you can dial in the slightest changes or reset a fence exactly, without a fuss. A shop-made dust port and coupling on the fences connects to a dust collector to keep things clean. And, this tabletop is a generous 28¼" x 48"—offering plenty of real estate for supporting long or large workpieces.

The routers hang directly from the table instead of on removable insert plates to provide a continuous work surface and no plate-leveling hassles. It also helps you wrestle those depth changes on plunge routers without the plates popping up. Since the routers are fixed to the table, an open leg base style keeps everything readily accessible underneath.

Tenoning operations on long workpieces won't be a balancing act anymore if you outfit your table with the horizontal routing attachment, also described here.

Making the Tabletop

Get this project under way by cutting the table (piece 1) to size and rounding off the corners with 2" radii. Go ahead and cut the supports and stringers (pieces 2, 3 and 4) while you are at the table saw.

Find and mark centerpoints for the router recesses using the Elevation Drawing on page 144. Drill a ⅛" hole through the table at both centerpoints to mark these spots.

Use a hand-held router and a flush-trim bit with a 1" cutting length to mill both router recesses. To do this, first make a template that matches your router base shape on a piece of ¾" MDF. Trace the base, cut out the shape with a jigsaw and sand the opening until the router base fits snugly in the template.

Before you start routing, you will need to mount your router to an oversized base plate so the router can span the template opening as you mill the recesses. We used a piece of ¼" clear acrylic about 10" square. Cut a clearance hole in this base plate for the flush-trim bit and drill the countersunk holes for mounting the router. Install the router on the plate.

To cut the recesses, mount the template on the table with double-sided tape, centering the template over one of the reference points you drilled. Rout the recesses in several passes of increasing depth, guiding the bit's bearing around the template rim and clearing out the inner waste. Rout both recesses ⅝" deep.

Bore a 1¾" bit clearance hole through the table at the drilled centerpoints. These holes are large enough to

Tabletop Exploded View

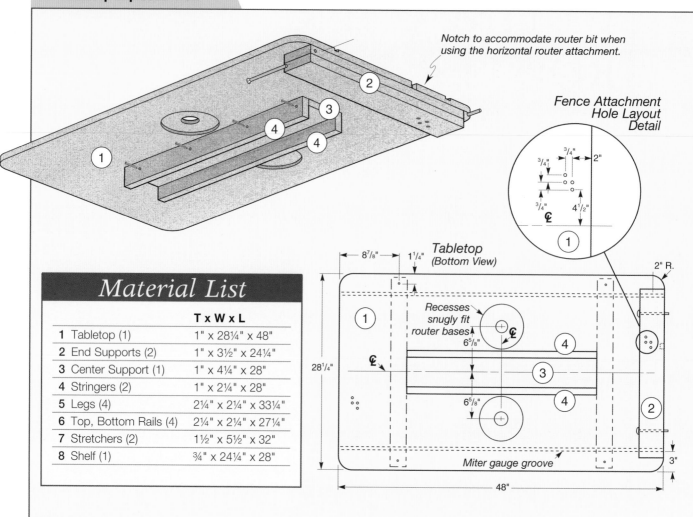

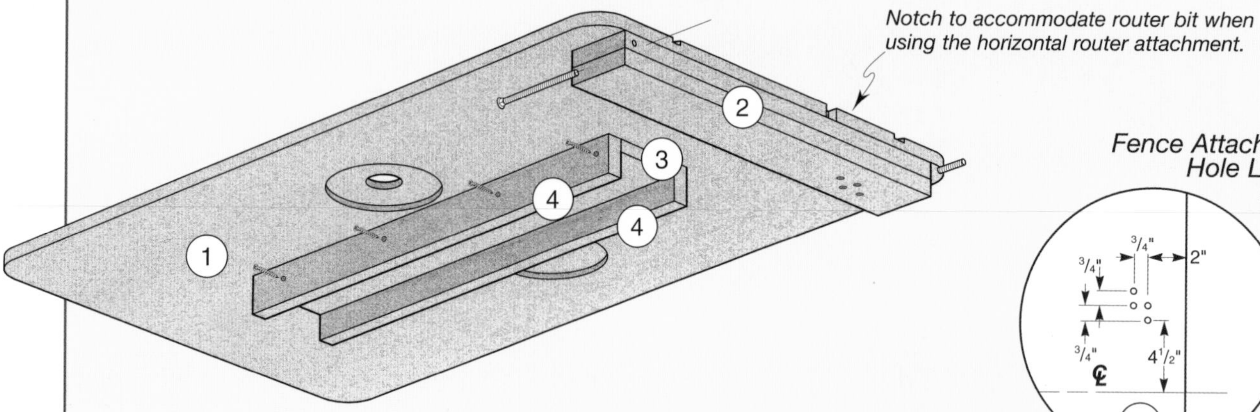
Notch to accommodate router bit when using the horizontal router attachment.
1
2
3
4
4

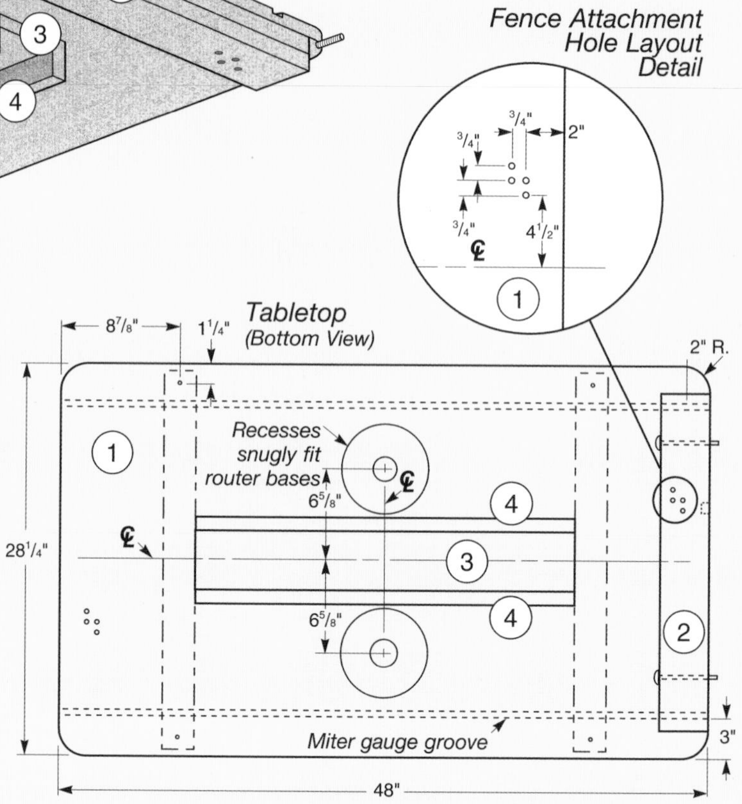
Fence Attachment Hole Layout Detail
3/4"
3/4"
2"
3/4"
4 1/2"
Tabletop
(Bottom View)
8 7/8"
1 1/4"
2" R.
Recesses snugly fit router bases
6 5/8"
6 5/8"
28 1/4"
Miter gauge groove
3"
48"
1
2
3
4
4

Material List

	T x W x L
1 Tabletop (1)	1" x 28¼" x 48"
2 End Supports (2)	1" x 3½" x 24¼"
3 Center Support (1)	1" x 4¼" x 28"
4 Stringers (2)	1" x 2¼" x 28"
5 Legs (4)	2¼" x 2¼" x 33¼"
6 Top, Bottom Rails (4)	2¼" x 2¼" x 27¼"
7 Stretchers (2)	1½" x 5½" x 32"
8 Shelf (1)	¾" x 24¼" x 28"

*Quick*Tip

Non-slip Options for Rules and Squares

A frustrating problem when drawing straight lines with a long rule or large carpenter's square is having the straightedge slip out of place, especially on uneven or vertical surfaces. Here are a couple of solutions to try. One option is to drill several small holes through the straightedge, sized just large enough to fit the shanks of bulletin-board push pins. Press the pins into the workpiece before drawing your line. The tiny holes left behind will be insignificant after a thorough sanding. Another remedy is to fix strips of sandpaper to the bottom of your square or straightedge with spray adhesive. A fine-grit paper will provide just enough bite to prevent shifting, and it leaves no evidence behind.

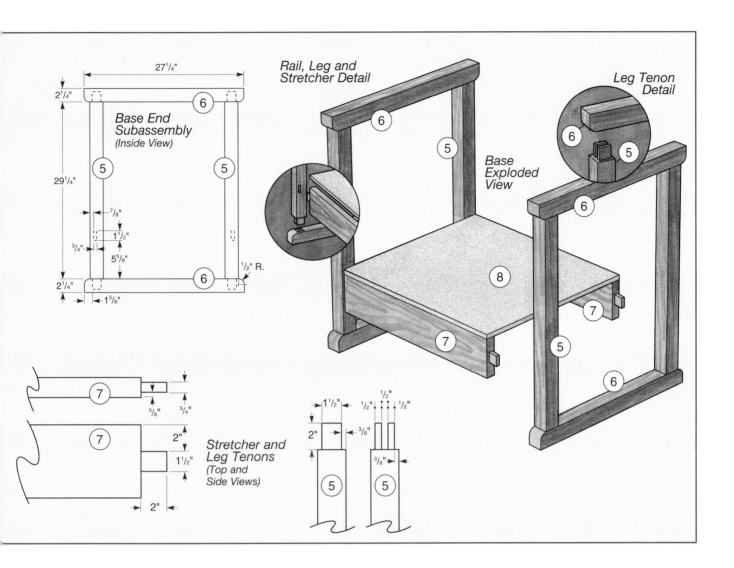

27¼"

2¼"

Base End Subassembly
(Inside View)

29¼"

⁷⁄₈"

1½"

¾"

5⅝"

2¼"

1⅜"

½" R.

Rail, Leg and Stretcher Detail

Base Exploded View

Leg Tenon Detail

⅜"   ¾"

2"

1½"

Stretcher and Leg Tenons
(Top and Side Views)

2"

1½"   ½"   ½"

2"   ⅜"

½"

⅜"

accommodate most common router bit diameters. Now use your routers' sub-bases as patterns for drilling countersunk mounting holes to hang them from the table.

With the recesses completed, refer to the Fence Attachment Hole Layout Detail, above, to lay out and drill four staggered ⁵⁄₁₆" holes on opposite ends of the tabletop. These should offer sufficient spacing to accommodate most router bit and fence adjustment needs.

Cut two dadoes along the length of the table into the top face to make miter gauge tracks. Inset them 3" from the table edges. Make the dado width and depth dimensions match your miter gauge bar.

Due to the length of the table, stiffen it by gluing and screwing the stringers (pieces 4) to the center support. Attach the brace assembly to the table's bottom face with epoxy and more screws.

Wrap up the top by attaching the end supports (pieces 2). These serve as mounts for the horizontal routing

Hog out the router base recesses *in the table by guiding a piloted flush-cutting bit against a template. An oversized acrylic base plate allows the router to skim over the template opening as you mill these recesses.*

Component Exploded Views

Router Table Fence Exploded View

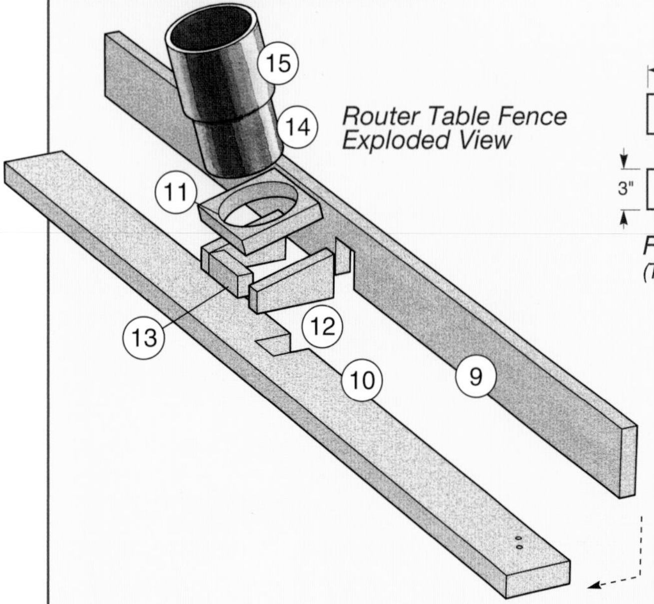
15
14
11
13
12
10
9

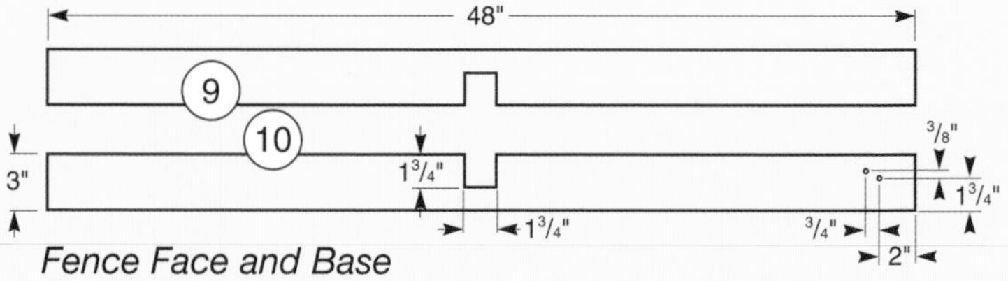
48"
9
10
3"
$1^3/_4$"
$1^3/_4$"
$^3/_8$"
$1^3/_4$"
$^3/_4$"
2"

Fence Face and Base

(Top View)

Horizontal Routing Attachment Exploded View

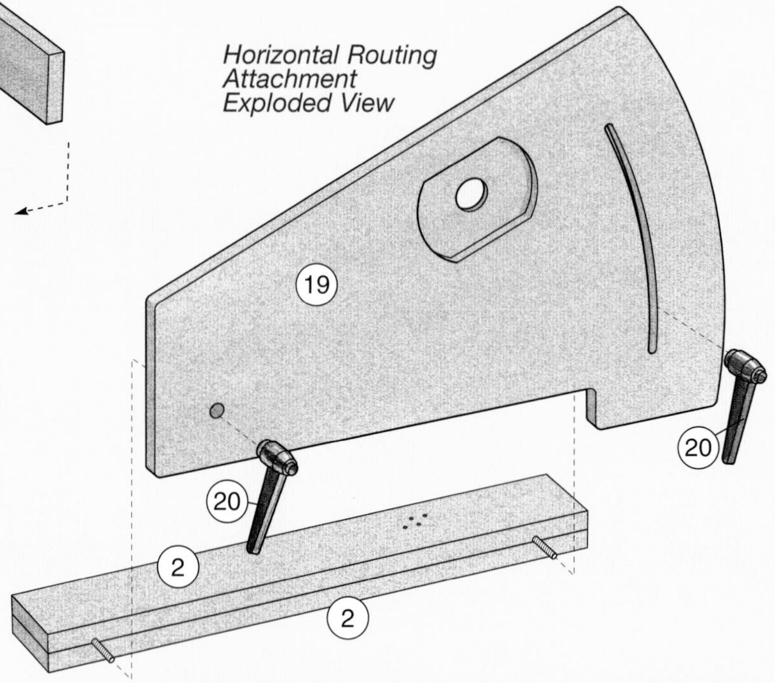
19
20
20
2
2

End Supports

(Top View)

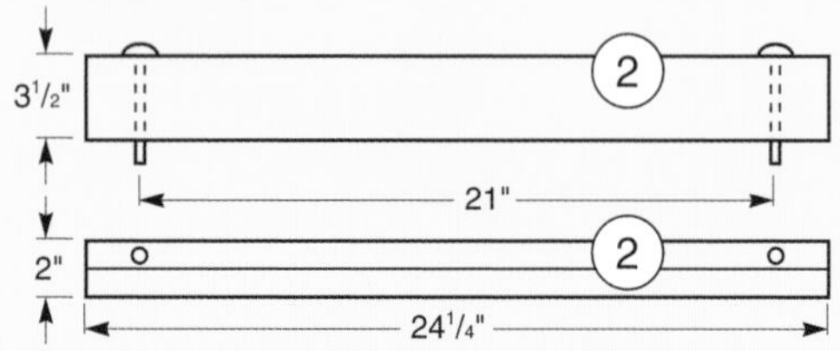
$3^1/_2$"
2
21"
2"
2
$24^1/_4$"

The end supports (pieces 2) are glued and screwed to the tabletop as shown in the Elevation Drawings on page 144.

Horizontal Routing Attachment

(Back View)

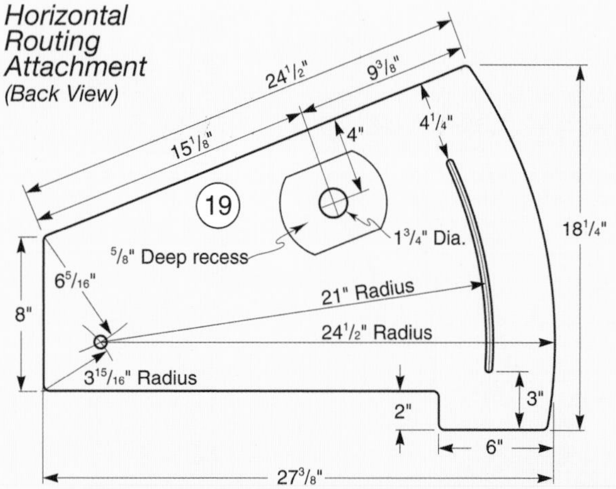
$24^1/_2$"
$9^3/_8$"
$15^1/_8$"
4"
$4^1/_4$"
19
$^5/_8$" Deep recess
$1^3/_4$" Dia.
$18^1/_4$"
$6^5/_{16}$"
8"
21" Radius
$24^1/_2$" Radius
$3^{15}/_{16}$" Radius
2"
3"
6"
$27^3/_8$"

Material List

	T x W x L
9 Fence Faces (2)	¾" x 3" x 48"
10 Fence Bases (2)	1" x 3" x 48"
11 Dust Port Tops (2)	¾" x 4" x 4¼"
12 Dust Port Sides (4)	¾" x 2" x 3$^{11}/_{16}$"
13 Dust Port Ends (2)	¾" x 1" x 2¾"
14 ABS Pipe Dust Port Insert (2)	3½" OD x 4½"
15 ABS Pipe Coupling (2)	4" OD x 3¼"
16 Micro-adjusters (2)	1½" x 1¼" x 3"
17 Knurled Adjuster Bolts (2)	¼"-20 x 2½"
18 T-knob Bolts (2)	¼"-20 x 1½"
19 Horizontal Routing Attachment	1" x 18¼" x 27⅜"
20 Ratchet Handles (2)	⅜" - 16 (female style)

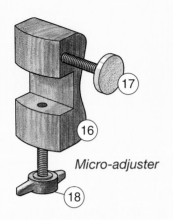

Micro-adjuster

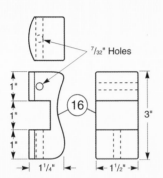

$^{7}/_{32}$" Holes

16

1"
1"
1"

3"

1$^{1}/_{4}$"
1$^{1}/_{2}$"

Micro-adjuster
(Side, Front and Top Views)

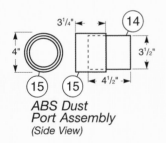

3$^{1}/_{4}$"

14

4"

3$^{1}/_{2}$"

15   15

4$^{1}/_{2}$"

ABS Dust
Port Assembly
(Side View)

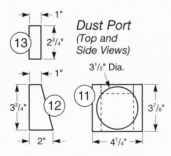

1"

13   2$^{3}/_{4}$"

Dust Port
(Top and
Side Views)

1"

3$^{1}/_{2}$" Dia.

3$^{3}/_{4}$"   12

11

3$^{7}/_{8}$"

2"

4$^{1}/_{4}$"

Cut the double leg tenons at the table saw with the workpieces clamped vertically to a tall tenoning jig.

attachment. Follow the Drawings on page 144 to locate and drill a pair of $^{3}/_{8}$" holes through the top end support for carriage bolts. Fasten the end support assembly flush with the end of the table, using glue and 2½" wood screws driven up from below to secure it. After the glue has cured, you'll need to extend the $^{5}/_{16}$" holes you drilled earlier (the fence attaching holes) through the end supports.

Finally, saw a 1¾" cutout in the table to provide for router bit clearance when using the horizontal routing attachment. Follow up with a quick sanding to ease the table edges.

Constructing the Base

The table base consists of a pair of leg and rail frames joined by two stretchers and a shelf. Start by building the end

frames. Cut the legs and rails to size (pieces 5 and 6). You can give the rails a bit of flair by rounding over the corners where they'll meet the legs.

Look to the Drawings on page 145 to locate and mark the mortises on the legs and stretchers. Use a Forstner bit to remove the majority of the waste and a sharp chisel to clean up the corners, or make these mortises any way you prefer. Once the mortises are completed, it's time to make the leg tenons. Nibble them to size at the table saw using a standard blade, with the legs clamped vertically against a shop-made tenoning jig. Make the tenon shoulders $^{3}/_{8}$" all around.

Dry-fit pairs of legs and rails together, shaving the tenons as necessary until they slip into the rail mortises with just a bit of resistance. Glue and clamp the end frames.

Turning the knurled bolt *in or out on these micro-adjusters makes it easy to move the fence in fractions of an inch or to locate an exact fence position again if needed. Simple and precise.*

Measure the diagonals and adjust the clamps until the frames are square.

While the frames are drying, cut the stretchers (pieces 7) to size and mill tenons on their ends to fit the leg mortises. Go ahead and cut the shelf (piece 8) to size as well.

Build the base framework by joining the stretchers and end frames together with glue and clamps. Assemble these parts on a flat surface to make sure the base does not twist when you clamp it tight. Fasten the shelf to the stretchers with 1¼" flathead wood screws driven into predrilled countersunk holes. Finish up by breaking the edges of the legs and rails with sandpaper to cut down on the chances for splinters later.

Next, set the tabletop on the base so the center support fits between the top rails, and adjust it until it overhangs the rail ends evenly. Drill four countersunk pilot holes down through the table and into the upper rails as shown in the Bottom View of the tabletop on page 144. Secure the tabletop with 2" flathead wood screws.

On to the Fences

The fence construction is fairly straightforward if you follow the Elevation Drawings on page 146. Build two fences so you'll have the flexibility of creating two different router setups.

Cut all the parts for both fences (pieces 9 through 13) now. Be sure to cut the 1¾" bit clearance slots in the fence faces and bases. We found that it's easier to make the dust port top pieces by first cutting the 3½"-diameter holes in larger stock, then sawing pieces 11 to their final size. Follow the fence Drawings to locate and drill the 5⁄16" lateral adjustment bolt holes.

Glue and clamp the faces and bases together, then build the dust ports by gluing pieces 11 through 13 in place. Center the dust ports around the bit clearance slots.

If you'll be connecting these fences to a 4" dust collector hose, make a coupling for each dust port from black ABS pipe. To do this, solvent-weld pieces 14 and 15 together. The smaller pipes will friction-fit into the fence dust port holes, and the larger coupling should slide snugly inside the hose.

Making the Fence Micro-adjusters

The fences mount to the table with a carriage bolt, washer and wing nut installed in the lateral adjustment holes. The opposite fence ends must be secured with a clamp. Since these fences can pivot on the carriage bolts, we've created micro-adjusters (pieces 16, 17 and 18) that allow you to shift the fences ever so slightly in relation to the bit. The photo on this page demonstrates how the micro-adjustment feature works. Essentially, a short T-knob bolt clamps the micro-adjuster to the table, and a top knurled bolt is then turned in or out to scootch the fence in either direction. Regardless of how you turn the knurled bolt, you'll need to slightly loosen the hand clamp that secures the fence in place to realign the fence with the micro-adjuster.

Make the micro-adjuster bodies from hardwood stock—laminating three strips of ½"-thick material in opposite grain directions. Rip and crosscut pieces 16 to size. Turn to your band saw to cut a notch in the wider faces of the micro-adjusters (to fit around the table edge). Use the Drawings on page 147 as guides for locating and drilling the two 7⁄32" through holes for the adjustment bolts. These drawings also illustrate how to shape the micro-adjusters on the drum sander to make them more comfortable to grasp.

Thread the bolts into their holes so the shorter T-bolt clamps the micro-adjuster in place, while the longer, knurled one adjusts the fence setting.

Horizontal Routing Attachment

If imitation is the purest form of flattery, I hope Patrick Spielman would be tickled by my adaptation of his horizontal routing attachment (piece 19). I found it in his book, *Router Jigs & Techniques.* In a nutshell, this handy accessory holds the router perpendicular to the table. It pivots up and down and locks in place with a couple of ratcheting handles (pieces 20). It's especially helpful for cutting mortises and tenons on long parts. It is so much easier to mill horizontally without having to stand pieces on-end to make the tenons. The attachment is also a handy way to mill raised panels with a vertical-style panel-raising bit.

Follow the Drawing on page 146 carefully to lay out and cut the router attachment. Use the same routing method you used earlier to make a router recess in this piece. Lay out and drill countersunk holes in the recess to mount your router, and bore a bit clearance hole. Drill the ⅜"-diameter pivot hole next. You'll need a trammel or circle-cutting jig to rout its curved slot with a ⅜"-diameter straight bit. Install the attachment on carriage bolts, using the ratchet handles.

Notice in the inset photo, top, how you can also use the micro-adjuster for tweaking the router bit height vertically with the horizontal attachment.

As a final convenience, and to help accommodate the fact that there is more than one router mounted to the table, mount a heavy-duty power strip to the table's leg.

Woodworker's Journal has published many router table designs over the years, and it's unlikely that this one will be the last. At this moment, though, I can't think of one more feature to add. But, our ingenious readers are sure to come up with even more!

This horizontal routing attachment *holds the router perpendicular to the table. Cutting tenons on long workpieces is a breeze when they're lying flat.*

QuickTip

Bevel Gauge Blade Spacer

Adding a simple spacer to the blade of your bevel gauge can help improve its accuracy when transferring and drawing angles. Equip the spacer with a small cleat that fits the blade slot to keep it lined up.

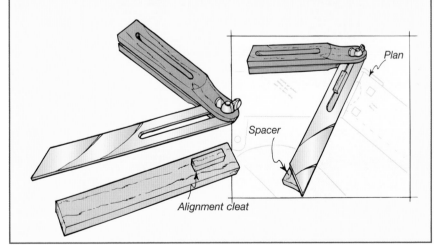

Plan

Spacer

Alignment cleat

by John English

So far, we've discovered that this milling machine will form a corner bridle, corner half-lap, standard dado, rabbeted dado, keyed miter, loose tenon, mitered half-lap, mitered slip joint, rabbet, round mortise, shouldered dado, slot dovetail, splined miter, tapered finger joint, through mortise, a tongue and groove…and we're still working on finding its limits.

BUILD A HORIZONTAL ROUTING SYSTEM

Turn your spare router into a versatile, horizontal milling machine featuring easy and accurate depth of cut, super-easy fence adjustment and above-the-table bit changes. It's a platform that will produce more than a dozen different joints (and counting!) safely and accurately.

All the horizontal routers we've seen have maximum adjustment between the bit and the table of just a couple of inches. This limits work on thick stock, panels, wide boards and other workpieces. For this project, I decided to avoid this limitation by going with a rotating fence, rather than simply moving the router up and down. That allows this system to take advantage of the unique geometry of an arc.

The router motor is mounted on a moving sled that provides incredibly quick and easy bit changes above the table. It also lets you adjust the depth of cut in a couple of seconds. The rotating horizontal fence delivers a huge range of bit-to-table adjustment: you can center the bit anywhere from almost 8" above the table to an inch below (which is great for working with wide bits), and change the setting in seconds. Add sliding tables to the machine, and you can nibble away a deep mortise or long tongue without ever adjusting the fence or bit height.

A Router Table at Heart

The heart of the machine is a router table to which the rotating fence and sliding motor mount are attached. This table is designed to be clamped to a workbench with the fence rotating down behind it. The first part to make is the table base (piece 1), which is cut

The router motor is mounted in a mobile base that slides back from the vertical fence. *This provides complete access to the router for bit changes. The same mechanism is used to set the depth of cut.*

to the size shown on the Material List on page 152. I used white melamine-coated particleboard—widely available at lumberyards. Seal the edges with heat-activated edge-banding tape (piece 2): a household clothes iron works well. Trim the edges with a sharp chisel and 220-grit sandpaper (Figure 1).

Cut the two router table sides (pieces 3) to size, then attach them to the base with 1¾" countersunk, pre-drilled screws, driven up through the bottom, as shown in the Exploded View

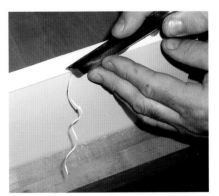

Figure 1: *Use a household clothes iron to apply plastic edge banding, then trim the excess with a sharp chisel and sandpaper.*

Sled *(Top View)*

2¼"

1⅞"

3⅛"

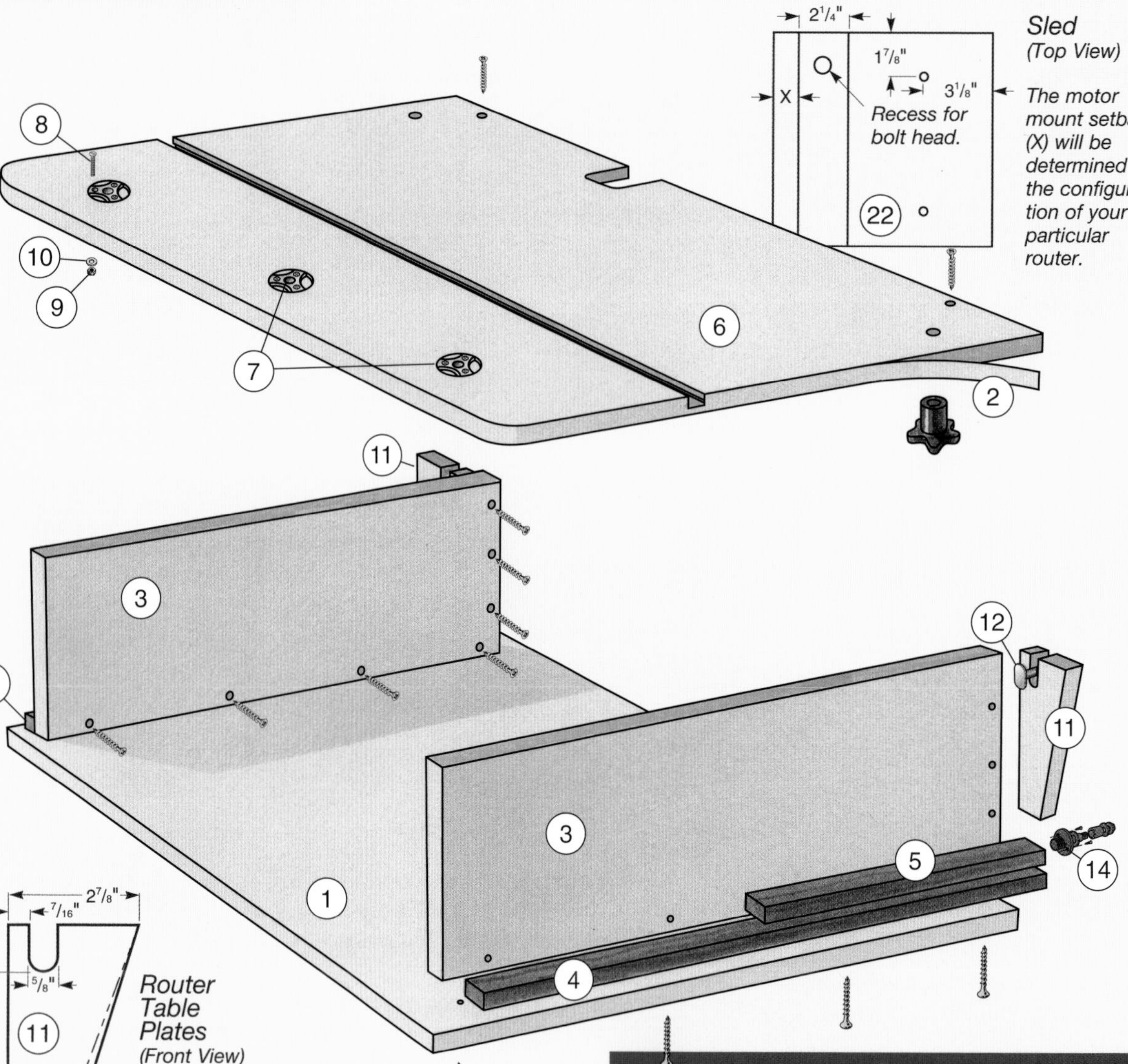

X

Recess for bolt head.

22

The motor mount setback (X) will be determined by the configuration of your particular router.

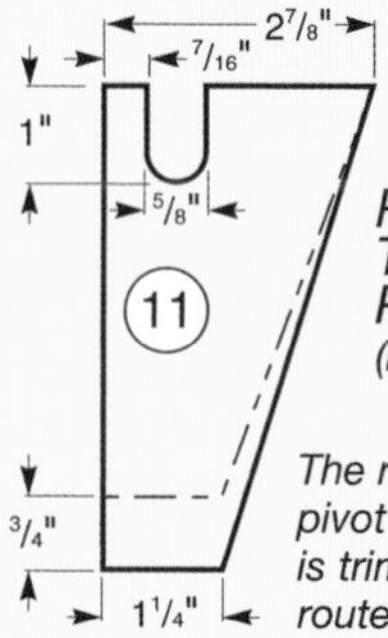

8

10

9

7

6

2

11

3

4

12

11

3

5

14

1

Router Table Plates *(Front View)*

2⅞"

⁷⁄₁₆"

1"

⅝"

11

¾"

1¼"

The router table plate on the pivot hinge side of the base is trimmed short to avoid the router table cleat (piece 5).

Router Table Top *(Top View)*

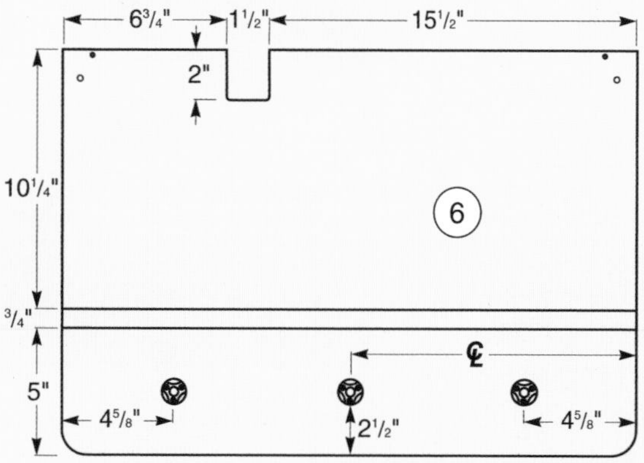

6¾"

1½"

15½"

2"

10¼"

6

¾"

5"

4⅝"

2½"

4⅝"

℄

Material List - Base

		T x W x L
1	Router Table Base (1)	¾" x 14½" x 21"
2	Edge Banding (2)	¹⁄₃₂" x ⅞" x 25'
3	Router Table Sides (2)	¾" x 5¾" x 14"
4	Router Table Braces (2)	¾" x 1¼" x 14"
5	Router Table Cleat (1)	¾" x 1¼" x 7"
6	Router Table Top (1)	¾" x 16" x 23⅝"
7	T-nuts (3)	⁵⁄₁₆" x 18
8	Stove Bolts (9)	To fit T-nuts x 1¼"
9	Stove Bolt Nuts (9)	To fit stove bolts
10	Washers (9)	Steel
11	Router Table Plates* (2)	¾" x 2⅞" x 5"
12	T-Bolts (17)	⁵⁄₁₆" x 2½"
13	Rotating Fence (1)	¾" x 25" x 21¼"
14	Pivot Hinge (1)	Rockler exclusive
15	Plastic Knobs (8)	⁵⁄₁₆" - 18

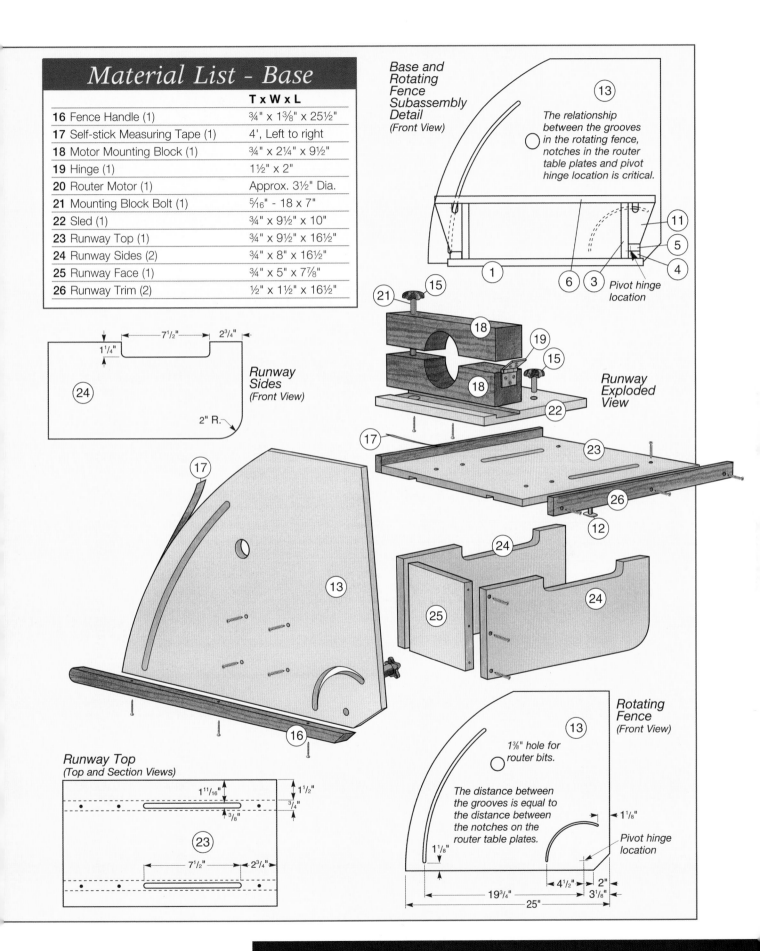

Material List - Base

	T x W x L
16 Fence Handle (1)	¾" x 1⅜" x 25½"
17 Self-stick Measuring Tape (1)	4', Left to right
18 Motor Mounting Block (1)	¾" x 2¼" x 9½"
19 Hinge (1)	1½" x 2"
20 Router Motor (1)	Approx. 3½" Dia.
21 Mounting Block Bolt (1)	5⁄16" - 18 x 7"
22 Sled (1)	¾" x 9½" x 10"
23 Runway Top (1)	¾" x 9½" x 16½"
24 Runway Sides (2)	¾" x 8" x 16½"
25 Runway Face (1)	¾" x 5" x 7⅞"
26 Runway Trim (2)	½" x 1½" x 16½"

Base and Rotating Fence Subassembly Detail
(Front View)

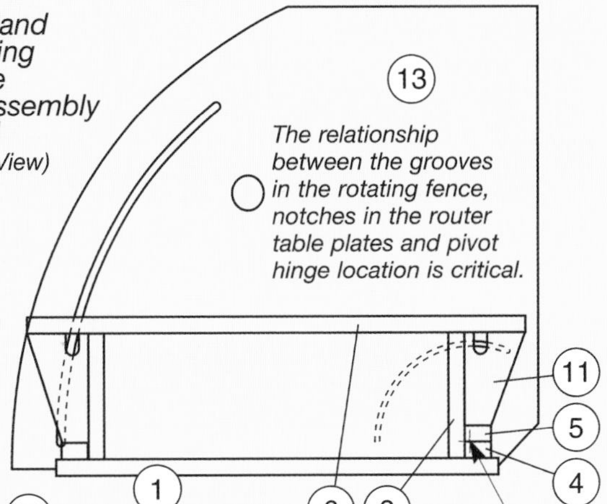

13
The relationship between the grooves in the rotating fence, notches in the router table plates and pivot hinge location is critical.
11
5
4
1
6
3
Pivot hinge location

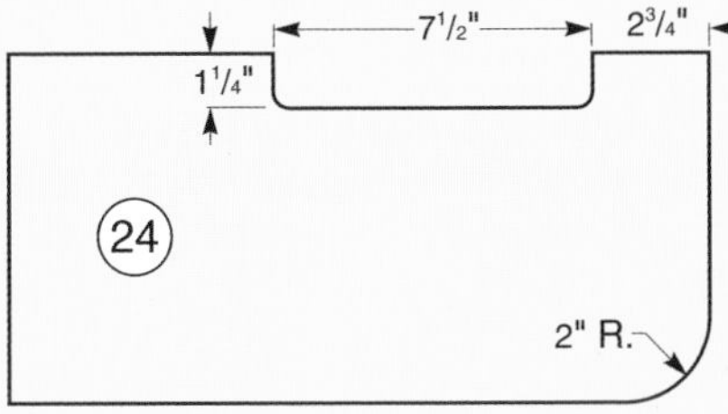

7 1/2"
2 3/4"
1 1/4"
24
2" R.

Runway Sides
(Front View)

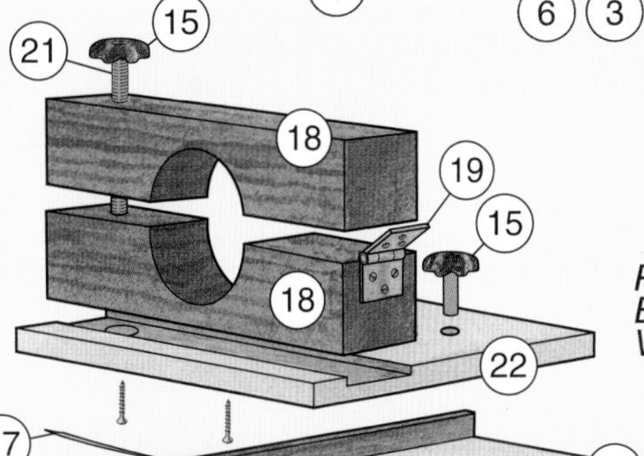

21
15
18
19
15
18
22

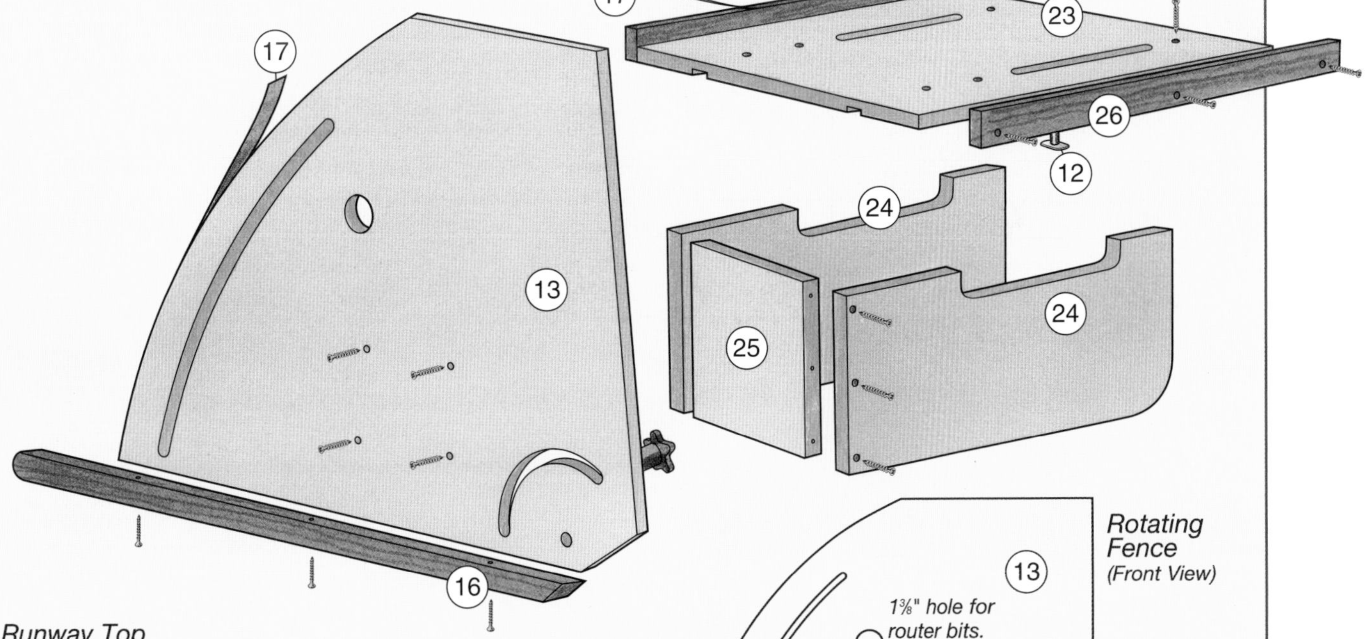

17
23
26
12
24
17
13
25
24
16

Runway Exploded View

Runway Top
(Top and Section Views)

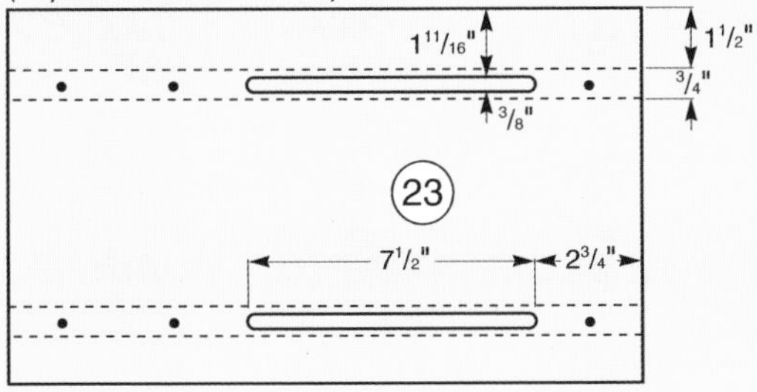

1 11/16"
3/8"
1 1/2"
3/4"
23
7 1/2"
2 3/4"

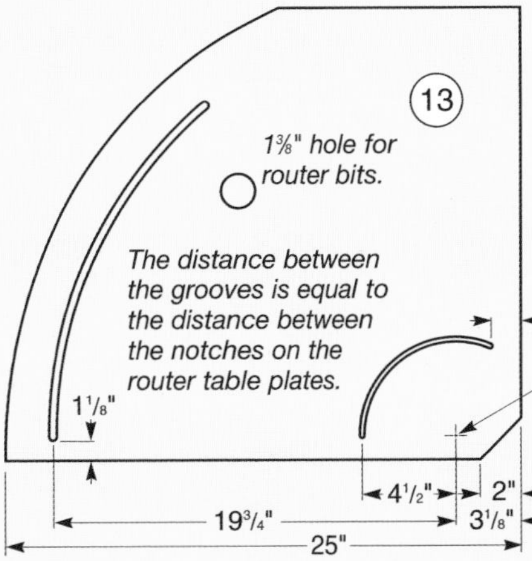

13
1⅜" hole for router bits.
The distance between the grooves is equal to the distance between the notches on the router table plates.
1 1/8"
1 1/8"
Pivot hinge location
4 1/2"
2"
19 3/4"
3 1/8"
25"

Rotating Fence
(Front View)

on page 152. Each of these two critical joints is reinforced with a hardwood brace (piece 4). Ease the outside front corner of each with a sander to avoid sharp edges. Attach them with three screws driven up through the table base and three more through each table side.

On the side of the table where the fence will be hinged, an additional short hardwood cleat (piece 5) is required. Chamfer one side and one end along the top edge; then glue and screw the cleat in place.

The top of the router table (piece 6) is cut to size; then its two front corners are radiused with a belt sander. Apply melamine tape to all four edges and trim it flush; then plow a groove across the top the same size as the guide bar on your table saw's miter gauge. Use the same setup to plow a couple of stopped, ¼"-deep grooves in the bottom face of the tabletop. These house the top edges of the sides as you glue and clamp the top to the sides. Do that assembly now.

After the glue is dry, embed three T-nuts (pieces 7) in the tabletop at the locations shown on page 152. Use a Forstner bit to counterbore holes for them so they sit just below the surface, as shown in Figure 2. Drill three holes for stove bolts, nuts and washers (pieces 8, 9 and 10) to secure the T-nuts: this method allows them to withstand more serious pressure than will the very small screws that come in the package.

The last elements of the router table are the two plates (pieces 11), which are attached at the back, outside the table sides. Each has a slot routed in it to accommodate a T-bolt head (see page 152) and another hole drilled for the bolt (piece 12). These are glued and screwed in place through the table sides and top: make sure the heads of the

Spin Doctoring

Often hardware is the solution to questions that you didn't even know to ask. Rockler Woodworking & Hardware's pivot hinge, shown below, was the perfect solution to a knotty problem: how to raise and lower the router smoothly and accurately. The hinge is unbelievably strong and allows the rotating fence (and its attached router) to move in a predictable arc.

Figure 2: *Three T-nuts embedded in the tabletop add versatility to the machine by allowing for the easy addition of jigs and hold-downs.*

screws going down through the top are totally below the surface.

Making the Rotating Fence
With the table completed, the next task is to make the melamine-coated fence (piece 13). On the table saw, cut it to the size shown in the Material List. Then, to lay out and cut the curve, we're

going to use the pivot point. Locate this point using the Rotating Fence Drawing on page 153, and drill a ½" hole at this location.

The fence rotates on a Rockler pivot hinge (piece 14) and is secured with two star knobs (pieces 15) that thread onto T-bolts protruding through arched slots in the fence. See the illustration of the hinge, left. To begin installing the hinge, use a Forstner bit to drill a recess in the back of the router table, as deep as the thickness of the large flange on the pivot hinge and centered on the square formed by the back ends of the brace and cleat. This is end grain, so a sharp 1⅜" bit is in order. Change to a ½" bit to complete the stepped hole.

Now counterbore the ½" hole you drilled earlier in the fence, following the instructions for the hinge. This is a 1" counterbore in the back of the fence. As the 1" bit no longer has a center to grab, drill a 1" hole in some scrap plywood and used this template over the hole to guide the Forstner bit.

Assemble the hinge and install the fence. Then slide the table to the edge of your workbench, so the fence can pivot, and draw the three arcs on the front face (for the two slots and the edge of the fence).

Cutting the Arched Slots
You can use the hole you drilled for the hinge as a pivot point to rout the grooves. To do this, you need to make a simple circle-cutting jig. Attach a router near one end of a 30"-long piece of scrap MDF. Chuck a ⅜" straight bit in the router, set the depth of cut for ¼", and plunge it through the scrap.

On the rotating fence, measure the distance from the center of the pivot hole to the center of one of the arched slots. Then, on the bottom of your circle-cutting jig, center a ½" hole exactly that distance from the center of the bit.

The pivot hinges come in pairs, so slide the serrated end of the second one into the hole you just drilled in the bottom of the jig. Slide the nylon sleeve into the ½" pivot hole in the fence and the threaded end of the hinge into the sleeve. On the rotating fence, mark the start and stop spots for each slot. Then turn on the router and take several passes to complete each slot.

When you're using the horizontal router table, the bits emerge through a 1⅜" hole in the fence. Find its location on page 153, drill the hole and chamfer the edges. Remove the corner of the fence, then cut the hardwood handle (piece 16) to size. Round over one end of it with a belt sander and attach the handle to the bottom of the fence with glue and countersunk screws. Then apply melamine tape to the other edges of the fence.

The handle makes it easy to control the fence and thereby make small adjustments in the height of the bit. Add part of a self-adhesive tape measure (piece 17) to the curved outer edge of the fence and you can keep track of these minute adjustments. The section of tape can begin and end at any measurement: all you're after is the ¹⁄₁₆" increment marks.

Building the Motor Block

The mounting block (piece 18) for your router is made up of three layers of ³⁄₄" x 4" x 20" hardwood, face-glued and clamped together. After the glue dries, dress all four sides on the jointer, then crosscut the block into two identical 9½" halves. Clamp them edge to edge (no glue lines on the visible top faces), and draw the radius of your router motor on the top face. Band-saw the two arcs and sand to the center of the line with a drum sander chucked in your drill press.

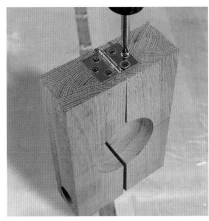

Figure 3: *After gluing up 1 x 4 stock and crosscutting it to make the block halves, join them together with a large surface-mounted hinge.*

Figure 4: *A pair of ¾" grooves in the bottom of the runway accommodates both the heads of the T-bolts and the tops of the runway sides.*

QuickTip

Half-lid Paint Striker

Next time you begin a paint job requiring a whole can of paint, remove the lid and use a hacksaw to cut it in two. Put one half aside for later, then slightly bend down the cut edge of the other and press it back in place atop the can. This half lid makes a sturdy brush shelf, and the cut edge can be used to strike excess paint from the brush.

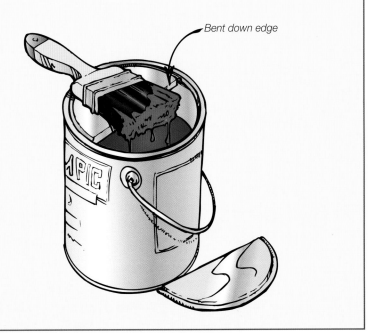

Bent down edge

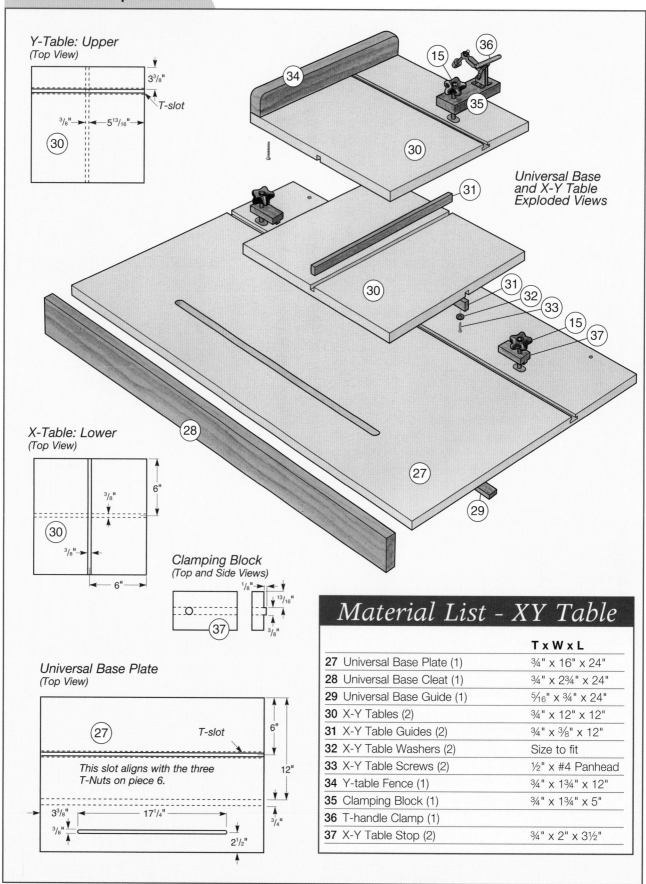

Y-Table: Upper
(Top View)

3³⁄₈"

T-slot

³⁄₈" — 5¹³⁄₁₆"

30

Universal Base and X-Y Table Exploded Views

X-Table: Lower
(Top View)

6"

³⁄₈"

30

³⁄₈"

6"

Clamping Block
(Top and Side Views)

¹⁄₈"

¹³⁄₁₆"

37

³⁄₈"

Universal Base Plate
(Top View)

27

T-slot

6"

This slot aligns with the three T-Nuts on piece 6.

12"

3³⁄₈"

17¹⁄₄"

³⁄₄"

³⁄₈"

2¹⁄₂"

Material List - XY Table

	T x W x L
27 Universal Base Plate (1)	¾" x 16" x 24"
28 Universal Base Cleat (1)	¾" x 2¾" x 24"
29 Universal Base Guide (1)	⁵⁄₁₆" x ¾" x 24"
30 X-Y Tables (2)	¾" x 12" x 12"
31 X-Y Table Guides (2)	¾" x ⅜" x 12"
32 X-Y Table Washers (2)	Size to fit
33 X-Y Table Screws (2)	½" x #4 Panhead
34 Y-table Fence (1)	¾" x 1¾" x 12"
35 Clamping Block (1)	¾" x 1¾" x 5"
36 T-handle Clamp (1)	
37 X-Y Table Stop (2)	¾" x 2" x 3½"

The versatility of this exceptional router system *is enhanced by the ease with which depth and height of cut are adjusted.*

Install a surface-mounted hinge (piece 19) on one end of the block, as shown in Figure 3. Then move to the jointer and take one pass along half of the inside face of each block, removing 1/16" of material. Start each cut at the arc and work away from the hinge. This offset will ensure a tight grip when you install the motor: the block will be full thickness at the hinge side, and 1/8" smaller at the other end.

Dry-fit the motor (piece 20) in the block and make any necessary adjustments for a perfect fit. Drill a 3/8"-diameter hole in the block for the bolt (piece 21) that secures the motor. Counterbore the head of this bolt so it's below the surface, slide it in place and thread a star knob on the other end. Tighten the knob to secure the motor.

Creating the Sled and Runway

After cutting the motor sled (piece 22) to size, plow a 2¼"-wide by 1/8"-deep

dado all the way across the top, to accommodate the bottom of the motor mount. Drill a 1⅜" hole in the dado to allow access to the head of the bolt. Then run a chamfering bit around this hole to remove the sharp edges. Glue and clamp the block into the dado and add three countersunk screws for good measure.

Drill two 5/16" holes through the sled at the locations shown on page 152. These will be used by T-bolts to lock the base in position during use.

The sled sits on a runway that is made up of a top, two sides, a face and two lengths of trim (pieces 23 through 26). Cut the top to size, then set up a router and fence to plow two 3/8"-wide stopped grooves in the top face, at the locations shown on page 153. Turn the part over, switch to a ¾" straight bit and set the depth of cut to 3/16". Then use a clamped-on fence to widen the slots to accommodate T-bolt heads. Make

these cuts the full length of the runway top, as they will house the runway sides (see Figure 4). Cut the sides to size and band-saw them to shape, then sand the edges. Attach them with glue and screws.

Screw the face of the runway subassembly in place between the

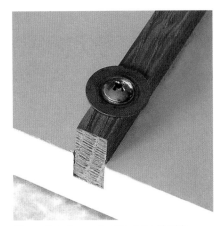

Figure 5: *In the underside of the Y-table (piece 31), a screw and washer in the hardwood guide run in the T-slot of the X-table to prevent lifting.*

sides. Then attach the two pieces of hardwood trim with countersunk screws and glue. Make sure the sled slides easily between the trim pieces: there should be no sloppiness, but no resistance, either.

Use two more T-bolts and star nuts to secure the sled on the runway. Then clamp the runway assembly to the rotating fence so the router chuck is visually centered in the opening in the fence and the top is parallel with the top of the fence. Secure the runway to the fence with four 2" countersunk screws driven through the fence and four 1⅜"-long screws through the runway face.

Adding Precision with X-Y Tables

While the horizontal router table is now fully assembled and operable, you can transform it into a precision milling machine by adding one or more pairs of X-Y sliding tables.

An X-table slides from left to right across the router table. A Y-table slides toward and away from the fence. If you control their travel (and thus control the length of cuts) with stop blocks, there's no limit to what this machine can do.

Begin by making a universal base. This attaches to the router table with a couple of T-bolts and star nuts and can be moved left or right to expand the options with your tabletop: it lets you place jigs, stops or hold-downs exactly where you need them.

The first part of the universal base is a plate (piece 27), cut to size from ¾" melamine. It should be exactly the depth of your router table, so place it on the table snug against the fence and mark the bottom edge where it overhangs the front edge of the table. Trim to this width, then edge-band the ends and back of the plate and trim off the excess tape.

Mill a T-slot across the plate's top surface at the location shown in the Drawing on page 156. Then switch to a ½" straight bit and rout a through, stopped groove that lines up above the three T-nuts you embedded in the router table. Attach a hardwood cleat (piece 28) to the front edge of the

Figure 6: *A hold-down clamp, secured by a T-bolt and star knob, keeps the workpiece tight against the fence of the Y-table, while a straight bit mills a tenon on the end of a cabinet rail.*

plate with glue and clamps. Screw a hardwood guide (piece 29) to the bottom face, lining it up with the miter gauge slot in the router table. Four countersunk screws will secure it.

Cut the X and Y-tables (pieces 30) to size and band all four edges. Plow a dado across the bottom face of the X-table, making it the same width as the smaller dimension of the T-slot you made in the universal base plate.

Install a hardwood guide (piece 31) in the dado with glue and clamps. Attach a washer and screw (pieces 32 and 33) to the bottom of the hardwood guide, as shown in Figure 5: this will lock into the T-slot and prevent the X-table from rising unexpectedly during milling operations. Then plow a T-slot in the top face of the X-table at the location shown on page 156.

Plow a T-slot in the top face of the Y-table at the location shown in the same drawing, then plow a dado in the bottom face and install a hardwood cleat, screw and washer. Attach a hardwood fence (piece 34) on top of the left edge of the table, using countersunk screws driven up through the table.

To clamp workpieces to either table, make a clamping block. This is a short length of hardwood (piece 35) with a hole drilled in it for a T-bolt and star nut (see Figure 6). Bolt a T-handle clamp (piece 36) to the hardwood block.

Since this table was originally designed, I've built several other specialty tables and jigs for this machine. I made some long X-Y tables to help facilitate edge-milling on long boards, such as chopping mortises in cabinet frames. There's also a special jig for milling mitered ends.

Once you realize how often you'll use this vertical router table, you may want to build a cabinet for it like we did to save on bench space.

QuickTip

Clear Protection for Shop Drawings

Professional woodworkers generally keep their drawings and notes on a clipboard, but even then the paper gets dog-eared and dirty. A piece of clear Plexiglas™, cut to 9" x 11" size, makes a great protector, but it also opens up a few other possibilities. By gluing a transparent ruler and protractor (both are available at office supply stores at very little cost) to the Plexiglas, you'll have an instant way to measure drawings, small parts and angles. Use a clear cyanoacrylate (instant) glue or epoxy to bond the parts.

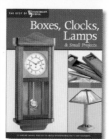
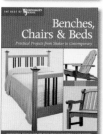

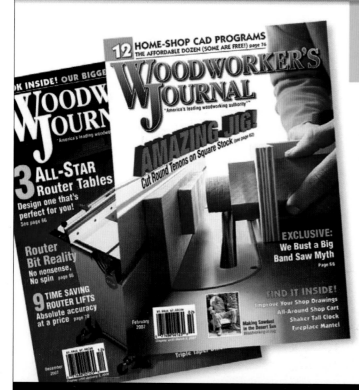